GCSE 9-1

geography

OCR B

T0346892

Revision Guide

Series editor
John Widdowson

Andy Crampton
Catherine Owen

OXFORD
UNIVERSITY PRESS

OXFORD

UNIVERSITY PRESS

Great Clarendon Street, Oxford, OX2 6DP, United Kingdom

Oxford University Press is a department of the University of Oxford. It furthers the University's objective of excellence in research, scholarship, and education by publishing worldwide. Oxford is a registered trade mark of Oxford University Press in the UK and in certain other countries

© Oxford University Press 2019

Series editor: John Widdowson

Authors: Andy Crampton, Catherine Owen

The moral rights of the authors have been asserted

Database right of Oxford University Press (maker) 2019

First published in 2019

British Library Cataloguing in Publication Data
Data available

978-0-19-843613 3

7 9 10 8 6

Paper used in the production of this book is a natural, recyclable product made from wood grown in sustainable forests. The manufacturing process conforms to the environmental regulations of the country of origin.

Printed and bound by CPI Group (UK) Ltd, Croydon, CR0 4YY

Acknowledgements

The publishers would like to thank the following for permissions to use copyright material:

Cover: Rob Hyrons/Shutterstock; **p8**: Chris Wildt/Cartoonstock; **p20**: NoDerog/iStockphoto; **p22**: Ymphotos/Shutterstock; **p23**: H3k27/ iStockphoto; **p32**: ZUMA Press, Inc./Alamy Stock Photo; **p36(r)**: Ben Kennedy/U.S. Geological Survey; **p36(l)**: NASA/Goddard Scientific Visualization Studio; **p37**: Heritage Image Partnership Ltd/Alamy Stock Photo; **p41**: Mohammed Seeneen/AP Images; **p42(l, r)**: NASA/ SCIENCE PHOTO LIBRARY; **p43(t)**: Louise Murray/Alamy Stock Photo; **p43(b)**: G.M.B. Akash/Panos Pictures; **p45**: Invisible Edit/ Shutterstock; **p48**: Ivy Close Images/Alamy Stock Photo; **p50(l)**: Derek Croucher/Alamy Stock Photo; **p50(r)**: NigelHigson/Getty Images; **p52**: FLPA/Alamy Stock Photo; **p54(t)**: Liquid Light/Alamy Stock Photo; **p54(b)**: Janet Baxter Photography (janetbaxterphotography.co.uk); **p62**: Skyscan Photolibrary/Alamy Stock Photo; **p64(t)**: Hoberman Collection/Alamy Stock Photo; **p64(b)**: Hufton+Crow-VIEW/Alamy Stock Photo; **p66**: Jeffdalt/iStockphoto; **p70**: Dekaro/iStockphoto; **p72**: Frans Lanting Studio/Alamy Stock Photo; **p73**: Courtesy of Samasati Retreat and Rainforest Sanctuary; **p78**: SeppFriedhuber/ iStockphoto; **p79**: Vladislav Gurfinkel/Shutterstock; **p83**: Mark Steward/Alamy Stock Photo; **p86**: David Hughes/Shutterstock; **p90**: David Bagnall/Alamy Stock Photo; **p92**: Dynasoar/iStockphoto; **p97**: Angus McComiskey/Alamy Stock Photo; **p98(b)**: Courtesy of John Widdowson; **p98(t)**: Askihuseyin/Fotolia; **p99**: Courtesy of John Widdowson; **p107**: John Panella/Shutterstock; **p110**: GavinD/ iStockphoto; **p114**: Eitan Simanor/Alamy Stock Photo; **p115**: Ulrich Doering/imageBROKER/Shutterstock; **p116**: Lynn Yeh/Shutterstock; **p119**: NASA; **p122**: Evgeniy Zhukov/Shutterstock; **p127**: Justin Kase zsixz/Alamy Stock Photo; **p128**: Jeffrey Blackler/Alamy Stock Photo; **p134**: United Archives GmbH/Alamy Stock Photo; **p135**: Travellight/Shutterstock; **p138**: Tyler Olson/Shutterstock; **p139(t)**: Dylan Garcia Photography/Alamy Stock Photo; **p139(b)**: Roger Hutchings/Alamy Stock Photo; **p140**: Xinhua/Alamy Stock Photo; **p141**: Mike Goldwater/Alamy Stock Photo; **p145**: Volodymyr Burdiak/Shutterstock; **p146**: Courtesy of Halvdan Jakobsen; **p148**: Photographer: Patrice De Villiers; Agency: Marcel Worldwide; **p149**: B Brown/Shutterstock; **p150(t)**: BlueSkyImage/Shutterstock; **p150(t)**: PeerPoint/Alamy Stock Photo; **p151**: VCG/VCG/Getty Images; **p153**: Minerva Studio/Shutterstock; **p156**: United States Geological Survey; **p161**: Bjanka Kadic/Alamy Stock Photo; **p163**: Londonstills. com/Alamy Stock Photo; **p166**: Jeffrey Blackler/Alamy Stock Photo; **p167**: Marcin Rogozinski/Alamy Stock Photo; **p169**: Zhao jian kang/ Shutterstock; **p171**: Imaginechina/Shutterstock; **p176**: Ordnance Survey © Crown copyright and Database rights 2019.

Artwork by Aptara Inc., Lovell Johns, Mike Parsons, and Q2A Media Services Inc.

Every effort has been made to contact copyright holders of material reproduced in this book. Any omissions will be rectified in subsequent printings if notice is given to the publisher.

Links to third party websites are provided by Oxford in good faith and for information only. Oxford disclaims any responsibility for the materials contained in any third party website referenced in this work.

Contents

Component 2: People and Society

Component 3: Geographical Exploration

Guided answers are available on the Oxford Secondary Geography website:
www.oxfordsecondary.co.uk/geography-answers

Please note this revision guide has not been written or endorsed by OCR. The answers and commentaries provided represent one interpretation only and other solutions may be appropriate.

Introduction: Helping you succeed

If you want to be successful in your exams, then you need to revise all you've learnt in your GCSE course! That can seem daunting – but it's why this book has been written. It contains key revision points that you need to prepare for exams for the OCR B GCSE 9–1 Geography specification.

Your revision guide!

This book is designed to help you revise for your three OCR B GCSE Geography papers. The OCR B GCSE 9–1 Geography specification has three components. Each component is assessed by an exam (Paper 1, 2, 3).

Each component is split into chapters. Each chapter has an introduction page, which contains an outline of:

- the exam paper you'll be taking
- the key questions and content that form the specification.

Each page of your revision guide has the following features:

You need to know – at the start of every page. This summarises the things you need to know for each theme.

Key learning points – a summary of the content found in the student book for each theme.

Six Second Summary – the essentials that you need to remember (like a ready-made flashcard).

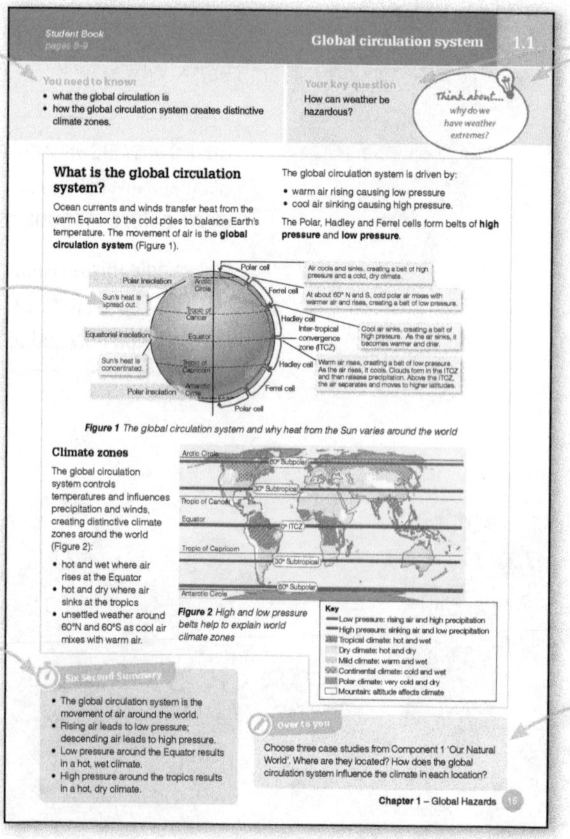

Student Book pages 8–9

Global circulation system 1.1

You need to know:
- what the global circulation is
- how the global circulation system creates distinctive climate zones.

Your key question
How can weather be hazardous?

Think about... why do we have weather extremes?

What is the global circulation system?

Ocean currents and winds transfer heat from the warm Equator to the cold poles to balance Earth's temperature. The movement of air is the **global circulation system** (Figure 1).

The global circulation system is driven by:
- warm air rising causing low pressure
- cool air sinking causing high pressure.

The Polar, Hadley and Ferrel cells form belts of **high pressure** and **low pressure**.

Figure 1 The global circulation system and why heat from the Sun varies around the world

Climate zones

The global circulation system controls temperatures and influences precipitation and winds, creating distinctive climate zones around the world (Figure 2):
- hot and wet where air rises at the Equator
- hot and dry where air sinks at the tropics
- unsettled weather around 60°N and 60°S as cool air mixes with warm air.

Figure 2 High and low pressure belts help to explain world climate zones

Six Second Summary
- The global circulation system is the movement of air around the world.
- Rising air leads to low pressure; descending air leads to high pressure.
- Low pressure around the Equator results in a hot, wet climate.
- High pressure around the tropics results in a hot, dry climate.

Over to you

Choose three case studies from Component 1 'Our Natural World'. Where are they located? How does the global circulation system influence the climate in each location?

Chapter 1 – Global Hazards 15

Your key question – the main question for each topic in the spec, which is split into sub-questions *(Think about)*. You should be able to answer these questions once you have revised.

Over to you – activities to help you learn the material for the exam and to make your revision more active.

Figure 1 *Your revision guide's key features*

Your revision

The content (1.1, 1.2 etc.) in this revision guide exactly matches the content for each theme in your *GCSE Geography OCR B* student book. Key content on each double page in the student book is summarised in a single page in this revision guide.

Topics you need to learn

Component 1: Our Natural World

This is all about physical geography and is assessed by Paper 1 in the exam.
It has **two** sections;

Section A: Questions on four topic areas – *Global Hazards, Changing Climate, Distinctive Landscapes and Sustaining Ecosystems.*

- For *Global Hazards* you have to know about **two** contrasting natural weather hazards and **one** tectonic event.
- For *Distinctive Landscapes* you have to know about **two** landscapes in the UK (**one** coastal landscape and **one** river basin).
- For *Sustaining Ecosystems* you need to know about **one** example of a sustainably managed area of tropical rainforest and **two** examples of sustainably managed polar environments (**one** small-scale example and **one** global example).

Section B: Questions about the physical geography fieldwork you have done and the geographical skills you have used. During your GCSE course, you should have done at least one day of physical geography fieldwork.

Component 2: People and Society

This is all about human geography and is assessed by Paper 2 in the exam.
It also has **two** sections:

Section A: Questions on four topic areas – *Urban Futures, Dynamic Development, UK in the 21st Century and Resource Reliance.*

- For *Urban Futures* you have to know about **one** city in an AC and **one** city in a LIDC or EDC. For each city you also need to know about **one** initiative to make it more sustainable.
- For *Dynamic Development* you have to know about **one** LIDC.
- For *UK in the 21st Century* you have to know about **one** UK economic hub and the UK's role in **one** global conflict.
- For *Resource Reliance* you have to know about attempts to achieve food security in **one** country.

Section B: Questions about the human geography fieldwork you have done and the geographical skills you have used. During your GCSE course, you should have done at least one day of human geography fieldwork.

Component 3: Geographical Exploration

This brings together physical and human geography in a decision-making exercise and is assessed by Paper 3 in the exam. It only has **one** section.

Questions could cover any of the topics you have studied in components 1 and 2, but it will probably not be based on a place or example you have studied. Instead, you will be given a Resource Booklet about a place or example you may not have studied. You will be expected to use your knowledge, understanding and geographical skills to complete the decision-making exercise.

A strategy for revision

However you look at it, revision can be hard work. You can make it easier for yourself by having a **strategy** (a plan).

Starting your revision

The worst bit of all is sitting down to start your revision. No one wants to start. You'll have to make yourself!

> **Make a checklist** of all the topics you have studied. A copy of the syllabus will help. Go through the notes in your book and make sure you have covered all the topics.

> **Break it down into chunks** for each topic. Each topic should have a key question, key words and case studies. Make sure you know what they are.

> **Find the gaps** in your notes and any themes, key words or case studies you haven't covered. Copy up the missing notes from a friend, or find the information elsewhere.

> **Spot your weak points** by going through the topics to identify the parts you are confident about and the ones that need extra work. You can build these into your three stages of revision (see page 11)

"We prefer to call this test 'multiple choice,' not 'multiple guess.'"

Figure 2 *The dangers of not revising!*

Make it active

Whatever revision you do, make it **active**. Don't just sit reading your notes and hope they sink in.

> **Use the revision guide** to help you. It includes a checklist of things... *You need to know*, *Six-second summaries* and *Over to you* activities. They're there to help you.

> **Make flashcards** for each theme. You could use the *You need to know* or *Six-second summary* ideas as your headings, or think of your own.

> **Make it visual** – some of us find it easier to revise things visually than by using words. Draw diagrams, maps and pictures to help you. Then add your own labels.

> **Summarise ideas** as lists or tables, using categories like good points/bad points, advantages/disadvantages, large scale/small scale – whatever helps you to understand.

> **Revise in a group** to make it more fun. Join with friends to test each other or practice doing questions together. More brains make light work!

Preparing for the exam

You began preparing for the exam from the moment you started your GCSE course. You may have been doing exam questions for the past two years, but practice makes perfect!

> **Know the command words** – make a list of them, such as *describe*, *explain*, *compare* and *evaluate* and know what they mean.

> **Understand how exams are marked** – which questions carry the most marks and how to reach the high levels. You can check mark schemes published on OCR's website.

> **Practice past exam papers** – the more you do the more you'll come to recognise the command words and different styles of questions.

> **Look at model answers** that are published by OCR. Go through the answers so that you know how the examiner marks the questions.

Using questions for revision

Your enquiring mind!

The OCR B GCSE Geography specification is also called 'Geography for Enquiring Minds'. It is based around key questions to help you to think like a geographer. Each topic has one or more key questions (Figure 3). You will find a key question at the top of each page in the Revision Guide. Use them to help with your revision.

Topic	Key question	Pages
Global Hazards	How can weather be hazardous?	15–24
	How do plate tectonics shape our world?	26–33
Changing Climate	What evidence is there to suggest climate change is a natural process?	35–45
Distinctive Landscapes	What makes a landscape distinctive?	48–52
	What influences the landscapes in the UK?	53–58, 61–64
Sustaining Ecosystems	Why are natural ecosystems important?	66–68
	Why should tropical rainforests matter to us?	69–73
	Is there more to polar environments than ice?	74–79
Urban Futures	Why do more than half the world's population live in urban areas?	81–87
	What are the challenges and opportunities for cities today?	88–92, 95–99
Dynamic Development	Why are some countries richer than others?	101–108
	Are LIDCs likely to stay poor?	109–117
UK in the 21st Century	How is the UK changing in the 21st century?	119–129
	Is the UK losing its global significance?	132–135
Resource Reliance	Will we run out of natural resources?	137–140
	Can we feed nine billion people by 2050?	141–151

Figure 3 *Key questions*

Key questions and sub-questions

Some of the key questions are big and might need a long answer. So, the specification also splits the questions into sub-questions. The *Think about* bubble alongside *Your key question* on each page gives you the sub-question. For example;

Key question: Are LIDCs likely to stay poor? Is split into **sub-questions**:

- How has an LIDC developed so far?
- What global connections influence its development?
- What development strategy is most appropriate?

If you can answer the sub-questions, it will help you to answer the key question.

Over to you

Choose one key question and find the relevant pages in this book. Also find the sub-questions in the *Think about* bubble on those pages. Write these questions down.

Before you revise try to answer the sub-questions and the key question. How well can you answer them?

After you revise try to answer the questions again. It should be easier this time. It's a good way to check your revision is working.

Making a revision timetable

Planning your revision

Revision doesn't just happen – for it to go well, it needs to be well planned! Here are some handy hints to help you plan.

> Two to three months before exams begin (so, probably during March), draw up a revision timetable. A plan for a school day is shown in Figure 4.

> Draw up a plan for your school holidays. Look at Figure 5 for an example plan.

> Divide up the time between the subjects and topics that you need to revise. Figures 4 and 5 assume you study ten subjects.

> In Figure 5, every revision day during the school holidays has three time slots – morning, afternoon, and evening. Use **two** of these on each day; give yourself some free time. Both timetables have one day and at least two evenings completely free.

> Split the three time slots in Figure 5 into three 50-minute chunks (see page 11).

Figure 4 *Revision timetable for term time (yellow blocks indicate free time).*

Time	Mon	Tues	Wed	Thurs	Fri	Sat	Sun
9 a.m. – 4 p.m.	Normal school day					Free day	Normal school homework
							Subjects 9 and 10
4–6 p.m.	Normal school homework						Free afternoon
6.30– 8 p.m.	Subjects 1 and 2	Subjects 3 and 4	Subjects 5 and 6	Subjects 7 and 8	Free evening		Free evening

Figure 5 *Revision timetable for school holidays (yellow blocks indicate free time).*

Time	Mon	Tues	Wed	Thurs	Fri	Sat	Sun
9 a.m. – 12 p.m.	Subject 1 (3 × 50-min sessions)	Free morning	Subject 5 (3 × 50-min sessions)	Subject 7 (3 × 50-min sessions)	Free day	Subject 9 (3 × 50-min sessions)	Free morning
2–5 p.m.	Free afternoon	Subject 3 (3 × 50-min sessions)	Subject 6 (3 × 50-min sessions)	Subject 8 (3 × 50-min sessions)		Free afternoon	Subject 10 (3 × 50-min sessions)
6–9 p.m.	Subject 2 (3 × 50-min sessions)	Subject 4 (3 × 50-min sessions)	Free evening	Free evening		Free evening	Flexible

A traffic-light approach to revision

You need to be smart about revision. There is no need to revise things you already know well! That would be a waste of time. It is better to spend your time on the things you are not sure about, or don't understand. That's where the three-stage traffic-light approach could help (Figure 6).

Stage 1 for the things that need most work (red), stage 2 for things that still need work but you are not so worried about (amber), and stage 3 for things you are confident about (green).

Figure 6 Three stages of revision – the traffic-light approach

Stage 1 Mending the gaps in your knowledge and understanding	Select a topic you're unclear about, where there are gaps in your notes or which you find more difficult. • Read through the topic using your own notes and also the student book. • Make a list of the key words. • Write a definition of each key word. Use your notes and the student book to help. • Then, you should be ready to go on to Stage 2.
Stage 2 Revising the topics you understood at the time, but may have forgotten	Select a topic that you understood but you still need to revise. • Read through the topic using your own notes and also the student book or revision guide. • As you read, copy the key question for the topic at the top of a sheet of paper. • Then, for the same topic in the revision guide, find the sub-questions in the *Think about* bubble next to the key question. Copy the questions on the same sheet, leaving large gaps under each question. • Now, write answers to the questions as far as you can, without looking at your notes or the student book. Don't worry about the ones you can't answer. • When you have finished you will see at a glance what you know and what you don't know. • For any gaps, go back and look at your notes and the student book. Then answer the questions again. • Identify your strengths and weaknesses. For topics you are confident about move on to Stage 3.
Stage 3 Revising topics you feel confident about	Select a topic you are already confident about or one of your strong topics from Stage 2. • Use the revision guide as a quick way to revise rather than read the student book again. If you discover any weak topics, go back to Stage 2. • Try to answer the practice questions from your student book. • Either, assess yourself using the mark schemes or, to make it more interesting, swap with a friend and mark each other's work, or ask your teacher to mark it. • Make sure you are confident about all your topics. Then you'll be ready for the exam!

Over to you

Go through the topics you have to revise, or even the themes within those topics. Rate them red, amber or green using the table above to guide you.

Just so you are sure, each chapter in the student book or revision guide covers a topic. Each double page in the student book, or single page in the revision guide, covers a theme.

Revising your case studies

Case studies are important in geography. At least one or two are sure to crop up in your exam so it is worth revising them well. There are not many to revise and Figure 7 lists them. Check to make sure you covered them in your geography lessons and that you revise them.

Figure 7 *Case study checklist*

Topic	Case study	Pages
1 Global Hazards	Weather hazard 1 – Typhoon Haiyan, 2013 Weather hazard 2 – Drought in the UK, 2012 Tectonic event – Nepal earthquake, 2015	22–23 24 31–32
2 Changing Climate	None	
3 Distinctive Landscapes	UK coastal landscape – Jurassic Coast UK river basin – Thames Basin	56–58 61–64
4 Sustaining Ecosystems	Sustainable management of tropical rainforest – ecotourism in Costa Rica	72–73
	Sustainable management of polar environments – small-scale example, whaling in the Arctic – global example, The Arctic and the Antarctic Treaty	77 76–78
5 Urban Futures	A city in an AC – Birmingham, UK A city in a LIDC or EDC – Istanbul, Turkey	88–92 95–99
6 Dynamic Development	A low-income developing country (LIDC) – Zambia	109–117
7 UK in the 21st Century	An economic hub – Cambridge The UK's role in a global conflict – the Middle East	129 133
8 Resource Reliance	Attempts to achieve food security in a country – Tanzania	144–147

One way to revise a case study is to create a **factfile**. It won't be exactly the same facts you need for each case study, but there are two basic formats – a **place** factfile or an **event** factfile.

Place factfile

- **Name** – what is the place called?
- **Location** – where is it? Which part of the world, which country, which region?
- **Area** – how big is it?
- **Physical geography** – what is the landscape like? What is the climate? What natural resources does it have?
- **Population** – what is the population? How is it changing? What is the birth/death rate? Which ethnic groups live there?
- **Economy** – what is wealth per person (GNP/capita)? What jobs do people do? What does it export or import? What is the economic growth rate?
- **Development** – what is average life expectancy? What is the literacy rate? What is the human development index (HDI)?

Event factfile

- **Name** – what was the event?
- **Time** – when did it happen? Which year, which month and date, what time?
- **Location** – where did it happen? Which part of the world, which country, which region?
- **Details** – what happened (give as much detail as you can)? Did it happen once, or more times? How frequently?
- **Causes** – what was the cause of the event? Was it natural or human? Could it have been avoided?
- **Impacts** – what were the short and long-term impacts on people? What were the economic, social and environmental impacts?
- **Responses** – how did people respond at the time? How did they respond later? What could be done to reduce the impacts next time?

 Over to you

Create a factfile for one of the case studies you have studied (Figure 7). It could be a place factfile or an event factfile, or you could do one of each.

Don't worry if you can't answer all the suggested questions for your case study. Some questions won't apply to all case studies. Just answer as many as you can. Is there any more information you could add, which is not included in the above factfiles?

Top tips for exam success

'Good luck' is what everyone will wish you for your exams. But, if you follow the advice below and revise for your exam, you won't need luck. Instead, you will be well-prepared, which is much better than luck.

Revise well. Lack of revision always catches up with you. GCSEs are tougher now than in previous years and it's important to know your stuff.

Know which topics to expect in each exam. For example, which exam tests physical or human geography and which topics, such as Global Hazards or Urban Futures, are on which paper.

Look at the marks so that you know roughly how much time to spend on each question and which questions carry the most marks (those are the questions you need to spend more time on).

Get your timing right. For example, Papers 1 and 2 are both 75 minutes long and carry 70 marks each. That's almost 1 mark a minute! If you spend 5 minutes on a 2-mark question that's probably too long.

Answer all the questions and don't leave any blanks. Even if you are unsure, write something. Try to use all the space for a 6-mark answer. A longer space indicates you need to write in detail.

Write in sentences where required. Single words or phrases are fine for a 1–2 mark question, but sentences are better than bullet points when a longer answer is required.

Give specific details, especially when answering questions about your case studies. Learn the names of places, facts and figures, to give you more of a chance of getting top marks.

Know the mark scheme and how questions are marked. Longer answers are marked in levels, based on quality. Level 1 is **basic** (no named places or examples), Level 2 is **general** (some key points), and Level 3 is **detailed** (giving facts, data and examples). Make sure you are in Level 3!

Use a timetable that gives you exactly which date and time each exam is on. Check and double-check to make sure you don't miss it!

Topic 1:
Global Hazards

Your exam

Global Hazards is part of Paper 1: Our Natural World. It is a 1 hr 15 min written exam and makes up 35% of your GCSE. The whole paper carries 70 marks (including 3 marks for SPaG).

There are two sections on the paper;

- Section A: questions on all the physical geography topics, including *Global Hazards*

- Section B: physical geography fieldwork

You will have to answer all questions on the paper.

Your revision checklist

Tick these boxes to build a record of your revision

Spec key question	Theme	1	2	3
How can weather be hazardous?				
Why do we have weather extremes?	1.1 Global circulation system			
	1.2 Extreme temperatures			
	1.3 Extreme winds			
	1.4 Extreme precipitation			
	1.5 Tropical storms and droughts			
	1.6 Tropical storms and extreme weather			
	1.7 Drought, El Niño and La Niña			
When does extreme weather become a hazard?	1.8 Typhoon Haiyan – a tropical storm			
	1.9 Typhoon Haiyan's path of destruction			
	1.10 Drought in the UK			
Fieldwork skills	1.11 Hazards fieldwork			
How do plate tectonics shape our world?				
What processes occur at plate boundaries?	1.12 Plate tectonics – shaping our world			
	1.13 Destructive and collision plate boundaries			
	1.14 Constructive and conservative plate boundaries			
	1.15 How earthquakes happen			
	1.16 Why volcanoes erupt			
How can tectonic movement be hazardous?	1.17 Earthquake disaster in Nepal – 1			
	1.18 Earthquake disaster in Nepal – 2			
How does technology have the potential to save lives in hazard zones?	1.19 Saving lives in earthquake zones			

You need to know:

- what the global circulation is
- how the global circulation system creates distinctive climate zones.

Your key question

How can weather be hazardous?

Think about...
why do we have weather extremes?

What is the global circulation system?

Ocean currents and winds transfer heat from the warm Equator to the cold poles to balance Earth's temperature. The movement of air is the **global circulation system** (Figure 1).

The global circulation system is driven by:

- warm air rising causing low pressure
- cool air sinking causing high pressure.

The Polar, Hadley and Ferrel cells form belts of **high pressure** and **low pressure**.

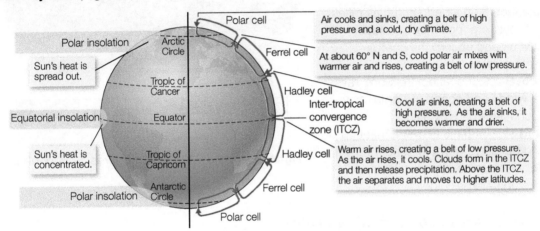

Figure 1 *The global circulation system and why heat from the Sun varies around the world*

Climate zones

The global circulation system controls temperatures and influences precipitation and winds, creating distinctive climate zones around the world (Figure 2):

- hot and wet where air rises at the Equator
- hot and dry where air sinks at the tropics
- unsettled weather around 60°N and 60°S as cool air mixes with warm air.

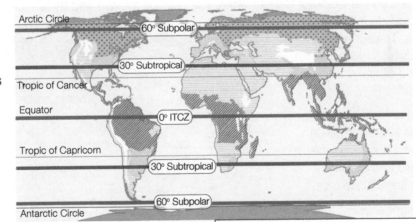

Figure 2 *High and low pressure belts help to explain world climate zones*

Key

— Low pressure: rising air and high precipitation
— High pressure: sinking air and low precipitation
▨ Tropical climate: hot and wet
☐ Dry climate: hot and dry
☐ Mild climate: warm and wet
▦ Continental climate: cold and wet
☐ Polar climate: very cold and dry
☐ Mountain: altitude affects climate

Six Second Summary

- The global circulation system is the movement of air around the world.
- Rising air leads to low pressure; descending air leads to high pressure.
- Low pressure around the Equator results in a hot, wet climate.
- High pressure around the tropics results in a hot, dry climate.

Over to you

Choose three case studies from Component 1 'Our Natural World'. Where are they located? How does the global circulation system influence the climate in each location?

You need to know:

- what affects temperatures around the world
- examples of extreme temperatures in contrasting countries.

Your key question

How can weather be hazardous?

Think about...

why do we have weather extremes?

What affects temperatures around the world?

Study Figure 1 and consider the following that affect temperatures:

- **Insolation**: the strength of the Sun's rays varies according to the angle at which they hit Earth.
- **Albedo effect**: high albedo surfaces reflect the Sun's rays (e.g. polar ice); surfaces with a low albedo absorb the energy (e.g. rainforests).
- **Cloud cover**: clouds reflect the Sun's rays.
- **Surface winds and ocean currents**: move heat around the world (Figure 2).
- **Land and sea**: water is slower to heat up than land but stays warm for longer.
- **Altitude**: air pressure is lower higher up, making temperatures colder.

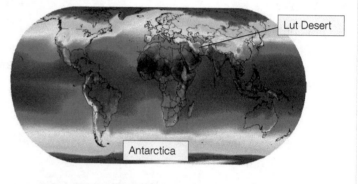

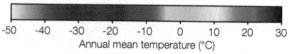

Figure 1 *Annual mean temperatures around the world*

Why are some areas hot and others cold?

The Lut desert in Iran is the hottest place on Earth (70.7 °C in 2005). This is because it is on the Tropic of Cancer where insolation is intense and there are no clouds to reflect the Sun's rays. The surface is dark lava which has a low albedo and absorbs the Sun's rays.

Antarctica is the coldest place on Earth (–89.2 °C in 1983) because the Sun's rays are less intense and ice on the surface reflects these rays.

Extreme temperatures in both areas are hazardous; no one lives there permanently.

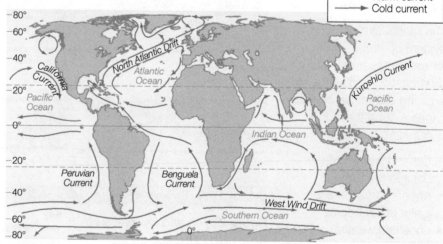

Figure 2 *Warm and cold ocean currents move heat around the world*

Six Second Summary

- The Sun radiates energy (insolation) which heats Earth's surface.
- Insolation is strongest at the Equator and weakest at the poles.
- Other factors influencing temperature include the albedo effect, clouds, winds, ocean currents and altitude.

Over to you

Look at Figure 1. What is the annual mean temperature along the west coast of South America? How does this compare to other locations at the same latitude? Suggest reasons for the differences.

You need to know:

- what affects winds around the world
- examples of extreme winds in contrasting countries.

Your key question

How can weather be hazardous?

Think about...
why do we have weather extremes?

What is wind?

Wind is the movement of air from an area of high pressure to one of low pressure. The greater the difference in pressure, the stronger the wind.

Why are some areas so windy?

Study Figure 1 and consider the following that affect wind around the world:

- **Trade winds** – blow from high pressure belts to low pressure belts.
- **Katabatic winds** – air flowing downhill, e.g. in Antarctica.
- **Jet streams** – strong winds in the atmosphere can affect mountain tops, e.g. Mt Everest.
- **Tornadoes** – very strong rotating winds, common in places such as 'Tornado Alley' in the USA.
- **Tropical storms** – large storms with strong rotating winds bring strong winds. The highest wind speed ever recorded was by Hurricane Olivia in 1996 on Barrow Island off the north-west coast of Australia.

The UK's wildest winds

The strongest winds in the UK are usually recorded on the mountain tops in the west. Coasts are also prone to high winds as there is less friction when winds pass over the sea and they not slowed down.

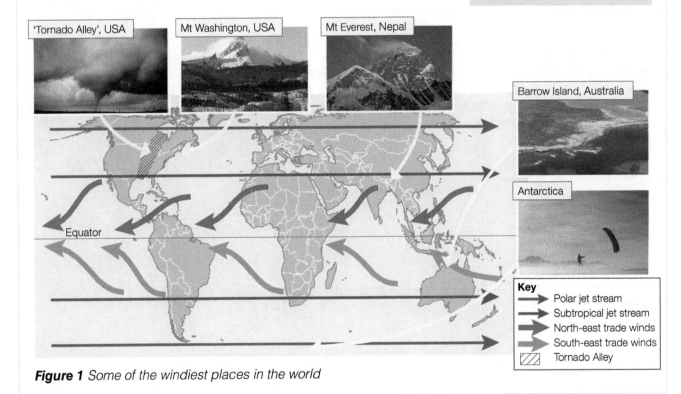

'Tornado Alley', USA

Mt Washington, USA

Mt Everest, Nepal

Barrow Island, Australia

Antarctica

Equator

Key

→ Polar jet stream
→ Subtropical jet stream
➤ North-east trade winds
➤ South-east trade winds
▨ Tornado Alley

Figure 1 *Some of the windiest places in the world*

Six Second Summary

- Wind is the movement of air from high to low pressure.
- Trade winds blow from high pressure belts to low pressure belts.
- Other types of strong winds include katabatic winds, jet streams, tornadoes and tropical storms.

Over to you

How are trade winds influenced by the global circulation system?

Think about...
why do we have
weather extremes?

What affects precipitation around the world?

Global scale: The global circulation system means that areas with low pressure have rising air and high levels of **precipitation**. Where warm air and cool air meet, **frontal rainfall** will be common. Where insolation is intense, air will become warm and rise, leading to **convectional rainfall**.

Regional scale: Coasts of continents can be particularly wet. If warm air from the sea is forced to rise over mountains, **relief rainfall** will fall (Figure 1).

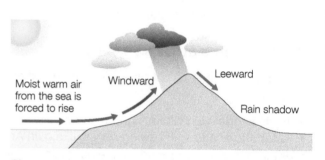

Moist warm air from the sea is forced to rise   Windward   Leeward   Rain shadow

Figure 1 *Relief rainfall affects precipitation patterns on a local and regional scale*

Why are some areas wet and others dry?

The Khasi Hills in northern India (Figure 2) are the wettest place on Earth (9300 mm of rain fell in July 1861). Wind blows over flat land in Bangladesh and is suddenly forced to rise, causing relief rainfall.

The Atacama Desert (Figure 2) in South America is the driest hot desert on Earth (average annual rainfall of 15 mm). It is in the **rain shadow** of the Andes mountains and is next to a cold ocean current, so there is no moist warm air to form clouds.

Antarctica is the driest cold desert because the air is so cold that it can hold very little water vapour.

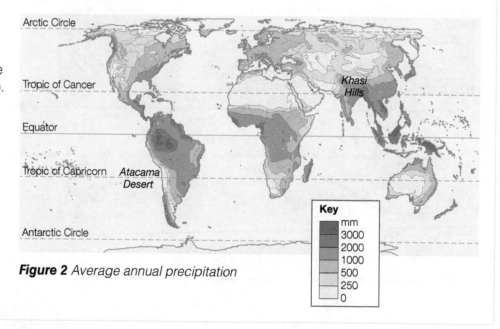

Arctic Circle

Tropic of Cancer

Equator

Tropic of Capricorn   *Atacama Desert*

Antarctic Circle

Khasi Hills

Key

| mm |
| 3000 |
| 2000 |
| 1000 |
| 500 |
| 250 |
| 0 |

Figure 2 *Average annual precipitation*

 Six Second Summary

- Precipitation is water falling from the atmosphere as rain, sleet, snow or hail.
- Areas of high pressure are dry whilst areas of low pressure are wet.
- Other factors affect precipitation, e.g. altitude.

Over to you

Look at Figure 2. What is the average annual precipitation in the UK? How does this compare to other areas at the same latitude? Suggest reasons for the differences.

You need to know:
- where tropical storms and drought are found
- how this may have changed over time.

Your key question

How can weather be hazardous?

Think about...
why do we have weather extremes?

Where do tropical storms and drought occur

Tropical storms are powerful rotating storms. They form over tropical oceans and move from east to west. They have wind speeds of over 120 km/h and can be up to 650 km across. They bring heavy rain.

Droughts are periods when there is much less precipitation than usual for the area, leading to water shortages. Drought is linked to long periods of high pressure.

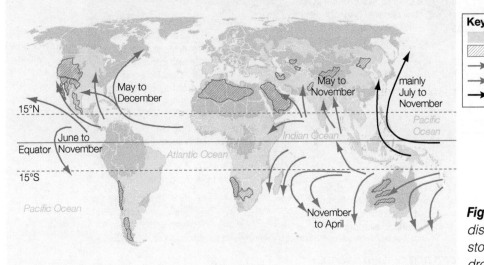

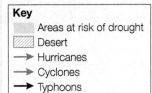

Figure 1 *Global distribution of tropical storms and areas where drought is a hazard*

How has the pattern of tropical storms and drought changed over time?

It is difficult to see a clear pattern of change in the pattern of tropical storms, but global warming may have an impact by increasing the temperature of the oceans.

The pattern of drought around the world has clearly changed (Figure 2). The severity of drought has increased since 1940, possibly because of changing rainfall and evaporation patterns, related to long-term climate change.

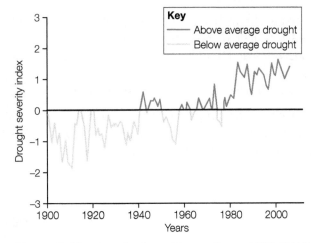

Figure 2 *Changes in drought over time, 1900–2010*

 Six Second Summary

- Tropical storms are powerful rotating storms that form over warm oceans.
- Droughts are periods when there is much less precipitation than usual.
- It is clear that the severity of drought around the world has increased.

Over to you

Look at Figure 2. Describe the changes in drought between 1900 and 2010.

You need to know:

- what causes tropical storms
- examples of extreme weather related to tropical storms.

Your key question

How can weather be hazardous?

Think about... 💡

why do we have weather extremes?

What causes tropical storms?

- Tropical storms can form when the ocean is over 26.5 °C and at least 60 m deep.
- The storm gets its energy from the moist warm air.
- These storms form between 5° and 15°N and also between 5° and 15°S of the Equator, where the **Coriolis effect** can start them spinning.
- Once a tropical storm reaches land it loses its energy supply and starts to die.

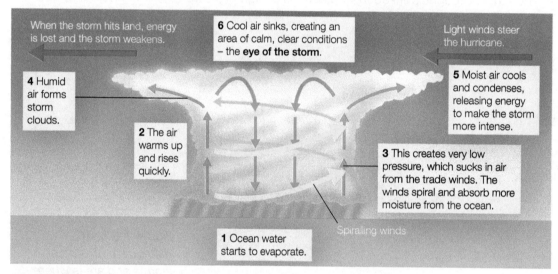

When the storm hits land, energy is lost and the storm weakens.

6 Cool air sinks, creating an area of calm, clear conditions – the **eye of the storm**.

Light winds steer the hurricane.

4 Humid air forms storm clouds.

5 Moist air cools and condenses, releasing energy to make the storm more intense.

2 The air warms up and rises quickly.

3 This creates very low pressure, which sucks in air from the trade winds. The winds spiral and absorb more moisture from the ocean.

Spiralling winds

1 Ocean water starts to evaporate.

Figure 1 *How tropical storms form and build in strength*

What extreme weather do tropical storms bring?

Tropical storms bring strong winds and heavy rainfall, which can cause **flash floods**, mudslides and **landslides**. Low air pressure raises sea levels leading to coastal flooding (Figure 2). This is known as a **storm surge**.

As well and endangering people and their homes, industries such as fishing, shipping, transport and tourism are vulnerable.

Storm surge: Low air pressure means high tides can flood inland.

Heavy rainfall: Torrential rain can lead to flooding, mudslides and landslides.

Strong winds: Trees, crops, buildings and power lines can be damaged by winds of over 120 km/h.

Figure 2 *Storm hazards and their consequences for people*

Six Second Summary

- Tropical storms form when oceans are over 26.5 °C and at least 60 m deep.
- They bring strong winds, heavy rainfall and coastal flooding.
- They cause damage to people's lives, homes and businesses.

Over to you

Outline two sources of energy for tropical storms.

You need to know:
- what El Niño and La Niña are
- how El Niño and La Niña are linked to droughts.

Your key question
How can weather be hazardous?

Think about... why do we have weather extremes?

El Niño and La Niña

These events are caused by changes in the sea surface temperature in a band across the Pacific Ocean.

- When the trade winds that blow from east to west are weaker, the surface temperature increases and causes the **El Niño** effect (Figure 1).
- When these winds are stronger, the temperature decreases, causing a **La Niña** effect.

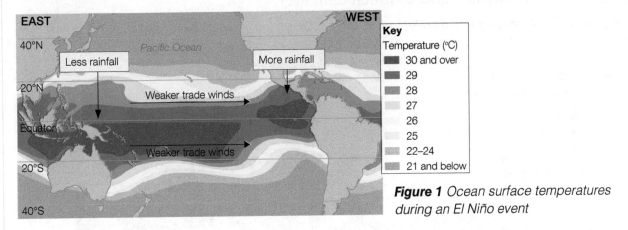

Figure 1 *Ocean surface temperatures during an El Niño event*

How are El Niño and La Niña linked to drought?

El Niño events result in less rainfall on the Australian/Asian edge of the Pacific Ocean and more on the North and South American edge (Figure 2). La Niña events reverse this.

During the 2015 El Niño event, Thailand experienced one of its worst droughts, which had major consequences for farmers, food prices and the economy.

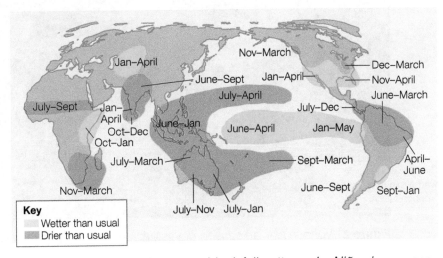

Figure 2 *Impact of El Niño on world rainfall patterns. La Niña also causes drought but in different areas, such as North and South America.*

Six Second Summary

- Surface temperatures in the Pacific Ocean are warmer during an El Niño event.
- El Niño and La Niña events affect global rainfall patterns.
- El Niño events can cause droughts on the Australian/Asian edge of the Pacific.

Over to you

What impact could El Niño droughts have on the people and environments in the areas it affects?

You need to know:

- what caused Typhoon Haiyan
- why the Philippines suffered such serious damage.

Your key question

How can weather be hazardous?

Think about... 💡
when does extreme weather become a hazard?

Causes of Typhoon Haiyan

Typhoon Haiyan formed over the Pacific Ocean in November 2013 at 7 °N (where it was affected by the Coriolis effect, the sea temperature was over 26.5 °C and depth over 60 m). It passed over little land (which would slow it down) and gained energy as it passed westwards over the warm ocean, becoming a category 5 storm on the Saffir–Simpson scale.

Why did Typhoon Haiyan cause so much damage?

The Philippines is an **emerging and developing country (EDC)** and is ranked 117 out of 187 countries in terms of development. The area hit by the typhoon was recovering from a recent earthquake. People were warned that a typhoon was coming, but many didn't have anywhere to go.

Total population	99.14 million
Population in rural areas	50.64%
GNI/capita (see spread 6.3)	$3470
Percentage below the poverty line	25.2%
Average life expectancy	69 years
Number of islands	7107

Figure 1 *Philippines factfile*

Typhoon Haiyan hit the Philippines in November 2013 causing 6300 deaths.

Heavy rain and wind speeds of 315 km/h caused widespread devastation.

Over 3 million people lived within 50 km of the typhoon's path.

Storm surges reached 6 m causing flooding up to 1 km inland.

Figure 2 *Typhoon Haiyan caused devastation and destroyed many homes*

⏱ **Six Second Summary**

- Typhoon Haiyan hit the Philippines in November 2013 causing widespread devastation and loss of life.
- The storm formed at 7 °N over the Pacific Ocean where it could be affected by the Coriolis effect.
- The Philippines is an emerging and developing country (EDC).

 **Over to you**

For an EDC you have studied, explain why it is difficult to prepare for tropical storms.

You need to know:

- primary and secondary consequences of Typhoon Haiyan
- emergency and long-term responses to this tropical storm.

Your key question

How can weather be hazardous?

Think about... when does extreme weather become a hazard?

What were the consequences of Typhoon Haiyan?

Primary consequences:

- Storm surge destroyed 90% of Tacloban city.
- Heavy rainfall led to flash flooding and landslides.
- Strong winds damaged buildings, trees and crops.
- Falling debris caused deaths and injuries.

Secondary consequences:

- People had no shelter, clean water or electricity.
- Roads were blocked by trees.
- 453 flights were cancelled.

Social consequences

- Over half a million families were made homeless.
- Over 6300 deaths left families devastated.
- Damage to 571 health clinics and hospitals.

Economic consequences

- $2.86 billion of damage was caused.
- 77% of farmers and 74% of fishermen lost their main source of income.

Environmental consequences

- Crops were damaged. • Trees were uprooted.
- A barge was punctured and 85 000 litres of oil leaked into the sea.

Figure 1 *Damage caused by Typhoon Haiyan*

Responses

Seven provinces were put under a 'state of national calamity' so that the price of vital goods could be controlled. **Emergency (short-term) aid** provided food, water, shelter and medical supplies (Figure 2). The United Nations appealed for £190 million for emergency aid and the WHO managed healthcare workers.

Attention then turned to **long-term aid**, recovery and development. Cash for work schemes paid local people to clean debris, repair **infrastructure** (water supply, roads etc) and replant mangroves around the coast.

Aid given	Who benefited
Food assistance	4 million people
Seeds	44 000 families
Fertiliser	80 000 families
Educational materials	420 000 children
Basic emergency shelter materials	500 000 households
Tools and materials to rebuild homes	55 000 people
Cash for materials and labour	40 000 people
Solar lanterns	50 000 families

Figure 2 *Some of the aid delivered in the first 100 days after Typhoon Haiyan*

Six Second Summary

- Primary consequences included flooding, damage to buildings and 6300 deaths.
- Secondary consequences included half a million families being left homeless.
- Emergency response focused on food, water and shelter; long-term response focused on recovery and development.

Over to you

For a tropical storm you have studied, explain the relative significance of social, economic and environmental consequences of the storm.

Case Study

You need to know:

- the causes and consequences of drought in the UK in 2012
- how people responded to this drought.

Your key question

How can weather be hazardous?

Think about... when does extreme weather become a hazard?

Causes of the 2012 drought

Droughts develop when reserves of water in soils, lakes and rivers are 'used up', without being refilled. Several factors contributed to the UK drought in 2012 (Figure 1):

- Low rainfall between April 2010 and May 2012 because of dry winds blowing from Europe.
- Warmer temperatures leading to higher evaporation rates.
- Dry soils made it difficult for water to soak in.
- High water usage and waste from leaking pipes.

Consequences of the drought

- Farmers found it hard to find water for crops and livestock.
- The environment was damaged by wild fires and extraction of water from rivers.
- Hosepipe bans made it more difficult to wash cars and water gardens.

Responses to the drought

- Water companies were allowed to extract water from rivers.
- Hosepipe bans were issued.
- Campaigns encouraged people to use less water in their homes.

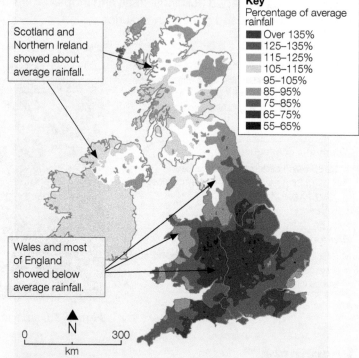

Figure 1 *Rainfall in the UK, April 2010 to March 2012*

Scotland and Northern Ireland showed about average rainfall.

Wales and most of England showed below average rainfall.

Key
Percentage of average rainfall
- Over 135%
- 125–135%
- 115–125%
- 105–115%
- 95–105%
- 85–95%
- 75–85%
- 65–75%
- 55–65%

⏱ **Six Second Summary**

- Causes of the 2012 drought in the UK included low rainfall, warm temperatures and dry soils.
- Consequences included a lack of water for crops, more wildfires and hosepipe bans.
- Water companies extracted water from rivers and encouraged people to use less water.

✏ **Over to you**

What are the costs and benefits of extracting water from rivers to maintain supplies during droughts?

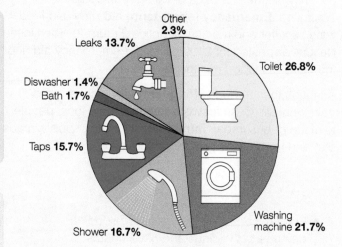

Other 2.3%
Leaks 13.7%
Diswasher 1.4%
Bath 1.7%
Taps 15.7%
Shower 16.7%
Toilet 26.8%
Washing machine 21.7%

Figure 2 *How do we use water in our homes?*

- how to carry out a questionnaire survey to test a hypothesis
- stages of the enquiry process.

Carrying out fieldwork to test a hypothesis

A **hypothesis** is a statement to be tested. You can use fieldwork to see if the hypothesis is true, false or needs to be changed. The hypothesis for this enquiry is:

'*Experiencing drought in the UK has raised awareness of the need to conserve water and has led to people changing their habits*.'

Using a questionnaire

Questionnaires need to be carefully designed to gather the data you need and avoid bias. Pilot (try out) your questionnaire to improve it, then conduct it with as large a sample size as possible. There are two types of question (Figure 1):

- **Closed questions**: the answer is one word or phrase, e.g. multiple choice (blue in Figure 1).
- **Open questions**: lengthy answers allow respondents to explain (orange in Figure 1).

Analysis, conclusion and evaluation of the enquiry process

Once you have formulated your hypothesis, designed your method (questionnaire) and conducted your research you can complete your enquiry by:

- analysis – using graphs, statistics and/or tables (Figure 2). Draw together your key findings and explain what they mean.
- conclusion – say if your hypothesis is correct, incorrect or needs changing based on your research findings.
- evaluation – consider your research and your methods. What went well? What could be improved?

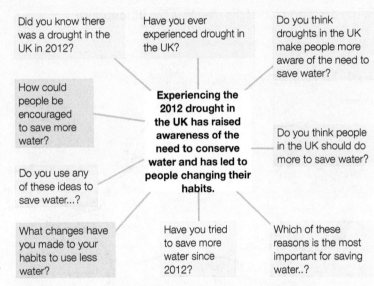

Figure 1 *Example closed (blue) and open (orange) questions for your questionnaire*

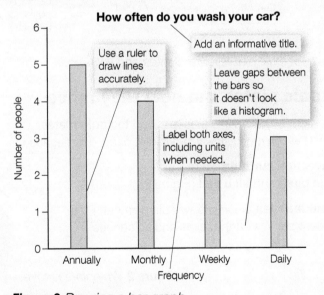

Figure 2 *Drawing a bar graph*

- A hypothesis is a statement to be tested.
- Questionnaire surveys must be carefully designed to collect the right data and reduce bias.
- The enquiry process involves choosing a hypothesis, designing a method, collecting data, analysis, drawing conclusions and evaluation.

Over to you

Justify the use of both closed and open questions in questionnaire surveys.

You need to know:

- the structure of Earth
- what tectonic plates are and how they move.

Your key question

How do plate tectonics shape our world?

Think about... what processes occur at plate boundaries?

The structure of Earth

Earth is made up of:

- **crust** – **continental** if on land; **oceanic** if under the ocean
- **mantle** – rock is close to melting point and flows slowly
- **core** – outer core is liquid; inner core is solid.

The crust and top of the mantle is the **lithosphere**.

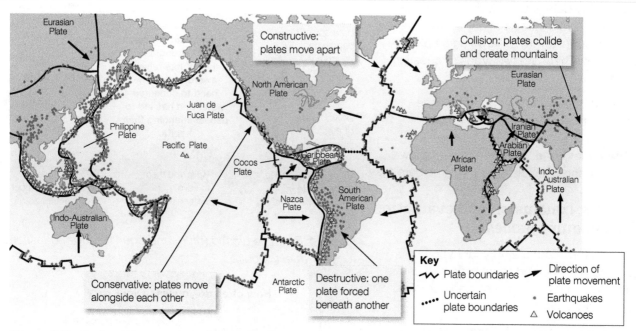

Figure 1 *Tectonic plates, earthquakes and volcanoes.*

Tectonic plates and how they move

Earth's crust is broken into pieces called **tectonic plates** (Figure 1) which move slowly in different directions because of:

- **convection currents**
- **ridge push** and **slab pull** (Figure 2).

Plate boundaries are where two plates meet. Plate movement causes earthquakes and volcanoes.

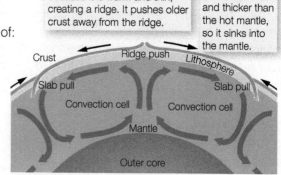

Ridge push: New crust rises because it is warm and thin, creating a ridge. It pushes older crust away from the ridge.

Slab pull: Old crust is cooler and thicker than the hot mantle, so it sinks into the mantle.

Figure 2 *Why plates move*

Six Second Summary

- Earth consists of a crust, mantle, outer core and inner core.
- The crust is broken into tectonic plates.
- These plates move due to convection currents, ridge push and slab pull.

Over to you

Describe the distribution of volcanoes using Figure 1.

26   **Chapter 1** – Global Hazards

Your key question

How do plate tectonics shape our world?

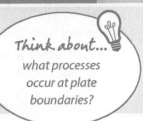

Think about...
what processes occur at plate boundaries?

Destructive plate boundaries

When an oceanic plate meets a continental plate the denser oceanic plate is forced under the continental plate – it is **subducted**. Subduction doesn't happen smoothly. The plates drag against each other and sometimes stick. An earthquake is caused when they jolt free and release energy (Figure 1).

As the plate subducts, seawater helps it to melt. The water makes it less dense and so it rises through cracks in the continental plate, and volcanoes form. **Fold mountains** are also found here (e.g. the Andes in South America).

When two oceanic plates meet, the denser one subducts and a deep trench forms, e.g. the Mariana Trench in the Western Pacific.

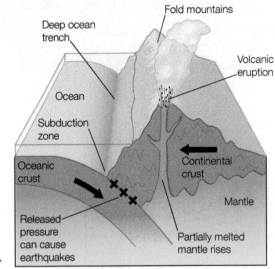

Figure 1 *Processes at a destructive boundary*

Collision plate boundaries

When two continental plates move towards each other, they collide, but do not subduct – they are less dense than the mantle beneath (Figure 2). The continental crust thickens and the surface lifts into fold mountains (e.g. the Himalayas, which are rising at 10 mm a year).

As there is no subduction, there are no volcanoes. But the pressure of the plates pushing together leads to faulting and earthquakes, such as the Nepal earthquake of 2015 (see 1.17–1.18).

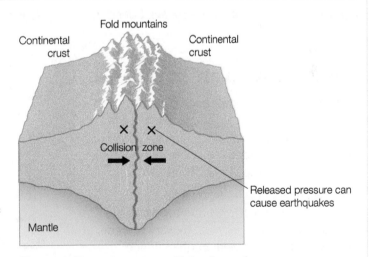

Figure 2 *Processes at a collision boundary*

Six Second Summary

- Destructive plate boundaries are found where an oceanic and a continental plate meet.
- The oceanic plate is subducted under the continental plate, causing an ocean trench, fold mountains, volcanoes and earthquakes.
- Collision plate boundaries are found where two continental plates meet, forming fold mountains.

Over to you

Why don't volcanoes occur at collision plate boundaries?

You need to know:

- The processes at work at constructive and conservative plate boundaries.

Your key question

How do plate tectonics shape our world?

Think about...
what processes occur at plate boundaries?

Constructive plate boundaries

When ocean plates pull apart, partially melted mantle rises up. This cools at the crust, forming new crust along a mid-ocean ridge. When parts of the mid-ocean ridge rise above the surface of the ocean, islands are formed (Figure 1).

When continental plates pull apart, the mantle rises and the plates above heat up and expand and bulge. Highlands form and, if the plate fractures, blocks drop, forming lowland (as in the Great African Rift Valley, Figure 2).

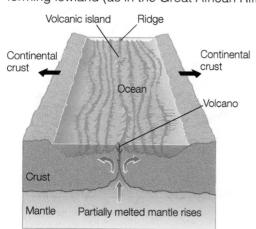

Figure 1 *Processes at a constructive boundary*

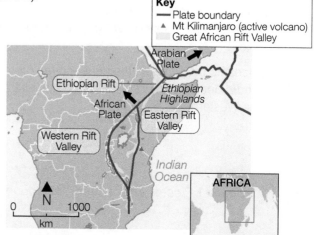

Figure 2 *Great African Rift Valley*

Conservative plate boundaries

Tectonic plates move past each other at conservative boundaries. The plates move in jerks. They can be locked together for years, then break free suddenly, causing an earthquake (e.g. the San Andreas Fault, Figure 3).

They can move in different directions, or in the same direction at different speeds. Large earthquakes are rare but can be very powerful as they are triggered near Earth's surface.

There are no volcanoes as there is no subduction.

Figure 3 *San Andreas Fault – a conservative plate boundary*

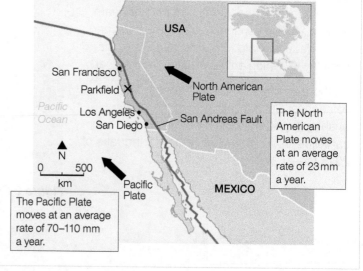

Six Second Summary

- Constructive plate boundaries are found where plates move apart.
- Semi-melted mantle rises up and cools to create new crust.
- Conservative plate boundaries are found where plates move alongside each other.

Over to you

Draw a diagram similar to Figure 1 that outlines the processes that take place at conservative plate boundaries.

You need to know:
- how the movement of tectonic plates causes shallow and deep focus earthquakes
- how earthquakes can be measured and predicted.

Your key question
How do plate tectonics shape our world?

Think about...
what processes occur at plate boundaries?

Causes of earthquakes

If plates stick, huge pressure can build up. When the plates break free or one plate gives way, the energy released causes an earthquake.

Deep focus earthquakes start 70–700 km below the surface. They occur at destructive plate boundaries and are very powerful, but the **seismic (shock) waves** spread out vertically and so a small area suffers the damage.

Shallow focus earthquakes start within 70 km of the surface. They occur at conservative boundaries, collision boundaries and the upper part of destructive boundaries (Figure 2). They are usually small in **magnitude** (amount of energy released) and most cannot be felt. But because the seismic waves spread out horizontally they can damage a large area.

Measuring and predicting earthquakes

Seismologists use seismometers to record the size of earthquakes. **Geographical information systems (GIS)** can be used to layer different information to predict which areas are at risk from earthquakes.

The magnitude of an earthquake is measured using the **Richter scale**. The **Mercalli scale** measures the effects and damage caused by an earthquake.

Figure 1 An earthquake on a fault

Figure 2 *Deep and shallow focus earthquakes at a destructive boundary*

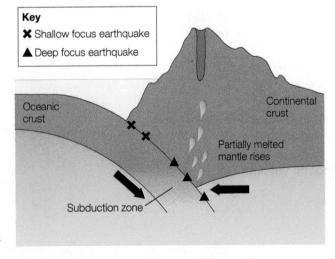

Key
✖ Shallow focus earthquake
▲ Deep focus earthquake

Oceanic crust

Continental crust

Partially melted mantle rises

Subduction zone

- Deep focus earthquakes start 70–700 km below the surface and occur at destructive plate boundaries.
- Shallow focus earthquakes start within 70 km of the surface and can be found at all types of plate boundaries.
- The Richter scale measures the magnitude of earthquakes.

Explain why both shallow focus and deep focus earthquakes can affect areas along destructive plate boundaries.

You need to know:

- How the movement of tectonic plates causes shield and composite volcanoes.

Your key question

How do plate tectonics shape our world?

Think about...
what processes occur at plate boundaries?

Shield volcanoes

Shield volcanoes are usually found at constructive plate boundaries where the mantle rises to the surface as the plates pull apart (Figure 1).

- Eruptions are gentle as the lava is runny.
- The quick-flowing lava cools to form a gently sloping volcano.
- Shield volcanoes are also found at **hotspots**, where **magma plumes** rise through the mantle and burn through where the crust is thin.

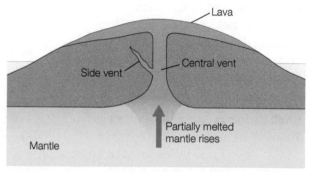

Figure 1 *A shield volcano where gentle eruptions gradually form a gently sloping mountain*

Composite volcanoes

Subduction takes place at destructive plate boundaries which can lead to volcanoes and earthquakes (Figure 2).

- The partially melted magma rises to the surface.
- The magma is viscous (sticky) and contains trapped sea water and hot gases.
- Steam and dangerous gases erupt violently from the resulting volcanoes.
- The sticky lava cools quickly, creating steep slopes.
- Layers of lava and ash create a **composite volcano**.

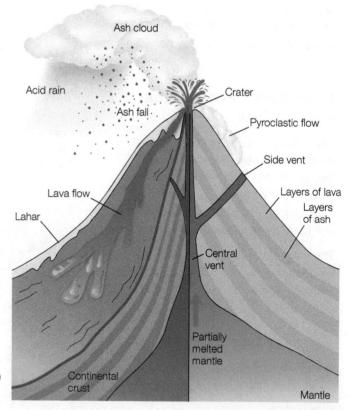

Figure 2 *Composite (layered) volcano*

- Shield volcanoes form at constructive plate boundaries and hot spots.
- The lava is runny and fast-flowing, forming gently sloping volcanoes.
- Composite volcanoes form at destructive boundaries; they are very explosive and the viscous lava forms steep slopes.

 **Over to you**

Explain the nature of volcanic activity at constructive plate boundaries.

You need to know:

- the causes of the 2015 earthquake in Nepal
- how aftershocks and landslides were linked to this earthquake.

Your key question

How do plate tectonics shape our world?

Think about... how can tectonic movement be hazardous?

Causes of the 2015 earthquake

Nepal is a mountainous country in the Himalayas. It is a **low-income developing country (LIDC)** (Figure 1). Geoscientists knew pressure was building up along the collision plate boundary in this area, but couldn't predict when the earthquake would happen.

On 25 April a magnitude 7.8 earthquake struck Nepal with no warning. The shallow earthquake had a focus 15 km below the surface and the fault line ran right under the capital city of Katmandu.

Aftershocks and landslides

The earthquake was followed by a large number of aftershocks, including one of a magnitude of 7.3 on 12 May. Steep slopes became unstable, leading to landslides – a landslide on 15 May flattened a village. Landslides blocked main roads, making it hard to reach areas affected by the earthquake. In all, 547 landslides were linked to the earthquake.

Total population	30 million
Population of Kathmandu	1.183 million
Population in rural areas	81.4%
GNI/capita (see spread 6.3)	$730
Percentage below the poverty line	25.2%
Average life expectancy	68 years
Literacy rate	64%

Figure 1 *Nepal factfile*

Figure 2 *Nepal Epicentre and aftershocks of the 2015 earthquake in Nepal*

Six Second Summary

- Nepal is an LIDC and was not prepared to deal with a major earthquake.
- Pressure which had been building up at a collision plate boundary was released as a 7.8 earthquake.
- The earthquake was followed by many aftershocks and 547 landslides.

Over to you

Outline the cause of the 2015 Nepal earthquake.

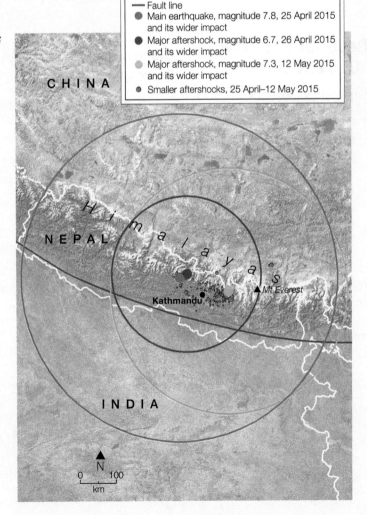

Key
— Fault line
● Main earthquake, magnitude 7.8, 25 April 2015 and its wider impact
● Major aftershock, magnitude 6.7, 26 April 2015 and its wider impact
● Major aftershock, magnitude 7.3, 12 May 2015 and its wider impact
● Smaller aftershocks, 25 April–12 May 2015

CHINA

Himalayas

NEPAL

Mt Everest

Kathmandu

INDIA

N
0   100
km

You need to know:
- the consequences of the 2015 earthquake in Nepal
- what the responses to the earthquake were.

Your key question

How do plate tectonics shape our world?

Think about... how can tectonic movement be hazardous?

Case Study

Consequences of the 2015 earthquake

Nepal, an LIDC, was badly affected by this large earthquake. Many poorly built buildings were destroyed which trapped and killed many people.

Primary consequences happened whilst the ground was still shaking, including buildings falling down, death and injury. **Secondary consequences** followed, including homelessness and lack of services (Figure 1).

Primary consequences

8635 people were killed.

19 009 people were injured.

Over 180 buildings were reduced to rubble in Kathmandu.

Historical and religious buildings were destroyed.

$10 billion of damage was caused.

Primary/Secondary consequences

Landslides in the mountains buried houses and cut off roads.

Secondary consequences

Thousands of homeless people had to sleep outside.

Schools, health facilities and government offices had to close.

People in Kathmandu struggled to return to their families in rural areas.

Landslides in the mountains buried houses and cut off roads.

Aftershocks threatened to destroy weakened buildings.

Figure 1 *Primary and secondary consequences of the earthquake*

Responses to the 2015 earthquake

Emergency aid included:

- **Non-governmental organisations (NGOs)** helped to support the injured and homeless.
- India quickly provided aid including 10 tonnes of blankets, 50 tonnes of water and 22 tonnes of food.

Long-term aid followed, including 'cash for work' projects which paid survivors to work on projects in their own communities.

One month after the earthquake people reflected on the responses

Less than 10% of the money spent on relief has come from overseas. I would like future international donations to be managed by my government. (*Nepal's Finance Minister*)

We have provided relief materials, services and goods. We don't give money to governments as they may be corrupt. (*International aid worker*)

There is a danger that children could be taken by traffickers. We need to keep an eye on children. (*Save the Children*)

The British Government has pledged £33m to help Nepal. £10m of this will be spent on primary health care and rebuilding hospitals. (*UK politician*)

We have provided food for 1.8 million people. This is one of our most complex operations because of the difficult terrain. (*World Food Programme*)

Six Second Summary

- Primary consequences included 8635 deaths and 19 009 injured.
- Secondary consequences included thousands of homeless people.
- Emergency aid such as food, water, shelter and medical help was provided by NGOs and countries such as India.

Over to you

What challenges faced those responding to the 2015 earthquake in Nepal?

You need to know:

- how building design can reduce earthquake damage
- how prediction and warning systems can reduce earthquake damage.

Your key question

How do plate tectonics shape our world?

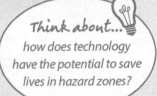

Think about...
how does technology have the potential to save lives in hazard zones?

Building to survive

If buildings are carefully designed, people inside stand a better chance of surviving an earthquake. Simple designs can be used to make buildings in LIDCs 'life safe' (Figure 1).

In **advanced countries (ACs)** 'earthquake proof' buildings minimise damage (Figure 2). Reducing damage in this way is called **mitigation**.

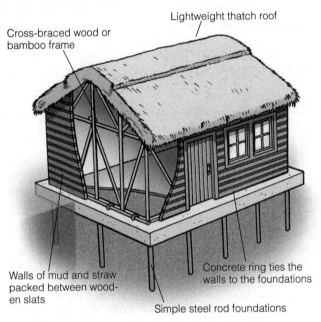

Cross-braced wood or bamboo frame

Lightweight thatch roof

Walls of mud and straw packed between wooden slats

Concrete ring ties the walls to the foundations

Simple steel rod foundations

Figure 1 Life-safe simple building design

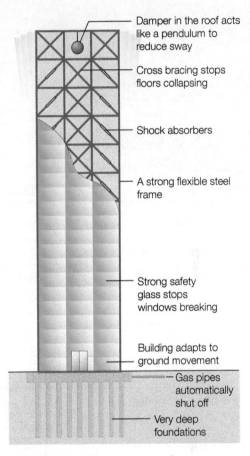

Damper in the roof acts like a pendulum to reduce sway

Cross bracing stops floors collapsing

Shock absorbers

A strong flexible steel frame

Strong safety glass stops windows breaking

Building adapts to ground movement

Gas pipes automatically shut off

Very deep foundations

Figure 2 Building to survive future earthquakes

Prediction and warning systems

Seismologists can't accurately predict earthquakes, but they can look for **seismic gaps**. Areas where there have been no earthquakes for a long time, and where pressure is likely to be building.

Once seismic waves start, 30-second warnings can be sent out.

It is vital that people are prepared by taking part in regular drills and carrying 'go bags'. These include, for example, first aid kit, food, water, torch, batteries, mobile phone, wind up radio, medicines, blankets, whistle and face mask.

Six Second Summary

- Life-safe buildings can be built in LIDCs using light roofing materials and firm foundations.
- ACs have the money to build very strong buildings to minimise damage.
- It is difficult to predict earthquakes and warn people, so it is important to carry out drills and carry 'go bags'.

Over to you

How can technology help to reduce earthquake damage in LIDCs?

Topic 2:
Changing Climate

Your exam

Changing Climate is part of Paper 1: Our Natural World. It is a 1 hr 15 min written exam and makes up 35% of your GCSE. The whole paper carries 70 marks (including 3 marks for SPaG).

There are two sections on the paper:

- Section A: questions on all the physical geography topics, including *Changing Climate*

- Section B: physical geography fieldwork.

You will have to answer all questions on the paper.

Tick these boxes to build a record of your revision

Your revision checklist

Spec key question	Theme	1	2	3
What evidence is there to suggest climate change is a natural process?				
What evidence is there for climate change?	2.1 Earth's changing climate			
	2.2 Evidence of climate change – 1			
	2.3 Evidence of climate change – 2			
Is climate change a natural process?	2.4 Natural causes of climate change			
	2.5 Human causes of climate change – 1			
	2.6 Human causes of climate change – 2			
Why is climate change a global issue?	2.7 Global impacts of climate change – 1			
	2.8 Global impacts of climate change – 2			
	2.9 Global impacts of climate change – 3			
	2.10 Impacts of climate change for the UK – 1			
	2.11 Impacts of climate change for the UK – 2			
Fieldwork skills	2.12 Climate change fieldwork			

You need to know:

- what the Quaternary period is
- how Earth's climate has changed during the Quaternary period.

Your key question

What evidence is there to suggest climate change is a natural process?

Think about... what evidence is there for climate change?

The Quaternary Ice Age

Earth is currently in the Quaternary period, which has lasted 2.6 million years. The Quaternary period is an **ice age** – an ice age is defined as any period of time when Earth has permanent ice sheets. Ice ages have very cold **glacial periods** that last for about 100 000 years, and warmer **interglacial** periods that last for about 10 000 years.

Earth's climate during the Quaternary period

Earth's temperature has mostly been colder than it is today but has fluctuated (gone up and down) a lot (Figure 1).

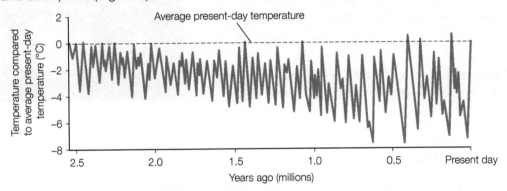

Figure 1 *Earth's temperature in the Quaternary Period*

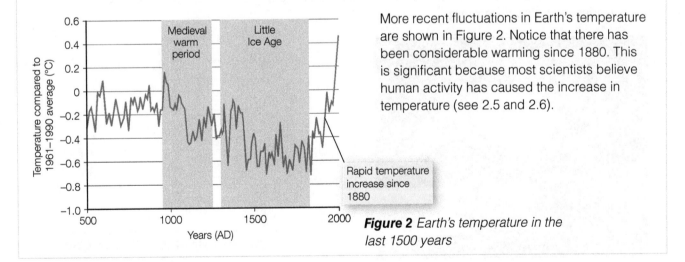

Figure 2 *Earth's temperature in the last 1500 years*

More recent fluctuations in Earth's temperature are shown in Figure 2. Notice that there has been considerable warming since 1880. This is significant because most scientists believe human activity has caused the increase in temperature (see 2.5 and 2.6).

Six Second Summary

- The Quaternary Period is the last 2.6 million years.
- Earth's climate has fluctuated in the Quaternary period but has mostly been colder than today.
- Earth's climate has warmed quickly since 1880.

Over to you

Study Figure 2. Write three or four sentences to describe the changes in Earth's temperature since AD 500.

You need to know:

- how ice cores and sea ice positions provide evidence of climate change
- whether this evidence is reliable.

Your key question

What evidence is there to suggest climate change is a natural process?

Think about...

what evidence is there for climate change?

Ice cores

Ice cores are long tubes of ice removed from the Arctic and Antarctic (Figure 1). Scientists study the gases trapped in each layer; lots of **carbon dioxide (CO_2)** means Earth's temperature was warmer that year.

- Ice cores provide climate evidence from up to 800 000 years ago.
- Each layer in the ice core is snow that fell in a particular year.
- Trapped in this snow is information about the climate.

Ice cores have been proved to be an accurate and reliable source of evidence because recent ice has been compared with other types of data, such as recorded temperatures.

Figure 1 *An ice core showing the different layers of ice; lighter colours are summer snow, darker colours are winter snow*

Sea ice positions

Satellite photos show the amount of the Arctic that is covered in frozen sea ice. The amount of sea ice varies throughout the year; the minimum amount is in September and the maximum is in March. Satellite photos show that the sea ice minimum is getting smaller. Scientists believe this is evidence of **global warming**.

Key

Average sea ice minimum, 1979–2012

Figure 2 *The sea ice minimum in September 2012*

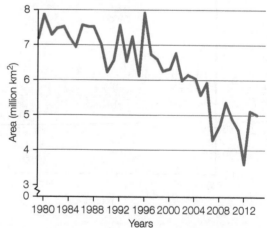

Figure 3 *The area in the Arctic covered by sea ice in September 1979–2014*

 Six Second Summary

- Gases trapped in ice cores give evidence of Earth's climate up to 800 000 years ago.
- Satellite photos of Arctic sea ice positions show the amount of Artic sea ice is getting smaller.

 Over to you

Write out an explanation of how ice cores provide evidence of climate change. Name specific gases in your explanation.

You need to know:

- how global temperature data provides evidence of climate change
- whether evidence from paintings and diaries is reliable.

Your key question

What evidence is there to suggest climate change is a natural process?

Think about...
what evidence is there for climate change?

Global temperature data

Weather stations record daily temperatures, allowing scientists to monitor the average global temperature each year. Records show Earth's climate is getting hotter. Nine of the ten hottest years since 1880 have been since 2002 (Figure 1).

Temperature data is reliable today, but data in the past was not collected with accurate equipment. The positioning of recording instruments (e.g. at the top of a hill) might also give misleading records of an area's real temperature.

Rank	Year	°C warmer than the average of all years
1	2014	0.69
2	2010	0.65
2	2005	0.65
4	1998	0.63
5	2013	0.62
5	2003	0.62
7	2002	0.61
8	2006	0.60
9	2009	0.59
9	2007	0.59

Figure 1 *Top ten hottest years, 1880–2014*

Evidence in paintings and diaries

Old paintings and diaries can give evidence of Earth's climate before temperature data was collected. We know London held a number of 'frost fairs' on the frozen River Thames between 1309 and 1814 from evidence of paintings and diary entries (Figure 2).

But paintings and diaries are not particularly reliable. They give evidence of day-to-day weather rather than Earth's climate. They are also just one person's interpretation of the weather.

Figure 2 *A 'frost fair' on the Thames at Temple Stairs, painted by Abraham Honduis, 1684*

Six Second Summary

- Global temperature data gives reliable evidence that Earth's climate is getting warmer.
- Old paintings and diaries give us unreliable evidence of periods of colder and hotter weather many years ago.

Over to you

Give one advantage and one disadvantage of using:

a global temperature data
b paintings and diaries

as evidence of climate change.

You need to know:

- how natural events like Milankovitch cycles, sun spots, and volcanic eruptions cause climate change.

Your key question

What evidence is there to suggest climate change is a natural process?

Think about...
is climate change a natural process?

Earth's climate changed many times before humans were alive. There are three main reasons for this: Milankovitch cycles, sun spots and volcanic eruptions.

1 Milankovitch cycles

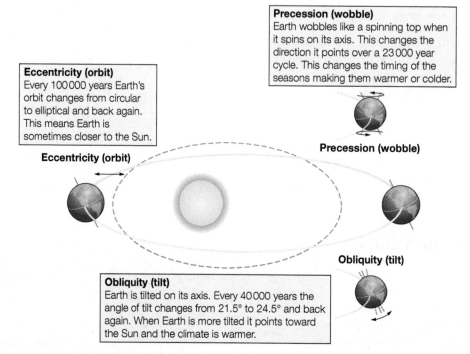

Precession (wobble)
Earth wobbles like a spinning top when it spins on its axis. This changes the direction it points over a 23 000 year cycle. This changes the timing of the seasons making them warmer or colder.

Eccentricity (orbit)
Every 100 000 years Earth's orbit changes from circular to elliptical and back again. This means Earth is sometimes closer to the Sun.

Precession (wobble)

Eccentricity (orbit)

Obliquity (tilt)

Obliquity (tilt)
Earth is tilted on its axis. Every 40 000 years the angle of tilt changes from 21.5° to 24.5° and back again. When Earth is more tilted it points toward the Sun and the climate is warmer.

Figure 1 *The Milankovitch cycles*

2 Sun spots

Magnetic storms cause temporary dark **sun spots** to form on the Sun. These give out more energy which warms Earth's climate. There is an 11-year cycle of sun spot activity moving from many to few sun spots and back again.

3 Volcanic eruptions

When volcanoes erupt they release huge amounts of dust containing things like ash and sulphur dioxide. If the volcano is large enough the dust will block enough of the Sun's energy to cool Earth's climate.

Six Second Summary

- Milankovitch cycles change Earth's distance from the Sun.
- Sun spots increase the amount of energy Earth receives.
- Volcanic eruptions block the Sun's energy.

Over to you

Try to summarise how Milankovitch cycles affect the Earth's climate in 25 words or less.

You need to know:

- the impacts that humans have on the atmosphere
- what the natural greenhouse effect is
- how humans have enhanced the greenhouse effect.

Your key question

What evidence is there to suggest climate change is a natural process?

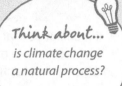

Think about...

is climate change a natural process?

The natural greenhouse effect

Naturally occurring gases like carbon dioxide and water vapour are called **greenhouse gases**. These gases act like the glass in a greenhouse and trap **radiation** (heat) from the Sun. Without these gases, radiation would reflect back out to space and Earth would be too cold for life to exist.

The enhanced greenhouse effect

Humans have added more greenhouse gases to the atmosphere. This means that more radiation is trapped and causes global warming. This is called the **enhanced greenhouse effect**.

Figure 1 *A greenhouse traps the Sun's heat*

Greenhouse gases

The main greenhouse gas causing the enhanced greenhouse effect is carbon dioxide (CO_2). This accounts for 60% of the enhanced greenhouse effect. It comes from things like cars and burning fossil fuels like coal to make electricity.

Other important greenhouse gases are:

- methane – from landfill sites and cows
- halocarbons – from refrigerators and air conditioning
- nitrous oxide – from fertilisers and car exhausts.

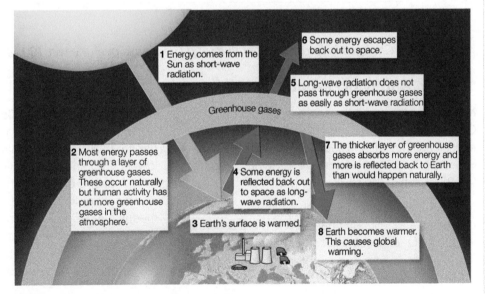

1 Energy comes from the Sun as short-wave radiation.

2 Most energy passes through a layer of greenhouse gases. These occur naturally but human activity has put more greenhouse gases in the atmosphere.

3 Earth's surface is warmed.

4 Some energy is reflected back out to space as long-wave radiation.

Greenhouse gases

5 Long-wave radiation does not pass through greenhouse gases as easily as short-wave radiation

6 Some energy escapes back out to space.

7 The thicker layer of greenhouse gases absorbs more energy and more is reflected back to Earth than would happen naturally.

8 Earth becomes warmer. This causes global warming.

Figure 2 *The enhanced greenhouse effect*

Six Second Summary

- Greenhouse gases occur naturally and trap radiation (heat) from the Sun.
- Human activity has put more greenhouse gases in the atmosphere trapping more radiation.
- The most significant greenhouse gas in carbon dioxide.

Over to you

Study Figure 2, focusing on the order of events in the enhanced greenhouse effect. Close the book and try to draw Figure 2 from memory.

You need to know:

- the countries that emit the most carbon dioxide
- why the lifestyle of people in advanced countries causes climate change.

Your key question

What evidence is there to suggest climate change is a natural process?

Think about...
is climate change
a natural process?

Carbon dioxide emissions and Earth's temperature

Look at Figure 1. The graph shows a clear link between the amount of CO_2 in the atmosphere and average global temperatures. Humans putting more CO_2 in the atmosphere is an important cause of climate change.

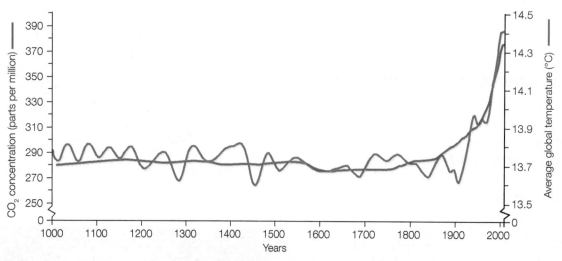

Figure 1 *Changes in Earth's temperature and CO_2 levels over the last 100 years*

The geography of carbon dioxide

Not all countries emit the same amount of CO_2. China emits the most – about 28% of global CO_2 emissions. The USA is second with about 15%. However, 1.4 billion people live in China compared to 320 million in the USA.

If we want to think about which countries are most responsible for climate change, it is more sensible to study CO_2 emissions per capita (per person).

Advanced countries (ACs), like the USA, Canada and Australia, emit the highest amount of CO_2 per capita. LIDCs, like Ethiopia and Rwanda, emit the lowest. People in ACs have lifestyles that use a lot of fuel and energy in things like cars, heating, electrical appliances and the food we eat. This means that ACs put the most greenhouse gases into the atmosphere per person.

Six Second Summary

- There is a strong link between rising global temperatures and the rising amounts of carbon dioxide (CO_2) in the atmosphere.
- China emits more CO_2 than any other country.
- The high energy lifestyle in ACs means they emit the most CO_2 per capita.

Over to you

List three reasons why advanced countries are to blame for the increased CO_2 in the atmosphere.

You need to know:

- a range of global social, economic and environmental impacts of climate change
- why climate change causes sea levels to rise and more extreme weather events.

Your key question

What evidence is there to suggest climate change is a natural process?

Think about...

why is climate change a global issue?

Rising sea levels

Climate change is making sea levels rise for three reasons.

- **Thermal expansion** – warmer water expands making sea levels rise.
- **Melting glaciers** – as glaciers melt more water is added to the oceans.
- **Melting ice caps** – as the ice in the Arctic and Antarctic melts more water is added to oceans.

Rising sea levels will flood low lying coastal areas, such as the Maldives in the Indian Ocean. In 2009 their government met under water to draw attention to rising sea levels (Figure 1).

The Maldives are affected in a number of ways.

- **Social**: People will have to move because of flooding (**climate change refugees**). More acidic sea water threatens fish numbers and food supplies.
- **Economic**: The cost of moving people and building flood defences. Jobs will be lost in the tourist industry.
- **Environmental**: Flooding destroys ecosystems. The sea water becomes more acidic because warm water absorbs more carbon dioxide.

Figure 1 *The Maldivian government meet under water in 2009*

Extreme weather

- Warmer oceans are making tropical storms more frequent and more severe.
- Higher global temperatures are making droughts and heatwaves more common. Recent weather events like Typhoon Haiyan in 2013 and heatwaves in Europe might be linked to climate change.
- Flooding and extreme weather is forcing people to move and become climate change refugees.

 Six Second Summary

- Climate change is causing sea levels to rise.
- There are social, economic and environmental impacts of rising sea levels.
- An increase in extreme weather events is linked to climate change.

 Over to you

Write two or three sentences that link social, economic and environmental effects of climate change in the Maldives.

You need to know:
- how climate change threatens food supplies
- how climate change is causing water shortages.

Your key question

What evidence is there to suggest climate change is a natural process?

Think about...
why is climate change a global issue?

Food supply

Climate changes (warmer temperatures, extreme weather and changing rainfall patterns) are affecting the amount of food that can be grown.

- Some parts of the world like Russia will be able to grow more food, but overall the amount of food grown worldwide will decrease.
- Crop **yields** (the amount of food grown per hectare) will be 22% lower in sub-Saharan Africa by 2050.
- In Vietnam, a reduction in rice production due to flooding may affect 1 million people and cost $17 billion.

Water shortages

Climate change will cause water shortages. 1 billion people might not have enough water by 2050. Warmer temperatures cause water shortages because:

- some areas have less rainfall
- some areas have very heavy rainfall which runs more quickly into oceans
- melting glaciers put freshwater stores into the oceans
- more freshwater evaporates.

Lake Chad is disappearing due to climate change – 30 million people rely on it for water. This has social, economic, and environmental effects (Figures 1 and 2).

Economic effects: less food and fish to sell meaning lower incomes.

Social effects: less drinking water; less water for crops meaning food production decreases; fewer fish; conflict between people over water.

Environmental effects: species die as lake habitat shrinks.

Figure 1 *Lake Chad in 1972*

Figure 2 *Lake Chad in 2007*

Six Second Summary

- Warmer temperatures are changing crop growing patterns and creating food supply shortages.
- Warmer temperatures are leading to water shortages.

Over to you

Learn one statistic about food shortages and one statistic about water shortages.

You need to know:

- how climate change threatens the survival of some species
- why climate change causes diseases that threaten human health.

Your key question

What evidence is there to suggest climate change is a natural process?

Think about...
why is climate change a global issue?

Plants and animals

Environmental impacts, such as warmer temperatures and changing rainfall patterns, mean the conditions that plant and animal species need to survive are changed, e.g. polar bears.

- Melting ice in the Arctic means they have to swim further for food.
- Declining seal populations also means there is less food available.
- Lack of food means polar bears do not produce as many cubs which threatens their survival.

Figure 1 *Reduced sea ice and declining seal populations are threatening polar bears*

Disease, health and food supplies

A **social impact** of climate change is an increase in the number of infectious diseases.

- Warmer temperatures mean insects like mosquitoes live longer and survive in parts of the world that used to be too cold for them (e.g. Europe).
- Increased flooding means diseases are spread in dirty water (Figure 2).

In Ethiopia coffee crops are threatened by the coffee berry borer beetle, which is thriving in the warmer temperatures. This has an **economic impact** because 700 000 people depend on coffee for their income.

Cholera

Typhoid

Hepatitis A

Dysentery

Figure 2 *Flooding causes water to be contaminated by human and industrial waste leading to disease*

Six Second Summary

- Some plants and animals are threatened with extinction due to warmer temperatures.
- The areas affected by diseases spread by insects and in polluted water will increase with climate change.

Over to you

Read this page again and make a note of all the places or regions of the world mentioned. List the effects of climate change on these places.

- a range of social, economic and environmental impacts of climate change on the UK
- the effects of rising sea levels, flooding and extreme weather on the UK.

What evidence is there to suggest climate change is a natural process?

Think about... why is climate change a global issue?

The UK's changing climate

The UK's climate is changing. Figures 1, 2 and 3 show the **environmental impacts** on the UK by 2050.

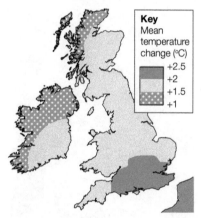

Key
Mean temperature change (°C)
+2.5
+2
+1.5
+1

Figure 1 *Average temperatures are expected to increase by 2050*

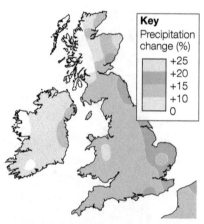

Key
Precipitation change (%)
+25
+20
+15
+10
0

Figure 2 *Winters are expected to be warmer and wetter by 2050*

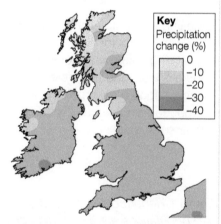

Key
Precipitation change (%)
0
–10
–20
–30
–40

Figure 3 *Summers are expected to be warmer and drier by 2050*

Coastal flooding

Rising sea levels mean many coastal areas are threatened with flooding. Flooding is an environmental impact that will cause economic and social impacts.

- Agriculture, manufacturing industry and infrastructure in coastal areas will be damaged. £120 billion of infrastructure is at risk (economic).
- More money will need to spent on coastal defences (economic).
- People will be forced to move and lose their jobs (social).

Extreme rainfall

More rainfall is expected in most parts of the UK. This will increase the number and severity of river floods. In July 2007, Tewkesbury had two months of rain in 14 hours. This had a range of impacts.

- 13 people died (social).
- 135 000 people had no water for 17 days (social).
- The flood cost local councils £140 million and the UK economy £32 billion (economic).
- Breeding grounds of lapwing and redshank birds were flooded (environmental).

Six Second Summary

- The UK will be warmer all year round with wetter winters and dryer summers.
- Rising sea levels will threaten coastal areas with flooding.
- Extreme rainfall will cause more river flooding.

Over to you

Draw a quick sketch of Great Britain and label how the climate will change by 2050.

You need to know:

- the problems and benefits of warmer temperatures.

Your key question

What evidence is there to suggest climate change is a natural process?

Think about...

why is climate change a global issue?

Problems with extreme heat

The UK will experience more extreme heat. This is an environmental impact that, in turn, leads to social and economic impacts:

- More people will die: the elderly and asthma sufferers will be particularly vulnerable. More bacteria will breed on food. By 2050 there will be an extra 9000 cases of illness caused by salmonella (social).
- More heat means more evaporation which, along with less rainfall, will lead to water shortages. This means there will be more hosepipe bans, less water for power stations and industry, and less water for growing crops (economic).

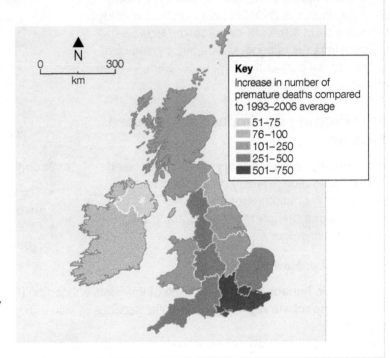

Key

Increase in number of premature deaths compared to 1993–2006 average

- 51–75
- 76–100
- 101–250
- 251–500
- 501–750

Figure 1 *Projected increases in early deaths in the 2050s compared to 1993–2006 average*

The benefits of warmer temperatures

The UK's climate is expected to be 1 °C–2.5 °C warmer by 2050. This can bring benefits.

- Fewer deaths due to cold (social).
- A better climate for tourism. An increase in tourism is good for the economy because more money is spent on things like hotels and days out (economic).
- Growing seasons will be longer, so more food may be able to be grown. Farmers will also be able to grow new types of crops, like olives and melons. The wine industry is benefiting from warmer temperatures (economic).

Figure 2 *Tourism will benefit from a better climate; a crowded UK beach in 2013*

 Six Second Summary

- There will be more heat-related deaths and disease, and also water shortages.
- Tourism and the wine industry will benefit from warmer temperatures.
- Possible increase in food production due to longer growing season.

 Over to you

Talk for one minute about the problems and benefits of warmer temperatures in the UK.

You need to know:

- the types of climate change issues that can be studied in the field
- a range of fieldwork methods.

Climate change and fieldwork

Many impacts of climate change, such as sea level rise or plant species change, happen over a long period of time. It is, therefore, not practical to study through a short fieldwork investigation. However, potential impacts of flooding, whether by sea level rise or coastal or river flooding, is an example of an issue that could be studied.

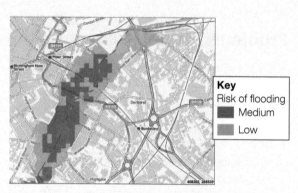

Figure 1 *Flood risk in central Birmingham*

Investigating the impact of increased flooding

Both **primary** and **secondary** data can be used in an investigation. Primary data is information you collect yourself through things like questionnaires. Secondary data is information collected by someone else.

Secondary data sources

- The Environment Agency has an interactive flood map identifying areas at risk (Figure 1).
- Online census data can help you understand the types of problems areas might face.

Primary data fieldwork activities

- **Economic impact survey**: Calculate of the costs of flooding (Figure 2)
- **Social impact survey**: Identify essential services at risk, e.g. hospitals, fire stations.
- **Annotated sketch/photo:** Annotate potential impacts on a sketch/photo.
- **Questionnaire:** Ask local people how they might be affected by flooding.
- **Role play:** Consider how different people might be affected, e.g. a pensioner living alone.

To calculate the cost of flooding, multiply:
A by £20 000
B by £30 000
C by £40 000
D by £30 000.
Add these figures together to get a total cost.

Street name	(A) Number of small houses and ground-floor flats	(B) Number of medium houses	(C) Number of large houses	(D) Number of businesses	Estimated cost of flooding to houses (£)	Estimated cost of flooding to businesses (£)	Total cost of damage (£)
Church Street	90	10	5	5	1 800 000 + 300 000 + 200 000 = 2 300 000	150 000	2 450 000
Priory Lane	50	20	0	0	1 000 000 + 600 000 = 1 600 000	0	1 600 000

Figure 2 *Economic impact survey*

 Six Second Summary

- Many impacts of climate change are difficult to study in a short piece of fieldwork.
- The potential impact of flooding is an example of an issue that could be studied.
- There are a range of fieldwork methods available.

Over to you

Identify an area near you that might be at risk of flooding. Take two photos to illustrate a potential economic impact and a potential social impact.

Topic 3:
Distinctive Landscapes

Your exam

Distinctive Landscapes is part of Paper 1: Our Natural World. It is a 1 hr 15 min written exam and makes up 35% of your GCSE. The whole paper carries 70 marks (including 3 marks for SPaG).

There are two sections on the paper;

- Section A: questions on all the physical geography topics, including Distinctive Landscapes
- Section B: physical geography fieldwork.

You will have to answer all questions on the paper.

Tick these boxes to build a record of your revision

Your revision checklist

Spec key question	Theme	1	2	3
What makes a landscape distinctive?				
What is a landscape?	3.1 Landscapes of the UK			
Where are the physical landscapes of the UK?	3.2 Upland and lowland landscapes			
	3.3 Geology and landscape			
	3.4 Climate and landscape			
	3.5 Human activity and landscape			
What influences the landscapes of the UK?				
What physical processes shape landscapes?	3.6 Shaping landscapes			
	3.7 Coastal landforms			
	3.8 River landforms			
What are the characteristics of your chosen landscapes?	3.9 The Jurassic Coast			
	3.10 Battered coastline			
	3.11 Coastline management			
Fieldwork skills	3.12 Landscape fieldwork – 1			
	3.13 Landscape fieldwork – 2			
	3.14 The Thames Basin			
	3.15 Landforms along the Thames			
	3.16 Flooding on the Thames			
	3.17 Flood threat to London			

You need to know:
- what a landscape is
- the differences between natural and built landscapes.

Your key question
What makes a landscape distinctive?

Think about...
what is a landscape?

What is a landscape?

A **landscape** is the view of an area of land. You can find either natural landscapes or built landscapes, but most landscapes contain *both* natural and human features. These features interact with each other. For example, people plant trees or rivers can flood buildings.

Very few landscapes are completely natural or human. A mountain may look completely natural but people may have planted the forest growing on it. A city may have been built but it still has a river flowing through it.

Landscape elements

The main elements of all landscapes are:

- physical (e.g. mountains or valleys)
- water (e.g. rivers or lakes)
- living (e.g. trees or grass)
- transitory (temporary) (e.g. weather or seasons)
- human (e.g. buildings and other land uses).

The cottage belonged to a farmer, a neighbour of John Constable.

The scene was painted on a bright summer's day.

Grassland is used for gazing sheep or cattle.

Trees grow naturally along the river bank.

The River Stour flows along the border of Suffolk and Essex.

The flat **floodplain** of the river is formed by silt and clay when the river floods.

Figure 1 *You can find all the landscape elements in* The Hay Wain, *a painting by John Constable*

🕕 **Six Second Summary**

- A landscape is the view of an area of land.
- There are natural and built landscapes.
- Most landscapes have both natural and human features.

✏ **Over to you**

Either look at the painting in Figure 1 *or* choose another landscape to look at. It could be a painting, a photo or even the view out of your window! Identify an example of each landscape element in your landscape. Describe the natural and human features and think of ways they interact with each other.

You need to know:

- the distribution of upland and lowland areas of the UK
- which areas of the UK were glaciated
- how ice changed the landscape.

Your key question

What makes a landscape distinctive?

Think about...
where are the physical landscapes of the UK?

Uplands and lowlands in the UK

The UK can be divided into **upland** and **lowland** areas. Uplands are found to the north and west (Scotland, Wales and northern England). Lowlands are found to the south and east (the rest of England). An imaginary line from the Bristol Channel to Flamborough Head in Yorkshire, divides the UK into uplands and lowlands (Figure 1).

How did glaciation change the UK landscape?

During the 2.6 million years of the current Quaternary Period, much of the UK has gone through several ice ages (periods of **glaciation** when it has been covered in ice) and warmer, interglacial periods.

Glaciation changed upland landscapes by:

- forming mountain peaks and ridges
- carving deep **U-shaped valleys**.

It also affected lowland landscapes by:

- freezing the ground and creating river valleys
- leaving behind **dry valleys** when the ice melted.

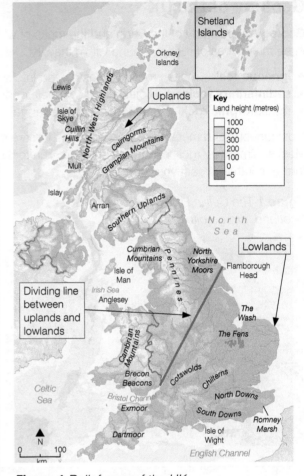

Figure 1 *Relief map of the UK*

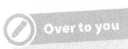
Six Second Summary

- The UK is divided into upland and lowland areas.
- Much of the UK has been glaciated during the Quaternary Period.
- Ice changed upland and lowland landscapes.

Over to you

On a blank map of the UK, draw lines to:

- divide the UK into upland and lowland areas
- show the limit of maximum glaciation

Then, annotate your map to describe the landscape in each area.

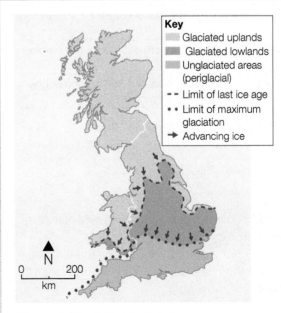

Figure 2 *Glaciation in Britain*

You need to know:
- the types of rock that make the land
- how rocks influence landscape.

Your key question
What makes a landscape distinctive?

Think about...
where are the physical landscapes of the UK?

Geology of the UK

Geology is the study of the Earth and the rocks of which it is made. There are three main types of rock, all found within the UK:

- **igneous rock** – molten rock that has cooled into solid rock made of crystals
- **sedimentary rock** – particles of rock or shell, deposited in layers
- **metamorphic rock** – rock that has been changed by heat or pressure.

Most igneous and metamorphic rocks in the UK are found in Scotland and Wales. Most sedimentary rock is found in England. The rocks tend to be younger, the further south and east you go.

Figure 1 *The Cuillin Hills on the Isle of Skye, Scotland, are granite*

Figure 2 *The South Downs in Sussex, England, are chalk*

Feature	Granite (Figure 1; The Cuillin Hills)	Chalk (Figure 2; The South Downs)
Formation	Igneous rock formed when molten rock cools slowly below the Earth's surface.	Sedimentary rock formed from layers of sea creatures that sink to the seabed.
Composition	Large crystals of different colour minerals.	Small particles of shells made from calcium carbonate.
Properties	A hard, impermeable rock that weathers and erodes slowly.	A soft, permeable rock that weathers and erodes easily.
Soils and farming	Forms infertile soil that is often boggy and no good for growing crops.	Forms fertile soil that is well-drained and good for growing grass and crops.

Figure 3 *Comparing granite and chalk*

 Six Second Summary

- The UK is made from igneous, sedimentary and metamorphic rock.
- Geology has a strong influence on the landscape.
- Granite and chalk are two rocks found in the UK with distinctive landscapes.

 **Over to you**

Draw quick sketches of the two photos in Figures 1 and 2. Annotate features of the two landscapes that help you to recognise they are made from granite and chalk.

You need to know:
- types of weathering and how they happen
- the influence of climate on the landscape.

Your key question
What makes a landscape distinctive?

Think about...
where are the physical landscapes of the UK?

Types of weathering

Weathering is the breakup of rocks, often due to the weather. Weathered rock may then be removed by erosion. Together, weathering and erosion slowly change the landscape. There are three main types of weathering:

- **mechanical weathering** – temperature changes cause rocks to break up, e.g. freeze-thaw weathering (Figure 1)
- **chemical weathering** – decomposition of rock, often caused by rainwater, e.g. dissolving (solution) of limestone
- **biological weathering** – breakup of rock due to the action of plants or animals.

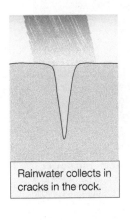

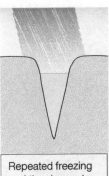
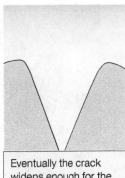

Rainwater collects in cracks in the rock.

When temperatures fall, the water freezes and expands to form ice.

Repeated freezing and thawing makes the crack bigger.

Eventually the crack widens enough for the rock to split apart.

Figure 1 *Freeze-thaw weathering*

Climate and weathering in the UK

The UK has a moderate climate, with not much extreme weather, so weathering usually happens slowly. The parts of the UK that experience most weathering are those with higher rainfall or more extreme temperatures (Figure 2).

Six Second Summary

- Rocks are broken up by mechanical, chemical and biological weathering.
- Variations in weather and climate in the UK influence the landscape.
- More weathering occurs in areas with higher rainfall or extreme temperature.

Over to you

For each segment of the UK shown on the map in Figure 2, say how likely it is that weathering will occur, and why.

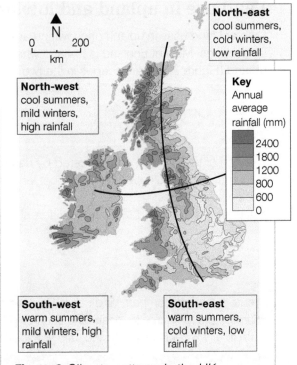

North-east
cool summers, cold winters, low rainfall

North-west
cool summers, mild winters, high rainfall

0 — 200 km

N

Key
Annual average rainfall (mm)

2400
1800
1200
800
600
0

South-west
warm summers, mild winters, high rainfall

South-east
warm summers, cold winters, low rainfall

Figure 2 *Climate patterns in the UK*

You need to know:
- the impact of human activities on the natural landscape
- the different land uses of upland and lowland areas.

Your key question
What makes a landscape distinctive?

Think about...
where are the physical landscapes of the UK?

Human activities in the landscape

Most of us live in towns and cities. It is obvious how people have changed the natural landscape here. But, even landscapes that appear natural have been changed (Figure 1).

Most of the natural woodland that once covered much of the UK was chopped down hundreds of years ago. New woodland has been planted in the past 100 years.

Wind farms are built on hill tops exposed to the wind.

Tourism is popular in upland areas. Tourists do activities like hill walking.

Forestry: Coniferous trees grow on better, well-drained land.

Farming: Sheep are grazed on hillsides and crops grown in valley bottoms.

Hunting: Poor quality land can be used to rear deer or grouse.

Hydro-electric power is generated by building a dam to create a reservoir.

Figure 1 Human activities in an upland area of the UK

Land use in upland and lowland areas

Different land uses in upland and lowland areas create distinctive landscapes. Most of England is lowland while most of Scotland is upland (Figure 2), so landscapes in the two countries differ.

Six Second Summary

- Much of the UK was once covered by natural woodland.
- Human activities have changed most landscapes in the UK.
- Upland and lowland areas have different land uses.

Over to you

Create a table to compare land use in England and Scotland. Estimate the % figures for each land use from Figure 2. Write them in a two columns like this to help you to learn them.

Land use	England	Scotland
Deciduous woodland	7%	3%

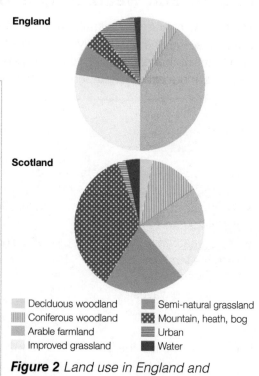

England

Scotland

- Deciduous woodland
- Coniferous woodland
- Arable farmland
- Improved grassland
- Semi-natural grassland
- Mountain, heath, bog
- Urban
- Water

Figure 2 Land use in England and Scotland

You need to know:
- the main agents of landscape change in the UK
- the physical processes involved in shaping the landscape.

Your key question
What influences the landscapes of the UK?

Think about...
what physical processes shape landscapes?

Landscape change in the UK

The UK landscape is constantly changing. There have been three main agents of change:

- **Rivers** flow on the land from their source to the sea.
- **Glaciers** once covered much of the country, like giant rivers of ice.
- **The sea** surrounds the coastline of the UK, making us an island.

Geomorphic processes

Similar physical processes happen in rivers, glaciers and at the coast, shaping the landscape (or geomorphology):

- **Erosion** wears away the land (Figure 1).
- **Transport** carries away the eroded material (see below).
- **Deposition** drops the transported material to build new land.

Erosion and **weathering** work together on steep slopes, leading to **mass movement**, such as landslides or land slumps.

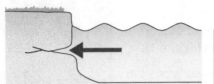
Hydraulic action: fast-flowing water or waves force air into cracks, splitting rock.

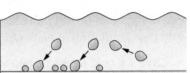
Attrition: pebbles bash into each other, wearing down into smaller, rounder particles.

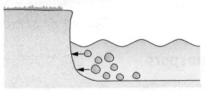
Abrasion: water picks up pebbles and smashes them against rock, wearing it away.

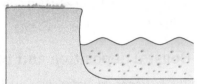
Solution: some rocks, like limestone, slowly dissolve in the water.

Figure 1 How rivers and waves erode the land

How rivers and waves transport material

- **Traction**: boulders and large stones are dragged along the river or seabed.
- **Saltation**: pebbles and small stones are picked up in water and dropped elsewhere.
- **Suspension**: tiny particles of sand and silt are carried by water.
- **Solution**: some rocks dissolve in water and are carried invisibly.

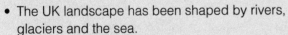
Six Second Summary

- The UK landscape has been shaped by rivers, glaciers and the sea.
- Erosion, transport and deposition are processes that change the landscape.
- Rivers and waves erode and transport material in similar ways.

Over to you

Create a glossary for geomorphic processes, or make individual revision cards for each process. Write a definition for all the processes highlighted on this page in bold.

You need to know:

- how geology can affect the shape of the coastline
- which landforms are created by coastal erosion, transport and deposition.

Your key question

What influences the landscapes of the UK?

Think about...
what physical processes shape landscapes?

The power of waves

The UK coastline is continually being shaped by the power of waves. The coastal landforms created depend on the type of rock, or geology.

- **Headlands** form where hard, more resistant rocks (e.g. granite) slowly erode.
- **Bays** form between headlands where soft, less resistant rock (e.g. clay) easily erodes.

Headland erosion

Headlands can go through stages of erosion, with new landforms at each stage (Figure 1).

- **Cave** – a hole formed when waves erode the base of the cliff.
- **Arch** – a gap formed when a cave wears all the way through a headland.
- **Stack** – a pillar of rock left in the sea when the roof of an arch collapses.

Figure 1 *Erosion of a headland*

Coastal deposition and transport

Waves transport material up the beach in the **swash** and back down again in the **backwash**.

Eroded material is then transported and deposited further along the coast (Figure 2).

- **Beach** – material, or sediment, deposited by waves.
- **Longshore drift** – movement of material along the beach due to the angle at which waves approach the coast.
- **Spit** – an extension of a beach across a bay or river mouth caused by longshore drift.

Figure 2 *Transport and deposition along the coast*

Six Second Summary

- Coastal landforms are influenced by geology.
- Headlands are eroded to form caves, arches and stacks.
- Longshore drift transports material along the coast and deposits it to form beaches and spits.

 Over to you

Draw a sketch of each of the two photos (Figures 1 and 2). Annotate your sketches to explain the formation of:

a a cave, an arch and a stack
b a beach and a spit. Draw an arrow to show the direction of longshore drift.

You need to know:

- the three stages of a river, from source to mouth
- the river landforms created by erosion and deposition.

Your key question

What influences the landscapes of the UK?

Think about...

what physical processes shape landscapes?

The stages of a river

As a river flows form source to mouth, it changes the shape of its valley by erosion and deposition, creating new landforms. The river itself also changes. A typical river goes through three stages – **upper**, **middle** and **lower** course (Figure 1).

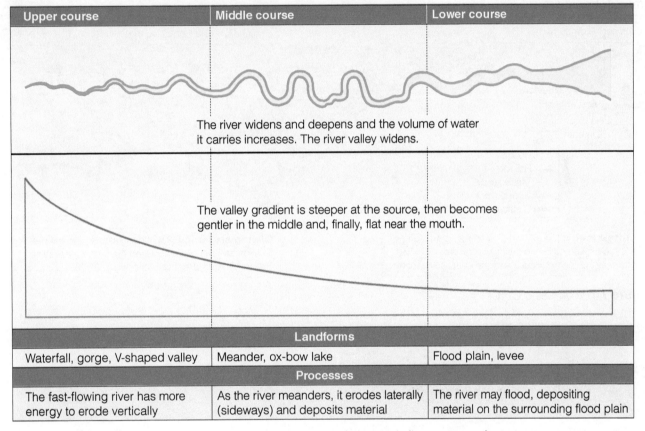

Upper course	Middle course	Lower course
	The river widens and deepens and the volume of water it carries increases. The river valley widens.	
	The valley gradient is steeper at the source, then becomes gentler in the middle and, finally, flat near the mouth.	

Landforms		
Waterfall, gorge, V-shaped valley	Meander, ox-bow lake	Flood plain, levee

Processes		
The fast-flowing river has more energy to erode vertically	As the river meanders, it erodes laterally (sideways) and deposits material	The river may flood, depositing material on the surrounding flood plain

Figure 1 *How a river changes from source (upper course) to mouth (lower course)*

 Six Second Summary

- Rivers go through three stages – an upper, middle and lower course.
- Rivers tend to erode in their upper course and deposit in their lower course.
- As a river flows from source to mouth, its valley shape and landforms change.

Over to you

Make your own table to summarise the changes that occur along the course of a river. You can lay your table out like this.

	Upper course	Middle course	Lower course
River (width, depth)			
Valley (width, gradient)			
Landforms			
Processes			

Case Study

You need to know:
- the location and landscape of the Jurassic Coast
- how geology has influenced the landscape
- some of the distinctive landforms along the coast.

Your key question
What influences the
landscapes of the UK?

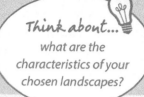
Think about...
*what are the
characteristics of your
chosen landscapes?*

Jurassic Coast

The Jurassic Coast stretches for 155 km along the south coast of England,
from Exmouth in Devon to Poole in Dorset. The coast is made of layers of
sedimentary rock which was formed millions of years ago (Figure 1).

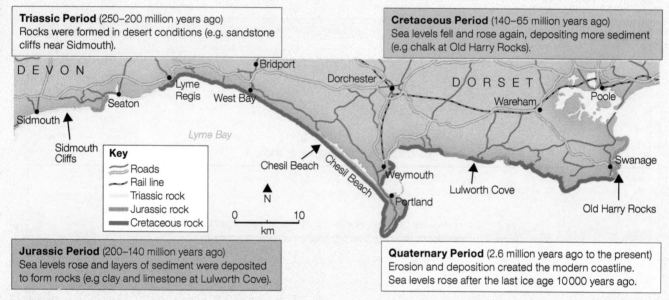

Triassic Period (250–200 million years ago)
Rocks were formed in desert conditions (e.g. sandstone
cliffs near Sidmouth).

Cretaceous Period (140–65 million years ago)
Sea levels fell and rose again, depositing more sediment
(e.g chalk at Old Harry Rocks).

Key
- Roads
- Rail line
- Triassic rock
- Jurassic rock
- Cretaceous rock

Jurassic Period (200–140 million years ago)
Sea levels rose and layers of sediment were deposited
to form rocks (e.g clay and limestone at Lulworth Cove).

Quaternary Period (2.6 million years ago to the present)
Erosion and deposition created the modern coastline.
Sea levels rose after the last ice age 10000 years ago.

Figure 1 *The Jurassic Coast*

Figure 2 *Lulworth Cove*

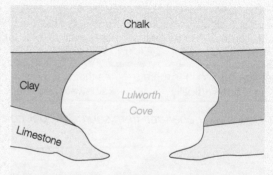

Figure 3 *Simple geological map of Lulworth Cove*

 Six Second Summary

- The Jurassic Coast is made of layers of
  sedimentary rock.
- The rocks date from the Triassic, Jurassic and
  Cretaceous geological periods.
- Erosion and deposition along the coast have
  created the landforms we see today.

 **Over to you**

Name four distinctive landforms along the
Jurassic coast. For each one say:

a whether it was formed by erosion or deposition
b which geological period it dates from
c what type of rock, or rocks, it is made of.

Case Study

The 2014 storm

A huge storm battered the Jurassic Coast of Devon and Dorset on 5 February, 2014. It had many impacts along the coast.

- The main railway line from Exeter to Plymouth was badly damaged at Dawlish and was closed for two months.
- Portland Bill, at the end of Chesil Beach, was cut off by floodwater and buildings were damaged.
- Cliffs at West Bay collapsed and the coastline retreated by a few metres.
- Lyme Regis was pounded by waves but coastal defences protected the town.

How climate change makes impacts worse

The storm could have been the result of climate change.

- Warming global temperatures lead to higher sea levels as ice sheets melt and seawater expands.
- A warmer atmosphere leads to more intense storms, which create larger, more powerful waves.
- More intense rainfall leads to greater weathering of cliffs, making rock falls and landslides happen more often.

The UK coastline

Climate change has an impact around the whole UK coast (Figure 1). The impact is greatest on coasts where cliffs are made of softer rocks or where low-lying land can flood.

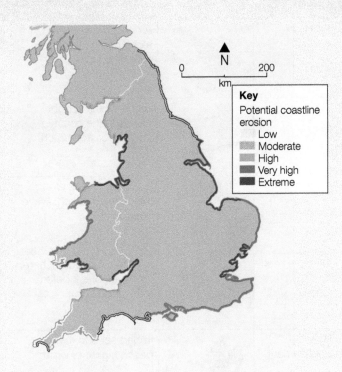

Figure 1 *Coastal erosion rates in England and Wales*

 **Six Second Summary**

- The Jurassic Coast was hit by a powerful storm on 5 February, 2014.
- The storm had damaging impacts at several places along the coast.
- Climate change could make the impact of storms worse around the UK coast.

Over to you

It is good to impress the examiner with your up-to-date knowledge. Do your own internet research into recent storms in the UK, since 2014. Find out:

a when did the storms happen?
b which stretches of coastline were affected?
c what damage was caused?

Case Study

You need to know:

- why coastlines need to be managed
- the engineering strategies used to manage the coast
- different shoreline management options

Your key question

What influences the landscapes of the UK?

Think about... what are the characteristics of your chosen landscape?

Coastal management strategies

Coastlines are managed to balance natural processes, such as erosion, against the need to protect people, property and infrastructure. Two types of strategy can be used (Figure 1):

- **hard engineering** works against natural processes
- **soft engineering** works with natural processes.

Shoreline management plans (SMPs)

Local councils are required to produce SMPs for their stretch of coastline. The main options are to:

- do nothing
- hold the line
- retreat the line
- advance the line.

Strategy	Drawing	Description	Advantage	Disadvantage
Sea wall		A concrete wall built along coast to protect cliffs or buildings	Protects against flooding	Expensive
Groynes		Barriers built at right angles to the coast to prevent loss of beach	Beach looks natural	Unattractive and prevents longshore drift
Rock armour		Boulders placed along the coast to absorb wave energy	Boulders are cheap	Unattractive
Offshore reef		Boulders placed offshore, so waves break before they reach coast	Beach looks natural	Difficult to maintain
Beach nourishment		Import sand to make beach higher or wider	Keeps beach natural	Requires maintenance
Managed retreat		Land is allowed to erode or flood naturally	Cheap and natural	Land and homes are lost

Figure 1 *Hard (red) and soft (green) coastal management strategies*

Six Second Summary

- Coastlines are managed to balance natural processes and the need to protect.
- They can be managed using hard- or soft-engineering strategies.
- Shoreline management plans are used to hold, retreat or advance the line, or to do nothing.

Over to you

Choose one place on the Jurassic Coast from Figure 1, 3.9. It could be a landform or a town. Decide on the best shoreline management plan and which engineering strategy you would use. You could choose more examples of coastal places to practice making decisions.

- how to plan a coastal fieldwork investigation
- the sort of questions you could investigate through fieldwork
- the methods you could use to carry out your investigation.

Planning a coastal fieldwork investigation

All fieldwork investigations, whether at the coast or not, should include these stages:

- Think of a suitable **question** or **hypothesis**.
- Choose the best **fieldwork methods** to help you to collect data to answer the question (Figure 1).
- **Process** and **present data**, including maps, graphs and diagrams.
- **Analyse** and **explain data** you have collected.
- **Draw conclusions**, using evidence, to answer the question.
- **Reflect** on the whole investigation and **evaluate** it.

The most important thing to remember when doing fieldwork, is to stay safe. To prepare for any fieldwork you should do a **risk assessment**.

Coastal fieldwork methods

- **Beach profile survey** – measure the gradient at different points along a beach.
- **Beach material survey** – measure shapes and sizes of material along a beach.
- **Wave survey** – measure the movement of pebbles along a beach.
- **Coastal management survey** – map management strategies used along the coast.
- **Cost/benefit analysis** – score the costs and benefits of different coastal strategies.

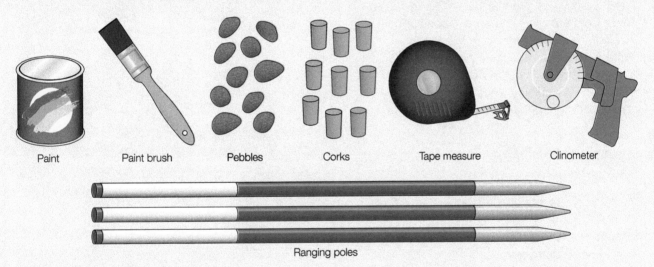

Paint   Paint brush   Pebbles   Corks   Tape measure   Clinometer

Ranging poles

Figure 1 Fieldwork equipment to use on a beach. How would you use each one?

- Fieldwork investigations should begin with a question or hypothesis.
- There are a range of fieldwork methods that can be used at the coast.
- Risk assessment is an important preparation for coastal fieldwork.

Plan a fieldwork investigation at the coast.

a Think of a question to investigate.
b Choose the fieldwork methods you could use.
c Suggest how you could use any of the fieldwork equipment in Figure 1.
d Write a risk assessment for any coastal fieldwork.

Fieldwork

You need to know:

- how to plan a river fieldwork investigation
- the sort of questions you could investigate through fieldwork
- the methods you could use to carry out your investigation.

Planning a river fieldwork investigation

There are good reasons for doing fieldwork on rivers (or coasts):

- You can see examples of geomorphic processes at work.
- There are opportunities for activities like measuring, counting and surveying.
- Rivers and coasts can both be fun – but you need to stay safe!

Not all rivers are suitable for fieldwork. Some factors to consider when choosing a river, or sites along a river, for fieldwork include:

- **the size of the river** – especially its width and depth
- **river flow** – not too fast, but not completely dry
- **land ownership** – so you can get access to the river.

River fieldwork methods

- **Channel survey** – measure the width and depth of the river at points along its length.
- **Flow survey** – measure the speed of water flowing along the channel.
- **River load survey** – measure shapes and sizes of the river's load along the channel.
- **Valley slope survey** – measure the gradient of the valley sides along the river.
- **Water quality survey** – assess water quality by counting living things in the water.

🕐 **Six Second Summary**

- Rivers and coasts both have advantages for doing fieldwork.
- There are a range of fieldwork methods that can be used on rivers.
- There are factors to consider when choosing a site on a river for fieldwork.

✏️ **Over to you**

Plan a fieldwork investigation on a river.

a Think of a question to investigate.
b Choose the fieldwork methods you could use.
c Explain the methods you would use.
d Write a risk assessment for any river fieldwork.

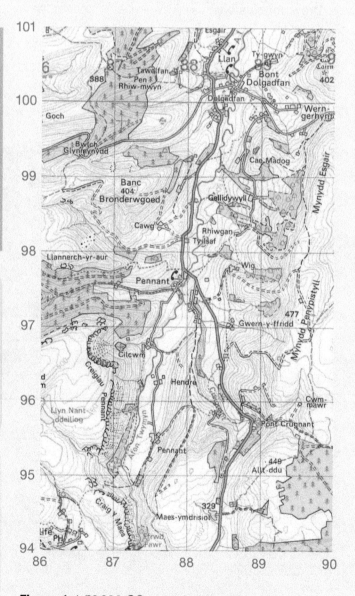

Figure 1 *1:50 000 OS map showing Afon Twymyn, a small river in Wales*

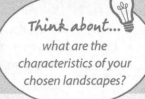

Case Study

You need to know:

- the main features of the Thames Basin
- the underlying geology of the area
- how people in London obtain their water.

Your key question

What influences the landscapes of the UK?

Think about...
what are the characteristics of your chosen landscapes?

The Thames Basin – key facts

- The River Thames is 346 km long from source to mouth (Figure 1).
- It rises in the Cotswold Hills and flows to the North Sea.
- It flows mainly over clay but its basin also has other rocks, including chalk.

- The river runs through the cities of Oxford, Reading and London.
- It is the most densely populated river basin in the UK, with 13 million people.

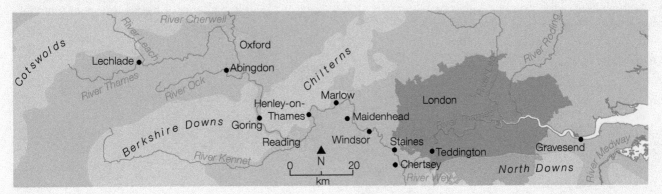

Figure 1 *Map of the Thames Basin*

London's water supply

South-east England is the driest region in the UK. Its growing population puts extra pressure on water resources.

- The River Thames alone is not able to meet the demand for water.
- So, London obtains 40% of its water from **groundwater**.
- Boreholes drilled through the clay supply groundwater from the underlying chalk **aquifer** (Figure 2).

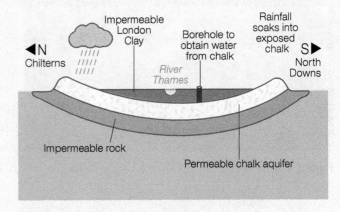

Figure 2 *Cross-section of the Thames valley*

Six Second Summary

- The River Thames flows 346 km from the Cotswolds to the North Sea.
- The Thames Basin is made of various rocks, including chalk and clay.
- London obtains much of its water from chalk, under the clay.

Over to you

Draw a sketch map of the Thames Basin to show:

a the source and mouth of the river
b four ranges of hills
c three cities
d eight tributaries.

Now, try to draw it again from memory.

You need to know:

- some of the landforms along the Thames
- the processes that creates these landforms
- how the river's gradient affects the creation of landforms.

Your key question

What influences the landscapes of the UK?

Think about...
what are the characteristics of your chosen landscapes?

Case Study

Meanders on the Thames

The Thames is a lowland river. Its gentle gradient means less downward erosion but more **lateral erosion**. This creates meanders as the river flows from side to side, across its valley (Figure 1).

- On the outside of the bend fast-flowing water erodes the bank to form a **river cliff.**
- On the inside of the bend slow-flowing water deposits its **load** to form a **slip-off slope.**

Figure 1 A meander on the Thames near Oxford

Rejuvenation on the Thames

Past sea level changes affected the river's gradient and its power to erode its valley (Figure 2).

- When sea level fell, the gradient increased and the river gained energy. It eroded downwards into its floodplain, forming **river terraces**.
- When sea level rose again, the gradient decreased and the river lost energy. It deposited more material to form a new floodplain.

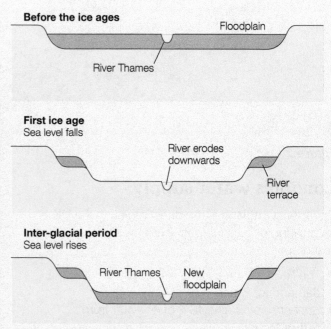

Figure 2 Formation of river terraces in the Thames valley

Six Second Summary

- The River Thames is a lowland river with a gentle gradient.
- The river meanders along its length due to lateral erosion.
- Past sea level changes rejuvenated the river, forming river terraces.

Over to you

Either
Draw a sketch to show how the shape of the meander in Figure 1 will change in the future. Annotate your sketch to explain the processes.
Or
Draw two more diagrams to add to Figure 2 to show what will happen to the river and valley if sea level falls, then rises again. Annotate the diagrams to explain.

You need to know:

- the causes of flooding on the River Thames
- what impacts floods can have
- how people attempt to reduce the flood risk.

Your key question

What influences the landscapes of the UK?

Think about... what are the characteristics of your chosen landscapes?

Floods west of London, 2014

The worst flooding along the River Thames for 40 years happened in February 2014, west of London. The village of Wraysbury and town of Staines were badly hit (Figure 1).

The floods followed a very wet winter in 2013/14. On 9 February water levels in the Thames were very high and more rain was forecast. The Environment Agency (EA) issued a flood alert, warning that property and lives were at risk.

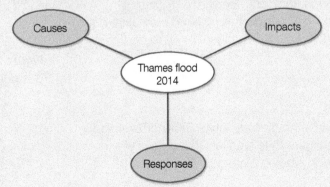

Jubilee River
Datchet
M4
Greater London
R. Thames
R. Thames
Heathrow Airport
Windsor
Twickenham
Wraysbury
A30
R. Thames
Staines
Bushy Park
Kingston
Virginia Water
M3
N
Shepperton
Surbiton

Key
Area covered by severe flood warnings
Lakes and reservoirs

0   5
km

Figure 1 Area of severe flood warnings along the Thames in February 2014

Causes	Impacts	Responses
• Over twice the normal winter rain fell in 2013/14. • The ground was saturated with water. • Buildings and roads increase the flow of water to rivers in urban areas. • A new, artificial channel on the Thames (the Jubilee River) speeds the flow of water, increasing the flood risk in Wraysbury and Staines	• Over 5000 homes and businesses were flooded in Wraysbury and Staines. • Some homes were damaged and people could not return for many months. • The cost of cleaning up after the floods was over £500m. • No lives were lost.	• The EA issued 14 flood alerts along the Thames. • People were evacuated from their homes by emergency services. • There are plans for a new flood relief channel on the Thames to reduce the flood risk west of London.

Figure 2 Causes, impacts and responses to 2014 floods west of London

Six Second Summary

- The River Thames flooded west of London in February 2014.
- The main cause of the flood was a wet winter, but human activities were also to blame.
- Building flood relief channels can reduce the flood risk in one place but increase the risk elsewhere.

Over to you

Draw a spider diagram like the one below. List the causes, impacts and responses to the Thames flood in 2014 on your diagram.

Causes — Thames flood 2014 — Impacts — Responses

You need to know:

- how London has been affected by past floods
- why the Thames Barrier is necessary
- how flood risk is managed at Barking Riverside.

Your key question

What influences the landscapes of the UK?

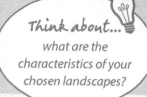

Think about...
what are the characteristics of your chosen landscapes?

Case Study

Flood protection for London

The last major flood in London was in 1928. Fourteen people died when the River Thames burst its banks. London escaped even worse flooding in 1953 when a storm surge in the North Sea pushed water up the river. Over 300 people drowned on the east coast.

The Thames Barrier was built in 1984 to protect London from flooding. Gates on the barrier can be raised to prevent tidal water reaching London (Figure 1). During the stormy winter of 2013/14 the barrier was closed more than 50 times.

There are proposals for a new, higher barrier to cope with predicted rise in sea level in the 21st century.

Figure 1 *The Thames Barrier*

Barking Riverside

A new residential development is being built in east London at Barking Riverside (Figure 2). The site is downstream of the Thames Barrier, so it gets no flood protection. Instead, flood risk is managed by:

- allowing water to spread naturally over the floodplain on the site
- including water as a feature of the development
- planting trees and grass to slow the rate that water filters into the ground
- building homes on raised land to protect them from flooding.

Six Second Summary

- London flooded in 1928 and almost flooded again in 1953.
- The Thames Barrier was built in 1984 to protect London from tidal flooding.
- Barking Riverside has no flood protection but the flood risk is managed.

Figure 2 *Barking Riverside, a new residential development beside the Thames*

Over to you

Draw an annotated sketch of Barking Riverside (using Figure 2) to highlight the ways in which flood risk is being managed.

Topic 4:
Sustaining Ecosystems

Your exam

Sustaining Ecosystems is part of Paper 1: Our Natural World. It is a 1 hr 15 min written exam and makes up 35% of your GCSE. The whole paper carries 70 marks (including 3 marks for SPaG).

There are two sections on the paper:

- Section A: questions on all the physical geography topics, including *Sustaining Ecosystems*

- Section B: physical geography fieldwork.

You will have to answer all questions on the paper.

Tick these boxes to build a record of your revision

Your revision checklist

Spec key question	Theme	1	2	3
Why are natural ecosystems important?				
What are ecosystems?	4.1 Ecosystems			
	4.2 Global ecosystems			
	4.3 More about biomes			
Why should tropical rainforests matter to us?				
What biodiversity exists in tropical rainforests?	4.4 Tropical rainforests			
Why are tropical rainforests being 'exploited' and how can this be managed sustainably?	4.5 The value of rainforests			
	4.6 Human impacts on rainforests			
	4.7 Costa Rica – sustainable rainforest management			
	4.8 Ecotourism in Costa Rica			
Is there more to polar environments than ice?				
What is it like in Antarctica and the Arctic?	4.9 Polar regions			
	4.10 Life in the Arctic			
	4.11 Human impacts in the Arctic			
How are humans seeking a sustainable solution for polar environments?	4.12 Sustainable management of whaling			
	4.13 Sustainable management of the Arctic			
	4.14 Towards an Arctic Treaty			

- what an ecosystem is
- how parts of an ecosystem are linked
- the stores and flows of nutrients, water and energy.

Your key question

Why are natural
ecosystems important?

Think about...
what are
ecosystems?

What is an ecosystem?

An **ecosystem** is a community of plants and animals, together with the environment in which they live. There are both living and non-living components in an ecosystem. All these components are interdependent (Figure 1).

Nutrients, water and energy

Nutrients, water and energy are stored and flow within an ecosystem.

- Nutrients are stored in **biomass**, **litter** and **soil** (Figure 2).
- Water is stored in the atmosphere, soil and biomass.
- Energy from the Sun is captured by **producers** (plants) through **photosynthesis**. They pass on this energy up the **food chain** to **consumers** (animals).
- Only a small proportion of the energy at the bottom of the chain reaches the top. Energy is lost at each level in the chain through heat, functions such as breathing and movement, excretion and wastage (uneaten food).

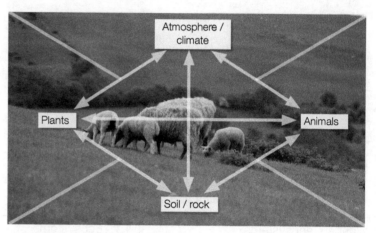

Figure 1 *A field of grazing sheep – an example of an ecosystem*

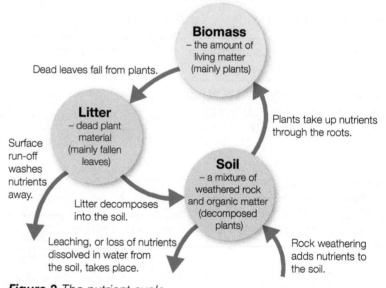

Figure 2 *The nutrient cycle*

 Six Second Summary

- An ecosystem includes both living and non-living components.
- All the components of an ecosystem are interdependent.
- There are stores and flows of nutrients, water and energy in an ecosystem.

Over to you

Draw a large copy of the links in an ecosystem from Figure 1. Write a sentence on each arrow to describe the links. For example: *animals breathe in oxygen from the atmosphere and breathe out carbon dioxide.*

You need to know:
- the global distribution of biomes
- how global climate influences their distribution
- the productivity of different biomes.

Your key question
Why are natural
ecosystems important?

Think about...
*what are
ecosystems?*

Global distribution of biomes

Natural ecosystems are found all around the world. At a large scale they are known
as **biomes** (Figure 1). In many parts of the world, natural ecosystems have been
replaced by cities and farmland.

Biomes include the natural **flora** (plants) and **fauna** (animals) you would expect to
find if there was no human intervention.

Temperature and rainfall are the most important factors that determine plant growth
in any part of the world. The distribution of biomes reflects the world's climate pattern.

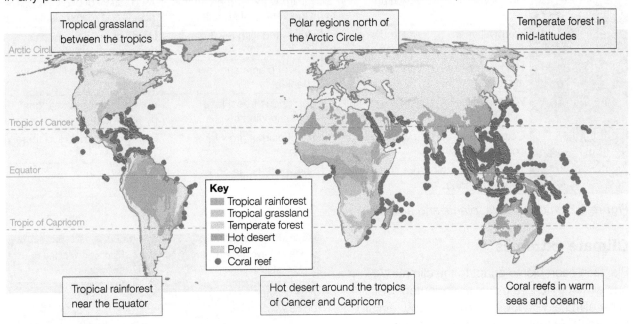

Tropical grassland between the tropics

Polar regions north of the Arctic Circle

Temperate forest in mid-latitudes

Tropical rainforest near the Equator

Hot desert around the tropics of Cancer and Capricorn

Coral reefs in warm seas and oceans

Key
- Tropical rainforest
- Tropical grassland
- Temperate forest
- Hot desert
- Polar
- ● Coral reef

Figure 1 *Some important world biomes*

Productivity of biomes

The most productive biomes, with the greatest biomass, often
grow in a hot, wet climate, such as tropical rainforest (Figure 2).

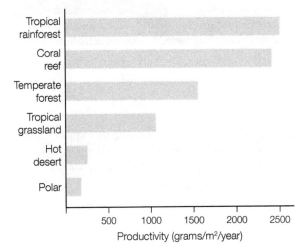

Figure 2 *Biome productivity measured by biomass*

Six Second Summary

- Natural ecosystems on a large scale
  are known as biomes.
- Their global distribution can be
  explained by climate patterns.
- The most productive biomes are
  often found in a hot, wet climate.

Over to you

Study the distribution of one of
the biomes in Figure 1. Then, from
memory, *either* describe its global
distribution, *or* draw its distribution
onto a blank world map. Do the same
for the other biomes.

You need to know:

- about global climate patterns
- the types of plants and animals found in each climate
- how plants and animals adapt to climate.

Your key question

Why are natural ecosystems important?

Think about...
what are ecosystems?

Global climate patterns

The global distribution of biomes closely mirrors the world's climate zones (Figure 1).

- At the Equator, the Sun is overhead, heating the ground strongly, causing moist air to rise, leading to heavy rain.
- At the poles, the angle of the Sun is low, providing little heat, so cold air sinks, producing little rain.

Biome	Temperature	Rainfall	Plants	Animals
Tropical rainforest	Hot all year	Very high	Tall trees forming a canopy, wide variety of species	Wide variety of birds, reptiles, insects and mammals
Tropical grassland	Warm all year	Wet and dry seasons	Grassland with few trees	Herds of grazing animals and hunters
Hot desert	Hot by day, cold at night	Very low	Lack of plants and few species	Animals adapt to live in dry conditions
Temperate forest	Warm summers, mild winters	Variable rainfall	Deciduous trees, lose leaves in winter	Animals adapt to seasons by hibernating
Tundra (in polar regions)	Cold winters, cool summers	Low rainfall	Small plants, grow in summer	Migrating animals live there in summer
Coral reef	Tropical and sub-tropical oceans	(not applicable)	Seaweed, algae and plankton	Coral and fish

Figure 1 *Biomes, climate, plants and animals*

Climate extremes

Plants in each biome adapt to the climate. At one extreme, tundra plants are adapted to a polar climate, with low temperature and rainfall (Figure 2). At the opposite extreme, tropical rainforest plants are adapted to a tropical climate that is hot and wet.

Plants have a short growing season.

Plants grow close to the ground.

Plants have small leaves and lose little moisture.

Plants grow slowly.

Figure 2 *Tundra plants in the polar region*

Six Second Summary

- Climate is affected by the angle of the Sun and circulation in the atmosphere.
- Plants and animals adapt to the climate in which they live.
- Tropical rainforest and tundra are two ecosystems at opposite climate extremes.

Over to you

Draw an empty table like the one in Figure 1, with five columns and seven rows. Copy the headings for each column and row. Then try to complete the information in each box from memory.

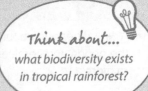
Where rainforest grows

Tropical rainforests cover about 5% of the Earth's surface but contain 50% of the world's **biodiversity** of living organisms. Rainforests grow north and south of the Equator, between the tropics of Cancer and Capricorn, in Asia, Africa, Australia and South America (Figure 1). All rainforests share similar characteristics (Figure 2).

Nutrient and water cycling

Nutrients and water both cycle rapidly in the hot, wet climate of tropical rainforest.

In the nutrient cycle:

- most nutrients are stored in biomass (mainly trees)
- soil is low in nutrients as they are quickly taken up by trees.

In the water cycle:

- the forest canopy intercepts heavy rain, protecting the soil
- water quickly evaporates and returns to the atmosphere, forming clouds.

Six Second Summary

- Tropical rainforest covers 5% of the Earth but contains 50% of its biodiversity.
- Trees in the rainforest grow tall to reach sunlight, forming a canopy.
- Nutrients and water are cycled rapidly in a hot, wet climate.

 **Over to you**

List all the characteristics of tropical rainforest. Explain each characteristic using one or more of these three facts:

a It is hot.
b It is wet.
c Plants need light.

For example, *trees grow tall because the climate is hot and wet and they try to reach sunlight.*

Manaus

Figure 1 *Climate in Manaus, in the Amazon rainforest of Brazil in South America*

Emergent trees grow tall to find sunlight.

Lianas and vines climb tall trees to reach sunlight

Canopy forms a continuous layer, blocking light.

Drip tips on leaves allow heavy rain to run off

An under-canopy of younger trees grows in the gaps.

Little light penetrates the canopy so few shrubs grow.

Buttress roots support the weight of tall trees

Top soil

Sub-soil

Bedrock

Soil profile
- Thin litter layer
- Shallow top soil
- Deep sub-soil
- Underlying rock weathers quickly

Figure 2 *Characteristics of tropical rainforest*

You need to know:

- how indigenous people live in the rainforest
- the goods and services which people obtain from rainforest

Your key question

Why should tropical rainforests matter to us?

Think about...

why are tropical rainforests being 'exploited' and how can this be managed sustainably?

Living in the rainforest

Around the world, about 60 million people live in areas with tropical rainforest. Many of them are **indigenous people** who have lived sustainably in the forest for thousands of years (Figure 1).

Food is obtained by hunting, gathering and fishing

Everyday items, such as clothes, rope, fuel, oil and glue are made from plants

Homes and boats are made from forest timber

Natural medicines from forest plants are used to cure diseases

Trees are chopped down and burnt to use the land for **shifting cultivation**. People cultivate a small area for a few years, then move on.

Figure 1 *Indigenous people in the Amazon rainforest, South America*

Why do people need rainforests?

People in other parts of the world also depend on goods and services from rainforests:

- goods are the products obtained from the rainforest
- services are the jobs that rainforests do.

The value of rainforest goods and services can be put under six headings:

- **Climate** – rainforests acts as a **carbon sink**, removing and storing CO_2 that would, otherwise, add to global warming.
- **Water** – rainforests filter water, purifying it before people drink it. They also act as a sponge to prevent floods and droughts.
- **Food** – many foods originally come from rainforests and some are still grown there.
- **Health** – many medicines are made from rainforest plants.
- **Energy** – hydro-electric power is produced by dams built on rivers in the rainforest.
- **Raw materials** – resources, like timber, rubber and oils, come from rainforests.

 Six Second Summary

- People have been living sustainably in rainforests for thousands of years.
- Rainforests provide the essential resources they need to live.
- People around the world depend on goods and services provided by rainforests.

 Over to you

Classify all the things that rainforests provide into two groups – **goods** and **services**. Now, divide them into the things that **local people need**, and things that people in **other parts of the world need**. You could draw a simple table with columns headed 'Goods' and 'Services' and rows headed 'Local' and 'Worldwide'.

You need to know:
- how rainforests can help economic development
- the ways in which rainforest are exploited
- why the rate of deforestation might be slowing down.

Your key question
Why should tropical rainforests matter to us?

Think about...

why are tropical rainforests being 'exploited' and how can this be managed sustainably?

Rainforests and economic development

Most of the world's rainforests are in **low-income developing countries** (LIDCs) and **emerging and developing countries** (EDCs). The largest area of tropical rainforest is the Amazon rainforest in South America. It covers an area half the size of Europe (Figure 1). Rainforests are used as a resource by LIDCs and EDCs, to be **exploited** for economic development.

Ways of exploiting rainforest

Rainforest exploitation has led to large-scale **deforestation** in some countries. Among the ways in which countries exploit forests are:

- **logging** – large trees are chopped down for timber, sometimes over a wide area
- **mineral extraction** – open-cast mining removes trees and soil from the surface rock, while drilling obtains oil and gas from deep below ground
- **agriculture** – trees are cleared for small-scale and large-scale farming, but soil quickly loses fertility
- **tourism** – avoids deforestation as tourists pay to visit the forest, helping the local economy.

Rainforests as 'natural capital'

Tropical rainforests are a form of 'natural capital' – a resource that, if used wisely, can provide an income for many years. Governments have begun to realise the value of rainforests, such as the goods and services they provide (see 4.5). The rate of deforestation in the Amazon has slowed down (Figure 2).

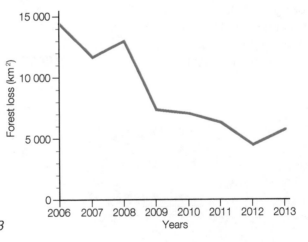

Figure 1 *The Amazon rainforest*

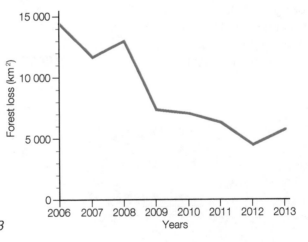

Figure 2 *Amazon deforestation, 2006–2013*

Six Second Summary

- Most of the world's rainforests are found in LIDCs and EDCs.
- Rainforest exploitation contributes to economic development in these countries.
- Rates of deforestation in the Amazon rainforest are slowing down.

Over to you

Weigh up the economic benefits and costs of deforestation.

a List the benefits from this page.
b What costs of deforestation can you think of? Make another list (don't forget the goods and services that rainforests provide (see 4.5).
c Which list is longer? How do your two lists help to explain the graph in Figure 2?

Case Study

You need to know:

- about the problem of deforestation in Costa Rica
- how the government protects rainforests
- the strategies used to manage forest sustainably.

Your key question

Why should tropical rainforests matter to us?

Think about...

why are tropical rainforests being 'exploited' and how can this be managed sustainably?

Costa Rica's rainforests

Costa Rica is a small country in Central America (Figure 1). It is home to 6% of the world's biodiversity and it attracts over 2 million tourists a year. They come to experience its tropical rainforests and variety of other ecosystems.

Until 1980, Costa Rica had one of the highest rates of deforestation in the world due to cattle ranching and agriculture. So, the government passed laws to stop deforestation. Today there are 28 **national parks** and **nature reserves** and 24% of the country's land area is protected.

Strategies for sustainable management

In addition to protecting areas, there are other strategies for sustainable management of rainforests.

- **Agroforestry**: trees and crops are grown together.
- **Afforestation**: trees are planted to replace the original forest that has been lost.
- **Monitoring**: satellite images are used to ensure that no illegal logging happens.
- **Selective logging**: trees are felled only when they reach a certain height.

Figure 1 *National parks in Costa Rica*

Key
- City
- National park
- Volcano
- Land over 1000 m

Figure 2 *Rainforest in Costa Rica*

Six Second Summary

- Costa Rica has 6% of the world's biodiversity and attracts 2 million tourists a year.
- Today, 24% of the country's land area is protected.
- A range of strategies are used for the sustainable management of forests.

Over to you

From memory, make a flashcard with key facts and figures about rainforests in Costa Rica.

Then make another flashcard giving four strategies for sustainable management of forests. In your own words, describe each strategy.

Case Study

You need to know:

- what ecotourism is
- sustainable features of ecotourism in the rainforest
- questions to ask when planning a sustainable holiday.

Your key question

Why should tropical rainforests matter to us?

Think about...
why are tropical rainforests being 'exploited' and how can this be managed sustainably?

Ecotourism

Ecotourism is sustainable tourism that aims to create local employment while conserving the natural environment.

Ecotourism differs from other types of holiday because it:

- does not damage the natural environment
- is on a relatively small scale
- consults with the local community
- benefits local people as well as tourists.

Samasati Nature Reserve is an example of ecotourism in the Costa Rican rainforest (Figure 1).

No mature trees destroyed

Buildings on stilts to allow drainage

Employs only local people

Blends with the landscape

Spring water for drinking

Uses sustainable timber

No heavy machinery

Recycles rainwater for bathrooms

Minimises energy use

Only biodegradable washing products

Figure 1 *Samasati Nature Retreat – an example of ecotourism*

	Questions to ask about your holiday
Travel Shop	Where will the money for my holiday go?
	What impact will my holiday have on the environment?
	How will the number of tourists affect the resort?
	What resources does my holiday use?
	How does my holiday affect natural ecosystems and wildlife?

Figure 2 *How sustainable are our holidays?*

 **Six Second Summary**

- Ecotourism aims to create local jobs and conserve the natural environment.
- Samasati Nature Retreat in Costa Rica is an example of ecotourism.
- We need to ask questions about our holidays to ensure they are sustainable.

Over to you

What five questions should you ask to ensure that your holidays are sustainable? Answer these questions for a holiday at Samasati Nature Retreat.

You need to know:

- where polar regions are found
- the similarities and differences between the Arctic and Antarctica
- some landscape features found in the two regions.

Your key question

Is there more to polar environments than ice?

Think about...
what is it like in Antarctica and the Arctic?

The Arctic and Antarctica

The Arctic and Antarctica are the two polar regions found around the North and South poles. They have many similarities, but also differences (Figure 1).

Landscapes in polar regions

Similarities	Differences
• Winters are long and dark with little sunlight (Figure 1). • The angle of the Sun is low in the sky, even in summer. • Much of the land surface is covered in ice. • Sinking air brings high pressure and dry conditions.	• The Arctic is mainly ocean, surrounded by land. In winter the ocean freezes but much of it melts in summer. • Antarctica is a continent surrounded by ocean. Temperatures rarely rise above freezing. • Polar bears live in the Arctic; penguins live in Antarctica!

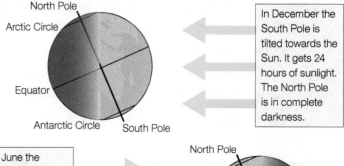

In December the South Pole is tilted towards the Sun. It gets 24 hours of sunlight. The North Pole is in complete darkness.

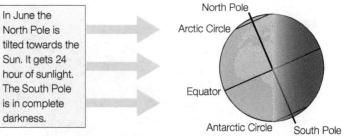

In June the North Pole is tilted towards the Sun. It gets 24 hour of sunlight. The South Pole is in complete darkness.

Figure 2 *Summer and winter at the poles*

Figure 1 *The Arctic and Antactica: similarities and differences*

Ice sheets cover most of the land in Antarctica and Greenland (in the Arctic). Further from the poles, temperatures rise above freezing in summer and tundra grows (Figure 2).

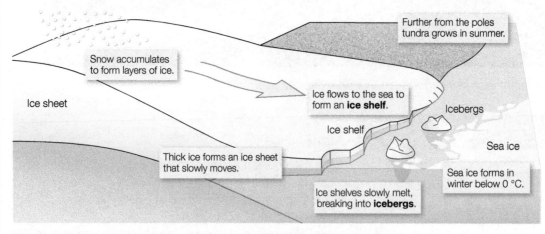

Further from the poles tundra grows in summer.

Snow accumulates to form layers of ice.

Ice sheet

Ice flows to the sea to form an **ice shelf**.

Icebergs

Ice shelf

Sea ice

Thick ice forms an ice sheet that slowly moves.

Ice shelves slowly melt, breaking into **icebergs**.

Sea ice forms in winter below 0 °C.

Figure 3 *Landscape features of the Arctic and Antarctica*

Six Second Summary

- Polar regions are found in the Arctic and Antarctica.
- There are many similarities, but also differences, between the two regions.
- Ice, on land and sea, is an important part of the landscape in both regions.

Over to you

Draw a flow diagram to show the links between *snow, ice sheets, ice shelves, icebergs, sea ice* and *ocean* in polar regions. Label the arrows on your diagram to explain the processes that link the features.

You need to know:
- about Arctic ecosystems in the ocean and on land
- how species are linked to each other within the ecosystem
- why soils in the Arctic are not good, even for building.

Your key question
Is there more to polar environments than ice?

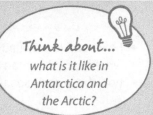
Think about...
what is it like in Antarctica and the Arctic?

Arctic ecosystems

The Arctic region includes both sea and land. There are two main types of ecosystem.

- The Arctic **marine ecosystem** is found in the ocean (Figure 1). There are many interdependent species within the **food web**. Energy flows up the food chain from producers to consumers. The top consumers are polar bears and whales.
- The tundra ecosystem grows on land. The producers are small, low-growing plants that grow only in summer. The consumers are migratory animals such as caribou, or birds such as geese and ducks

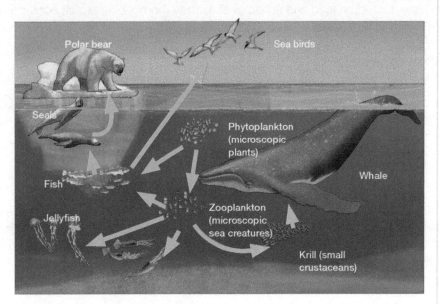

Figure 1 The Arctic marine food

Arctic soils

Arctic soils are generally thin and poor quality so few plants can grow.

- The underlying rock weathers slowly because of low temperatures.
- **Permafrost** is the part of the ground that remains frozen all year, even when air temperature rises above 0 °C.
- The **active layer** is the upper layer of soil that thaws in summer.
- Modern homes are built on stilts so that they do not melt the permafrost, which would cause buildings to collapse.

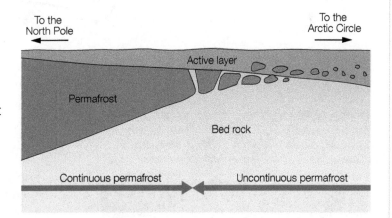

Figure 2 Arctic soil

Six Second Summary

- The Arctic Ocean and surrounding land both support ecosystems.
- The marine ecosystem has a food web with polar bears as top consumers.
- Soils in the Arctic are frozen at increasing depths closer to the North Pole.

Over to you

How would you explain to someone who has never studied the Arctic:

a how we know other species live in the Arctic Ocean, not just polar bears?
b why people who live in the Arctic build their homes on stilts?

You need to know:

- how people exploited the Arctic in the past
- what modern human activities happen there
- how these activities threaten the Arctic environment.

Your key question

Is there more to polar environments than ice?

Think about...
what is it like in Antarctica and the Arctic?

Case Study

Human activities in the Arctic

- Inuit people have lived sustainably in the Arctic for hundreds of years. They hunted on land and fished at sea. They did not overexploit ecosystems.
- From the 18th century onwards, Europeans came to hunt the large numbers of seals and whales. Some species were driven almost to extinction.
- Modern human activities threaten the Arctic (Figure 1). They include:
  - fishing
  - mineral exploitation
  - drilling for oil and gas
  - shipping routes
  - tourism.

Global warming is also leading to disappearance of Arctic sea ice.

Threats from oil and gas exploration

The seabed of the Arctic Ocean is one of the world's largest remaining untapped reserves of oil and gas. Drilling could be a threat to the marine ecosystem (Figure 2).

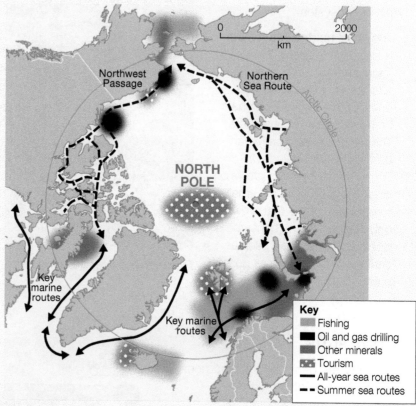

Figure 1 *Modern human activities in the Arctic*

Oil spills in the Arctic could be impossible to clean up in icy water.

Recovery for the ecosystem will be slower at low temperature.

Response to an oil spill will be slow because there are few ports nearby.

Fish and animal species are at risk of disturbance by drilling.

Figure 2 *Drilling for oil in the Arctic*

 **Six Second Summary**

- Inuit people have lived sustainably in the Arctic for hundreds of years.
- Modern human activities and global warming are a threat to the Arctic.
- Drilling for oil and gas could be particularly damaging in the Arctic.

Over to you

Explain the threat from each modern human activity in the Arctic.

You need to know:

- why whaling became unsustainable in the 20th century
- about international efforts to control whaling
- how whaling can be managed more sustainably.

Your key question

Is there more to polar environments than ice?

Think about... how are humans seeking a sustainable solution for polar environments?

A history of whaling

People have hunted whales in the Arctic for centuries. The Inuit hunted for whales, one at a time, for their oil, meat and bones. Small-scale whaling like this was sustainable.

During the 20th century, whaling was on an industrial scale. Factory ships harvested whales in large numbers. They were used in the production of margarine, chemicals, cosmetics and animal feed.

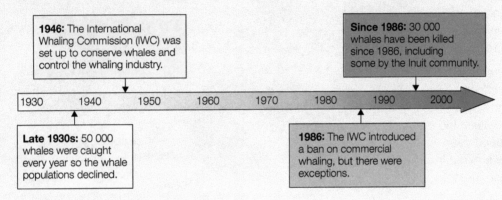

1946: The International Whaling Commission (IWC) was set up to conserve whales and control the whaling industry.

Since 1986: 30 000 whales have been killed since 1986, including some by the Inuit community.

1930   1940   1950   1960   1970   1980   1990   2000

Late 1930s: 50 000 whales were caught every year so the whale populations declined.

1986: The IWC introduced a ban on commercial whaling, but there were exceptions.

Figure 1 *Timeline of whaling in the 20th century*

A case-study of sustainable management: Clyde River

In 2008, Clyde River on Baffin Island became Canada's first marine wildlife sanctuary. The indigenous Inuits killed a bowhead whale in 2014, the first Inuit hunt in over 100 years in Clyde River. This was supported by Greenpeace, who argued that small-scale hunting can be part of a sustainable management strategy.

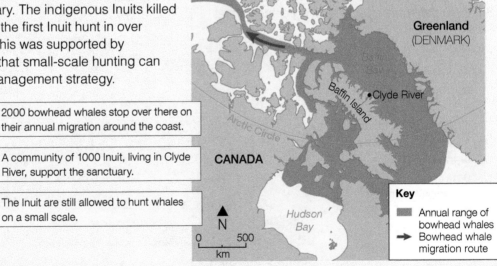

2000 bowhead whales stop over there on their annual migration around the coast.

A community of 1000 Inuit, living in Clyde River, support the sanctuary.

The Inuit are still allowed to hunt whales on a small scale.

Key

Annual range of bowhead whales

→ Bowhead whale migration route

Figure 2 *Clyde River on Baffin Island, northern Canada*

Six Second Summary

- Whaling on an industrial scale became unsustainable in the 20th century.
- The IWC conserves whales and banned commercial whaling in 1986.
- Clyde River is a marine wildlife sanctuary where whaling is managed sustainably.

Over to you

Weigh up the arguments for and against commercial whaling, by making two lists. Why might sustainable management of whaling be the best option?

Case Study

You need to know:
- what makes the Arctic a fragile environment
- the international agreements which help to protect the Arctic
- about the proposal for an Arctic Sanctuary.

Your key question
Is there more to polar environments than ice?

Think about...
how are humans seeking a sustainable solution for polar environments?

Threats to the Arctic

The Arctic is a **fragile environment** – one that is easily damaged by human activities. It includes the largest remaining area of **wilderness** in the northern hemisphere. Only a small part of this area is protected (Figure 1).

Perhaps, the greatest threat to the Arctic is from global warming. More sea ice melts in the Arctic Ocean each year and it could be ice-free in summer by the mid-21st century.

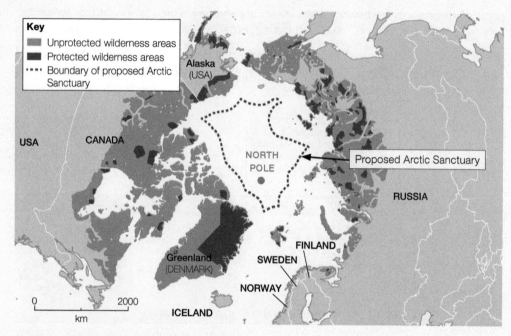

Key
- Unprotected wilderness areas
- Protected wilderness areas
- Boundary of proposed Arctic Sanctuary

Alaska (USA)

USA

CANADA

NORTH POLE

Proposed Arctic Sanctuary

RUSSIA

FINLAND

SWEDEN

Greenland (DENMARK)

NORWAY

ICELAND

0   2000
km

Figure 1 *Wilderness areas in the Arctic*

A case-study of sustainable management: the Arctic

Unlike Antarctica, there is no treaty to protect the whole of the Arctic. But there are some international agreements that help (Figure 2).

Now ...
- The **Arctic Council**, set up in 1996 to protect the Arctic environment, but it has no legal powers.
- The **Paris Agreement**, signed by 195 countries in 2015, is a legally binding agreement to limit global warming.

... and in the future?
The proposal for an **Arctic Sanctuary** where harmful human activities would be banned, including:
- no fishing
- no exploration or drilling for oil or gas
- no mining on the seabed
- no military activity
- strict controls on shipping.

Figure 2 *A polar bear on sea ice in the Arctic*

Six Second Summary
- The Arctic is a fragile environment with large areas of wilderness.
- The Arctic Council aims to protect the environment but has no legal powers.
- The proposal for an Arctic Sanctuary would ban harmful human activities.

Over to you

Draw a sketch map of the Arctic Ocean.

a Locate and mark eight countries.
b Mark and label the area proposed for an Arctic Sanctuary.

You need to know:
- why an Arctic treaty is needed
- the main features of the Antarctic Treaty
- how an Arctic treaty might differ from the Antarctic Treaty.

Your key question

Is there more to polar environments than ice?

Think about...

how are humans seeking a sustainable solution for polar environments?

Why an Arctic treaty?

The 1961 Antarctic Treaty protects the environment in Antarctica. It has become one of the most successful international treaties and was strengthened in 1998 by the Environmental Protocol (Figure 1).

The Arctic faces environmental threats and may need a treaty of its own. The main threats are:

- global warming is melting sea ice
- resource exploitation, like drilling for oil
- pollution from other parts of the world
- populations of Arctic species are declining.

The Antarctic Treaty

- Bans military bases and weapons testing.
- Allows scientific research, but results must be shared.
- Bans nuclear explosions and nuclear waste.
- No country can own Antarctic territory.

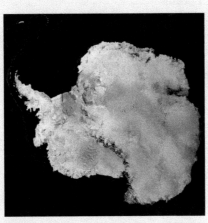

The Environmental Protocol

- Bans mining.
- Bans killing or interfering with wildlife.
- All waste must be removed.
- Controls fishing.
- All activities must be assessed for environmental impact.

Figure 1 *The 1961 Antarctic Treaty and 1998 Environmental Protocol*

Differences between the Arctic and Antarctica

- The Arctic is an ocean surrounded by land. Antarctica is a continent surrounded by ocean.
- Indigenous people live in the Arctic. Only scientists live in Antarctica.
- Arctic land has ice and tundra. 98% of Antarctica is covered by ice
- The eight countries in the Arctic control their own land and seabed. No one owns Antarctica.
- There is resource exploitation and military activity in the Arctic. Neither are allowed in Antarctica.

 Six Second Summary

- The Antarctic Treaty is one of the most successful international treaties.
- The Arctic may need a similar treaty to protect it from environmental threats.
- There are differences which might make an Arctic treaty harder to agree.

 Over to you

Write bullet points for an Arctic treaty, based on the Antarctic Treaty. Which parts of the treaty might be the same? What differences would there be?

Topic 5:
Urban Futures

Your exam

Urban Futures is part of Paper 2: People and Society. It is a 1 hr 15 min written exam and makes up 35% of your GCSE. The whole paper carries 70 marks (including 3 marks for SPaG).

There are two sections on the paper:

- Section A: questions on all the human geography topics, including *Urban Futures*

- Section B: human geography fieldwork.

You will have to answer all questions on the paper.

Your revision checklist

Tick these boxes to build a record of your revision

Spec key question	Theme	1	2	3
Why do more than half the world's population live in urban areas?				
How is the global pattern of urbanisation changing?	5.1 An urban world			
	5.2 Super-sized cities			
	5.3 How cities began and grew			
What does rapid urbanisation mean for cities?	5.4 The urban explosion			
	5.5 Slumming it			
	5.6 Urban trends in the UK			
	5.7 The future of cities			
What are the challenges and opportunities for cities today?				
What is life like for people in a city?	5.8 Birmingham on the map			
	5.9 Come to Birmingham			
	5.10 Explore Birmingham			
	5.11 Unequal Birmingham			
Fieldwork skills	5.13 Urban fieldwork – 1			
	5.14 Urban fieldwork – 2			
	5.15 Istanbul on the map			
	5.16 Expanding Istanbul			
	5.17 Explore Istanbul			
	5.18 At home in Istanbul			
How can cities become more sustainable?	5.12 Sustainable Birmingham			
	5.19 Congested Istanbul			

You need to know:
- what urbanisation is
- the proportion of people around the world living in urban areas
- the rates of urbanisation in each continent.

Your key question
Why do more than half the world's population live in urban areas?

Think about...
how is the global pattern of urbanisation changing?

Urbanisation around the world

Urbanisation is the growth in the proportion of people living in cities. Over half the world's population now live in cities (Figure 1). It is expected to be 60% by 2030 and 70% by 2050.

The most urbanised countries are mainly **advanced countries** (ACs). Urbanisation rates in these countries are now slowing down. The most rapid urbanisation now happens in **emerging and developing countries** (EDCs) and **low-income developing countries** (LIDCs).

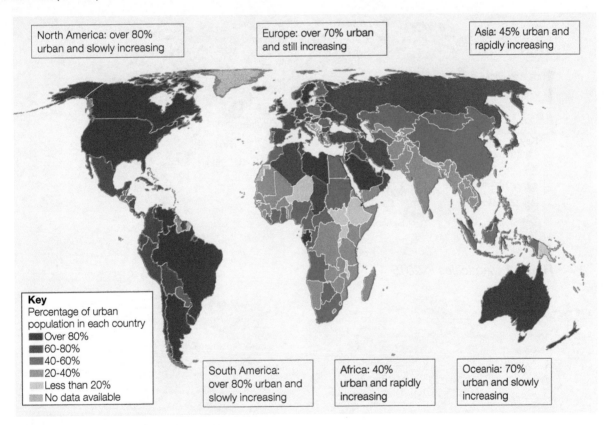

North America: over 80% urban and slowly increasing

Europe: over 70% urban and still increasing

Asia: 45% urban and rapidly increasing

Key
Percentage of urban population in each country
- Over 80%
- 60-80%
- 40-60%
- 20-40%
- Less than 20%
- No data available

South America: over 80% urban and slowly increasing

Africa: 40% urban and rapidly increasing

Oceania: 70% urban and slowly increasing

Figure 1 *Urban population by country*

Six Second Summary

- Over half the world's population live in cities and the proportion is growing.
- Most ACs are more urban but urbanisation rates are slowing down.
- Most EDCs and LIDCs are less urban but urbanisation rates are higher.

Over to you

Draw a simple world sketch map with six continents – it could be as simple as six circles. Label the continents. Then, devise a way to show how urban each continent is, *and* how the rate of urbanisation is changing in each one. Use a colour key and/or symbols to show the information. Your map will help you to remember the information.

You need to know:

- the difference between a megacity and a world city
- where the world's megacities are found
- why cities grow into megacities or world cities.

Your key question

Why do more than half the world's population live in urban areas?

Think about...
how is the global pattern of urbanisation changing?

Megacities and world cities

Megacities are cities with a population over ten million. Most of the world's megacities are now in Asia (Figure 1). The factors that cause cities to grow into megacities include:

- natural population increase
- migration
- coastal location
- economic development.

World cities are the most important cities in the global economy. They are hubs for international trade and for global communications networks.

Not all megacities are world cities, or the other way round. The top two world cities are London and New York, but London is not a megacity.

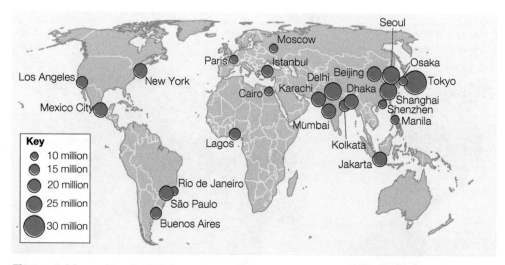

Figure 1 *Megacities in 2015*

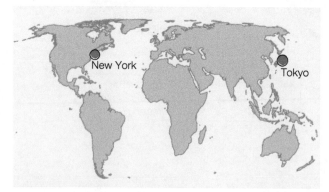

Figure 2 *Megacities 1950*

Figure 3 *Megacities 1975*

 Six Second Summary

- Megacities are cities with over 10 million people. They are mainly found in Asia.
- World cities are the most important cities in the global economy.
- The top two world cities are London and New York.

Over to you

Study the map in Figure 1. Only one city has over 30 million people. Which one? How many cities have over 25 million people? Make a list. Now, do the same for cities with 20, 15 and 10 million people, each time adding more cities to the list.

Now, hide your list. How many megacities can you name?

You need to know:

- how cities began and grew
- some of the key events in urbanisation over the centuries
- the main functions of cities and how these have changed.

Your key question

Why do more than half the world's population live in urban areas?

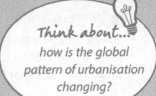

Think about...
how is the global pattern of urbanisation changing?

Cities and their growth

People have been living in cities for thousands of years (Figure 1). The first cities grew in fertile river valleys, such as the Nile in Egypt. The surplus food they produced allowed people to stop farming and settlements to grow.

The modern growth of cities began with the Industrial Revolution in Britain in the 19th century. Migration brought people to cities from the countryside to work in factories. Similar growth happened in Europe and North America.

Urban functions

Cities have many functions which can change over time. The first cities were a place for people to trade and exchange ideas. Since then, they have developed other functions (Figure 2), such as:

- market
- employment
- administration
- defence
- entertainment
- religion
- transport hub
- residential
- culture.

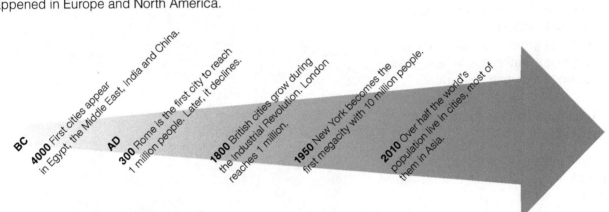

Figure 1 *Timeline of urban growth*

(Timeline labels:)
BC
4000 First cities appear in Egypt, the Middle East, India and China.
AD
300 Rome is the first city to reach 1 million people. Later, it declines.
1800 British cities grow during the Industrial Revolution. London reaches 1 million.
1950 New York becomes the first megacity with 10 million people.
2010 Over half the world's population live in cities, most of them in Asia.

(Photo labels: The Shard, London Bridge, St Paul's Cathedral, The City of London, The River Thames, The Tower of London)

Figure 2 *London's skyline today*

Six Second Summary

- People have been living in cities for thousands of years.
- Farming and industry played an important role in the development of cities.
- Cities have many functions which can change over time.

Over to you

Identify London's key functions, both past and present, from the photo in Figure 2. What other functions could you add from what you know about London?

You need to know:
- where people live in Africa
- reasons for urban growth in Africa
- push and pull factors for rural-urban migration.

Your key question
Why do more than half
the world's population
live in urban areas?

Think about...
*what does rapid
urbanisation mean
for cities?*

Cities in Africa

Africa is the world's least urbanised
continent, but also the one that is
urbanising most rapidly. About 40% of
Africa's population lives in cities (Figure 1)
and the numbers rise every day.

The two main factors in urban
growth are:

- **rural–urban migration**: the
  movement of people from the
  countryside to cities, due to **push**
  and **pull factors**
- **internal growth**: natural increase in
  urban population due to birth rates
  being higher than death rates.

Push factors for rural–urban migration

Push factors that force or encourage
people to move from the countryside
to cities include:

- few job opportunities
- poor access to services
- low or declining incomes
- rural overpopulation
- poor transport
- civil war
- natural disasters
- climate change
- food shortage.

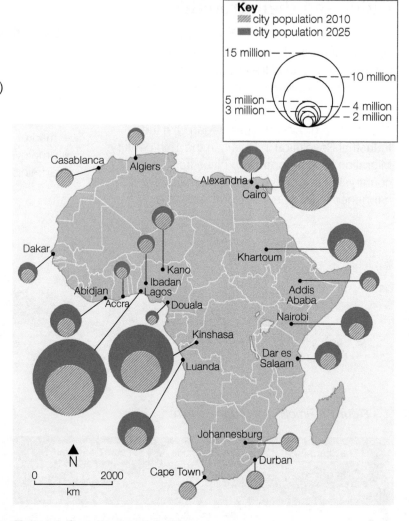

Key
city population 2010
city population 2025
15 million
10 million
5 million
3 million
4 million
2 million

Figure 1 *Growth of Africa cities*

Six Second Summary

- Africa is the world's least urbanised continent with
  40% living in cities.
- Urban growth is due to rural–urban migration and
  internal growth.
- A range of push and pull factors lead to rural–urban
  migration.

Over to you

Without referring to this book, write a list
of as many push factors for rural–urban
migration as you can remember. Then
make another list of pull factors you can
think of. Some will be the opposite of the
push factors. Now, check with the book.

You need to know:
- what a slum is
- where slums are found and why they grow
- what are the hazards of living in a squatter settlement.

Your key question
Why do more than half the world's population live in urban areas?

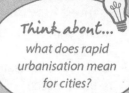
Think about...
what does rapid urbanisation mean for cities?

Consequences of urbanisation

One of the consequences of rapid urbanisation has been the development of **slums**.

A slum is a crowded urban area where people live in inadequate housing with poor living conditions. It can be either an old urban area where buildings have deteriorated, or a **squatter settlement** where people build their own homes on any available land (Figure 1).

Most slums are found in LIDCs or EDCs, where cities grow faster. Slums grow because of:

- rural–urban migration – more people arrive all the time
- unemployment – people cannot afford decent housing
- poor urban planning – not enough homes for new residents
- poor **infrastructure** – inadequate transport, power and water supply.

Landslips destroy buildings on steep hillsides

Fires spread easily in dense urban areas

Earthquakes destroy poor quality buildings

Unreliable electricity supply

Sewage overflows to pollute rivers and water

Air and water pollution from uncollected waste

Disease spreads because of poor sanitation

Figure 1 *Hazards of living in a squatter settlement*

Six Second Summary

- A slum is a crowded urban area with poor housing and living conditions.
- Most slums are found in LICDs and EDCs where there is rapid urbanisation.
- In squatter settlements people build their homes on any available land.

Over to you

Identify the hazards of living in a squatter settlement in Figure 1. For each one, explain why living in a squatter settlement makes the hazard more likely.

You need to know:
- what happened to UK cities in the 20th and early 21st centuries
- about suburbanisation, counter-urbanisation and re-urbanisation
- the causes and consequences of these processes

Your key question
Why do more than half the world's population live in urban areas?

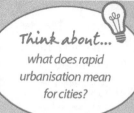
Think about...
what does rapid urbanisation mean for cities?

Suburbanisation in the 20th century

During the 20th century, the main process in the UK was not urbanisation, but **suburbanisation**. People moved out from city centres to new residential areas, or suburbs (Figure 1).

The consequence of this was **urban sprawl** and large areas of green land were built on. There was concern that cities were growing too large and eating up the countryside. So, in 1947, the government introduced the idea of a **green belt**, areas around cities on which no further building is allowed.

Counter-urbanisation and re-urbanisation

- **Counter-urbanisation** – during the second half of the 20th century cities were in decline. People moved to the countryside, small towns or the seaside. The urban population fell.
- **Re-urbanisation** – since the 1980s, people have been moving back into cities. Urban population has been growing again (Figure 2). This happened because **urban regeneration** helped to bring cities back to life.

Less crowded and congested
Less polluted
Cheaper land and house prices
'Better' quality of life

Figure 1 *Suburban housing in the UK; reasons for moving to the suburbs*

Rank	City	Population change, 2004–13	Change (%)
1	Milton Keynes	36 200	16.5
2	Peterborough	24 900	15.2
3	Swindon	27 600	14.8
4	Luton	24 400	13.3
5	Cambridge	14 300	12.7
60	Middlesbrough	4 300	0.9
61	Grimsby	1 300	0.8
62	Burnley	700	0.4
63	Blackpool	500	0.2
64	Sunderland	–4 000	–1.4

Figure 2 *Fast and slow-growing cities in the UK, 2004–2013*

 Six Second Summary

- The main process in UK cities in the 20th century was suburbanisation.
- Later in the 20th century came counter-urbanisation, then re-urbanisation.
- Having been in decline, the populations of most UK cities are growing again.

Over to you

What are the causes and consequences of suburbanisation, counter-urbanisation and re-urbanisation in UK cities. Create a table like this for your answer.

	Causes	Consequences
Suburbanisation		
Counter-urbanisation		
Re-urbanisation		

You need to know:

- how much of the world's population will be urban in 2050
- what are the opportunities and challenges of living in cities
- where the biggest cities will be in future.

Your key question

Why do more than half the world's population live in urban areas?

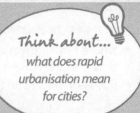

Think about...
what does rapid urbanisation mean for cities?

Urban opportunities and challenges

By the year 2050, 70% of the world's population will live in cities (Figure 2). Globally, there is no sign of urbanisation coming to an end. People move to cities because of the opportunities, but there are also challenges.

Metacities

In future, there are likely to be more **metacities** – cities with a population of more than 20 million people. Most of them will be in China or India. One metacity in China could have a population of 120 million!

Urban opportunities	Urban challenges
• Better quality of life • Longer life expectancy • More employment • Squatter settlements – a place to build a new home • More sustainable because things are within easy reach	• Greater inequality • Segregation of rich and poor • Slums (including squatter settlements) create hazards • Overpopulation • Environmental damage and pollution

Figure 1 *Opportunities and challenges of urban life*

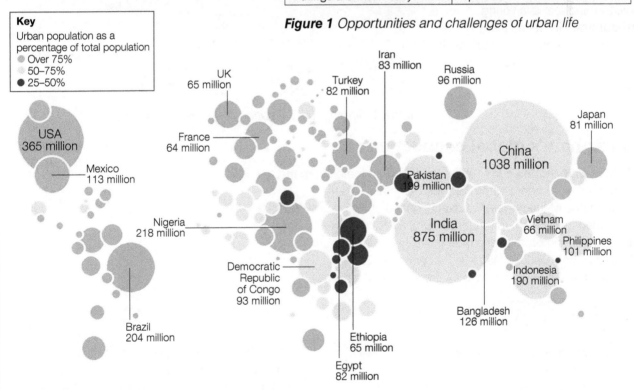

Key
Urban population as a percentage of total population
- Over 75%
- 50–75%
- 25–50%

USA 365 million
Mexico 113 million
Brazil 204 million
UK 65 million
France 64 million
Nigeria 218 million
Democratic Republic of Congo 93 million
Turkey 82 million
Iran 83 million
Russia 96 million
Egypt 82 million
Ethiopia 65 million
Pakistan 199 million
China 1038 million
India 875 million
Bangladesh 126 million
Indonesia 190 million
Vietnam 66 million
Philippines 101 million
Japan 81 million

Figure 2 *The world's predicted urban population in 2050*

Six Second Summary

- 70% of the world's population will live in cities by 2050.
- People move to cities for the opportunities, but there are also challenges.
- In future there will be more metacities with over 20 million people.

Over to you

Study Figure 2. Describe how urbanised each continent will be by 2050. Write a short summary for each continent, e.g. *Most countries in Europe will be over 75% urban. The largest urban population will be in the UK with 65 million people.*

Case Study

You need to know:
- where Birmingham is located
- how the city's role is changing
- Birmingham's connections with the wider world.

Your key question
What are the challenges and opportunities for cities today?

Think about...
what is life like for people in a city?

Birmingham's changing role

Birmingham is in the West Midlands (Figure 1). It is the second largest city in the UK, after London. Its population is about 1.1 million.

Birmingham began as a Saxon village over a thousand years ago. It grew into a city during the 19th century, with the development of manufacturing industry. It was once known as 'the workshop of the world'. In recent years, manufacturing has declined.

Today, Birmingham is a young, **multi-cultural** city. It has many global connections and has reinvented itself as a city of culture and shopping.

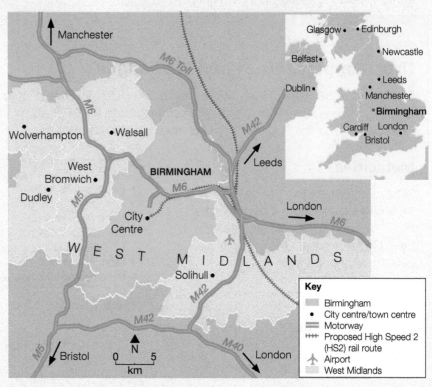

Figure 1 *Birmingham's location in the West Midlands*

Birmingham's global connections

- Workers were recruited from Asia and the West Indies from the 1950s.
- Migrant workers from Eastern Europe came after 2004.
- Home to one of the largest Pakistani communities in the world.
- It has the largest Irish community in England.
- Thousands of international students study in Birmingham.
- Cadbury's chocolate is made with cocoa from Ghana.
- Jaguar Land Rover is owned by Tata, an Indian company.

Six Second Summary

- Birmingham is the UK's second largest city with 1.1 million people.
- The city grew during the 19th century with the development of factories.
- Today, it is part of the West Midlands region with many global connections.

Over to you

Show Birmingham's global connections on a world map. Draw arrows to connect Birmingham to each place and label them. This will also help you to learn where other places in the world are.

You need to know:

- how Birmingham's population has changed
- why the population grew and then declined
- the make-up of Birmingham's population today.

Your key question

- What are the challenges and opportunities for cities today?

Think about...
what is life like for people in a city?

Birmingham's changing population

In 1700 Birmingham was a small market town of 10 000 people. Rural–urban migration led to rapid population growth in the 19th and early 20th centuries. It reached a peak of just over 1.1 million people by 1950 (Figure 1).

Birmingham is now one of the most diverse cities in the UK. The character of the city is changing with new cultures, languages and shops. It also has a young population, with more people under 40 and fewer over 40 than the average for England (Figure 2).

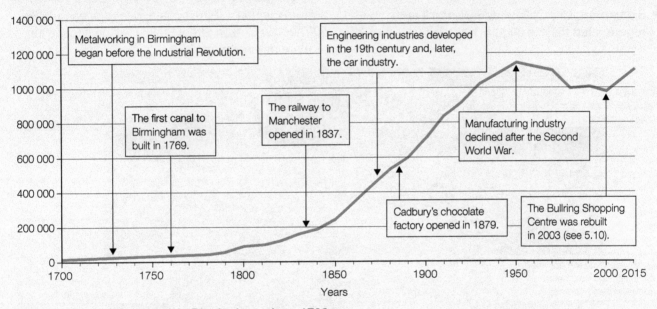

Figure 1 *Population change in Birmingham since 1700*

Six Second Summary

- Birmingham grew from a small market town to an industrial city in 200 years.
- The population grew as industry developed, then fell as industry declined.
- Today, Birmingham has a younger, more diverse population than the UK average.

Over to you

Learn Birmingham's populations in both 1700 and 1950. Then, from memory, draw a graph to show how population changed between those dates. What has happened to Birmingham's population since 1950? Explain the changes shown on your graph.

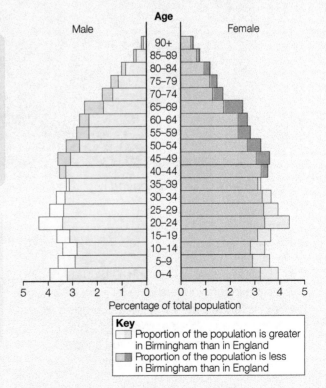

Figure 2 *Birmingham/England population comparison*

Case Study

You need to know:
- how Birmingham city centre is changing
- about the new Bullring and other regeneration projects
- how the Bullring has helped to regenerate the city centre.

Your key question
What are the challenges and opportunities for cities today?

Think about...
what is life like for people in a city?

The Bullring Shopping Centre

- The Bullring was Birmingham's historic market place.
- In the 1960s it was redeveloped into a large, concrete shopping centre surrounded by an urban ring road.
- By the 1990s it was run down and choked by traffic.
- Birmingham City Council demolished it and **regenerated** the site (Figure 1).

More city centre regeneration projects

- **Brindleyplace** – an area around the old canals in the city centre, including the National Indoor Arena and International Convention Centre.
- **Library of Birmingham** – opened in 2013 and is the largest public library in the UK. It helped to change the city's image.
- **High Speed 2 (HS2)** – a new high-speed railway from London to Birmingham, due to open in 2026. The new Curzon Street Station will be a focus for more regeneration.

Europe's largest city centre, retail-led, urban regeneration project, opened in 2003.

This 1960s block has been refurbished and converted from offices to luxury flats.

Once cut off by the ring road, the Bullring is now better connected with the city.

Pedestrianised streets bring more shoppers, making it feel safer, especially at night.

Buses and trains provide easy access for visitors. There is no need to travel by car.

The centre includes 160 shops, two department stores and public art galleries.

Figure 1 *The Bullring today*

- The Bullring was a run-down, 1960s shopping centre in Birmingham.
- It was regenerated in 2003 as Europe's largest, retail-led, urban regeneration project.
- The new Bullring has improved shopping, access, quality of life and safety.

Over to you

Think about the ways in which the new Bullring has helped to improve:

a shopping   **b** access to the city centre
c peoples' quality of life   **d** safety.

Try to write down at least two ways in which each has improved.

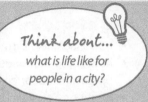

You need to know:

- that inequality is a challenge for Birmingham
- the pattern of inequality in the city
- how different indicators of deprivation are linked.

Your key question

What are the challenges and opportunities for cities today?

Think about...
what is life like for people in a city?

Case Study

Inequality in Birmingham

One of the main challenges for Birmingham, like other cities, is **inequality**. It can be seen in the different levels of wealth or **deprivation** that exist within the city. Birmingham is divided into small areas, or **wards**. Wealth and deprivation vary between one ward and another.

There are many indicators of wealth or deprivation, including,

- unemployment (Figure 1)
- educational achievement
- child poverty
- household income
- housing quality
- access to services
- crime rates
- environmental quality.

Housing provision

House prices reflect inequality in cities.

- Wealthy people, on high incomes, can afford high house prices, so they move to the least deprived areas, e.g. Sutton Four Oaks.
- Poorer people, including the unemployed, may not be able to afford a house and are more likely to rent their home. They live in more deprived areas, e.g. Sparkbrook (Figure 2).

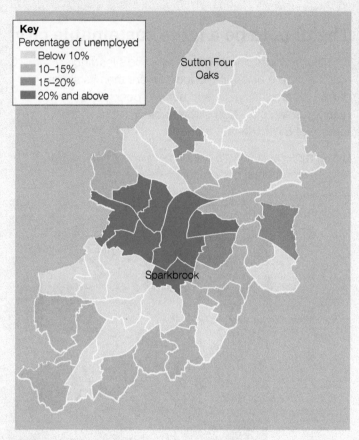

Figure 1 *Unemployment in Birmingham*

Key
Percentage of unemployed
- Below 10%
- 10–15%
- 15–20%
- 20% and above

Six Second Summary

- Inequality is a challenge for Birmingham, as it is for other cities.
- Wards near the city centre are more deprived than those further away.
- House prices reflect inequality and people live in areas they can afford.

Over to you

Draw a large spider diagram with 'Deprivation' at the centre. Add indicators of deprivation around it. Explain the connection between each indicator and deprivation, e.g.
Unemployment – people who are unemployed have lower incomes, making them more deprived.

	Sparkbrook	Sutton Four Oaks	Birmingham
Unemployment (%)	24.5	3.1	12.0
Economically active or at work (%)	48	81	68
Working age population with no qualifications (%)	49.7	20.9	37.1
Pupils with five GCSEs, A*–C (%)	51	74	58
Children living in poverty (%)	49	7	34
Average household income (£)	21 000	40 000	31 000
Households with income less than £15 000 (%)	46	12	27
Households with income over £35 000 (%)	12	47	27

Figure 2 *Comparing wealth and deprivation in Sparkbrook and Sutton Four Oaks*

You need to know:

- how cities, like Birmingham, can be more sustainable
- how being more sustainable can bring more opportunities for cities
- about one sustainable initiative in Birmingham.

Your key question

What are the challenges and opportunities for cities today?

Think about...
how can cities become more sustainable?

Case Study

The plan to be a more sustainable city

Birmingham was once one of the world's leading manufacturing cities. It produced more than its share of carbon emissions. Now, it aims to become 'a leading green city'. One sustainable initiative is the Library of Birmingham, opened in 2013 (Figure 1).

Being more sustainable brings new economic, social and environmental opportunities.

Opportunities such as:

- a new greener economy, specialising in low-carbon technology
- through better planning which uses fewer resources and is more efficient
- people become fitter and healthier by living a more sustainable lifestyle.

Built on brownfield site, reusing the land.

95% of waste material from the site was recycled.

250 builders employed to reduce local unemployment.

Ground-source heating and cooling minimises carbon emissions.

Energy consumption minimised by using natural daylight and ventilation.

Uses less water by harvesting and recycling rainwater.

A roof garden attracts wildlife and improves biodiversity

Good public transport connections and cycle storage space.

Figure 1 *The Library of Birmingham*

 **Six Second Summary**

- Birmingham was a manufacturing city but now aims to be a 'green city'.
- Being more sustainable brings new economic, social and environmental opportunities.
- The Library of Birmingham, opened in 2013, is one sustainable initiative.

Over to you

Complete a table like this to show the economic, social and environmental benefits of being a more sustainable city. Think about each of the four sustainable themes. Try to fill as many of the boxes as you can, e.g. *energy could bring economic benefits from manufacturing solar panels.*

Sustainable theme	Economic	Social	Environmental
Energy			
Resources			
Transport			
Biodiversity			

You need to know:

- how to plan an urban fieldwork enquiry
- the sort of questions you could investigate through fieldwork
- the methods you could use to carry out your enquiry.

Planning an urban fieldwork enquiry

Urban fieldwork enquiries, like other fieldwork enquiries, should include these stages;

- Think of a suitable **question** or **hypothesis**.
- Choose the best **fieldwork methods** to help you to collect data to answer the question.
- **Process** and **present data**, including maps, graphs and diagrams.
- **Analyse** and **explain data** you have collected.
- **Draw conclusions**, using evidence, to answer the question.
- **Reflect** on the whole investigation and **evaluate** it.

Urban fieldwork methods

Urban role play – look at an area through the eyes of different types of people.

Annotated sketch/photo – draw a sketch or take a photo and annotate it.

Environmental quality survey – give a score to different environmental features (Figure 1).

Questionnaire – ask people about their experiences and opinions.

Traffic/pedestrian survey – count the number of vehicles or pedestrians going past.

Land-use mapping – complete an outline map to show how each area is being used.

URBAN ENVIRONMENTAL QUALITY SURVEY

Name of site: Birmingham Bullring
General description: Large, modern shopping centre built in 2003

	Quality being assessed	High +2	OK +1	Av 0	Poor −1	Bad −2	
General	Vibrant, interesting place	/					Empty, uninteresting place
	Variety of natural features					/	No natural features
	Feels safe, light and busy	/					Feels unsafe, dark and quiet
	Clean environment	/					Dirty environment
Buildings	Well designed	/					Poorly designed
	In good condition		/				In poor condition
	Large, spacious buildings		/				Small, cramped buildings
	No vandalism	/					Extensive vandalism

Figure 1 Urban environmental quality survey

 Six Second Summary

- Urban fieldwork enquiries should begin with a question or hypothesis.
- There are a range of fieldwork methods that can be used in urban areas.
- One commonly used method is an urban environmental quality survey.

 Over to you

Plan an urban fieldwork enquiry that you could do with the help of an environmental quality survey.

a Think of a suitable question or hypothesis.
b Say how an environmental quality survey would help you to answer your question or investigate your hypothesis.
c What other fieldwork methods could you use?

Fieldwork

You need to know:

- the difference between primary and secondary data
- how both types of data help in an urban fieldwork enquiry
- what you could investigate about urban change.

Primary and secondary data

Fieldwork involves the collection of **primary data**, for example, by doing surveys, sketches or maps. Sometimes, you also need to use **secondary data**, from other sources such as the internet, newspapers or books.

	Count or tally Make a mark for each person who passes, up to a total of 100. Turn your total into a percentage.
White, including white British, Irish and European	卌 卌 卌 卌 卌 卌 卌 卌 卌 卌 卌
Asian, including Pakistani, Indian, Bangladeshi and Asian British	卌 卌 卌 卌 卌
Black, including West Indian, African and Black British	卌 卌
Chinese and British Chinese	//
Mixed race and other ethnic groups	卌 ////

Figure 1 Population survey

Investigating urban change

Urban change is one topic to investigate doing fieldwork. You could investigate the question, '*How is the population of the urban area changing?*', or the hypothesis, '*The proportion of ethnic minorities in the urban area is increasing*'.

To carry out the investigation you would need to collect primary data about the population now (Figure 1). You would also need secondary data about the population in the past (Figure 2).

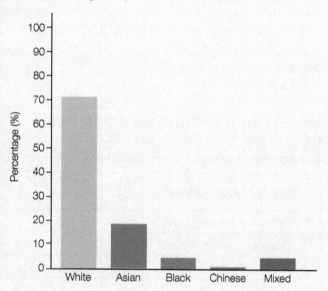

Figure 2 Population of Birmingham by ethnic groups from 2001 census

More questions and hypotheses about urban change

Why is the land use in the urban area changing?
How is the urban area becoming more sustainable?

Land use in the urban area is changing because more housing is needed.
Transport improvements are making the urban area more sustainable.

 Six Second Summary

- Primary data is information you collect yourself by doing fieldwork.
- Secondary data is information you obtain from other sources.
- To investigate urban change you will need to use primary and secondary data.

 **Over to you**

Plan a fieldwork enquiry about urban change using both primary and secondary data.

a Choose one question or hypothesis to investigate about urban change.
b Suggest one or two fieldwork methods you would use to collect primary data.
c Say what secondary data you would need and where you could find it.

You need to know:

- where Istanbul is located
- the history of the city and its different names
- the city's importance in the Ottoman Empire.

Your key question

What are the challenges and opportunities for cities today?

Think about...
what is life like for
people in a city?

Istanbul's location

Istanbul, in Turkey, has a unique location. It is the only city to span two continents – Europe and Asia (Figure 1). The city lies on the Bosphorus Strait that links the Black Sea and Sea of Marmara.

Istanbul is one of the world's fastest-growing cities, with a population of 15 million. It now stretches along the coast of the Sea of Marmara east and west of the Bosphorus.

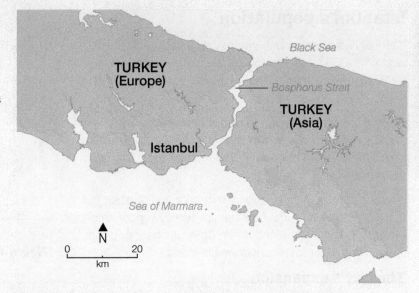

Figure 1 *Istanbul's location in both Europe and Asia*

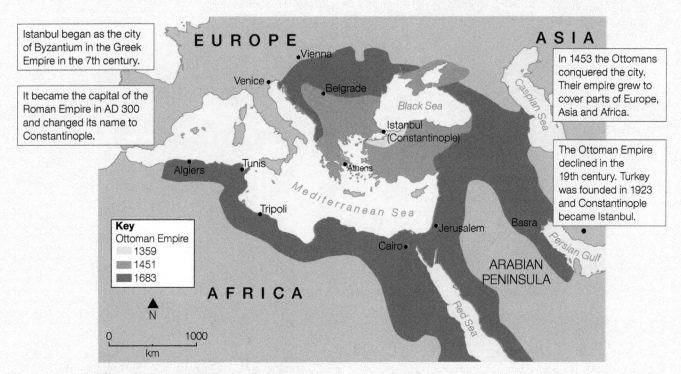

Istanbul began as the city of Byzantium in the Greek Empire in the 7th century.

It became the capital of the Roman Empire in AD 300 and changed its name to Constantinople.

In 1453 the Ottomans conquered the city. Their empire grew to cover parts of Europe, Asia and Africa.

The Ottoman Empire declined in the 19th century. Turkey was founded in 1923 and Constantinople became Istanbul.

Key
Ottoman Empire
- 1359
- 1451
- 1683

Figure 2 *A brief history of Istanbul*

Six Second Summary

- Istanbul lies on the Bosphorus Strait between Europe and Asia.
- The city was previously called Constantinople and, before that, Byzantium.
- Constantinople was at the heart of the Ottoman Empire until 1923.

Over to you

Draw a sketch map to show the location of Istanbul. Start by copying the labels from the map in Figure 1. Then draw your own map, without the book, with only the labels to help you.

You need to know:
- how Istanbul's population has grown
- the reason for its population growth
- how the size and shape of the city has changed.

Your key question
What are the challenges and opportunities for cities today?

Think about...
what is life like for people in a city?

Case Study

Istanbul's population

Istanbul has always been one of the largest cities in the world. In 1950 it had a population of almost one million, and by 2015 it was about 15 million (Figure 1). It is expected to reach 20 million by 2025.

Most of the growth is due to **national migration**. Migrants come to Istanbul from other parts of Turkey for jobs in the city. Only 29% of Istanbul's population was actually born in the city.

There is not much international migration to Istanbul, but it is growing as a tourist destination. Turkey is now among the world's most popular tourism destinations... and the Turkish city that most tourists visit is Istanbul!

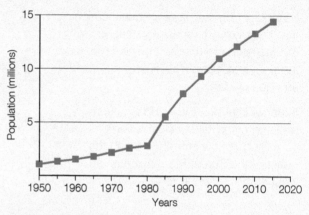

Figure 1 *Population growth in Istanbul, 1950–2015*

The city's expansion

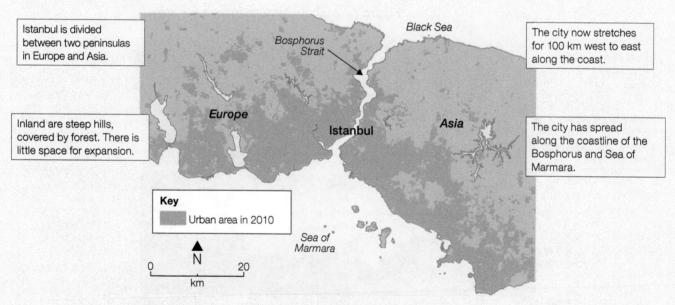

Istanbul is divided between two peninsulas in Europe and Asia.

The city now stretches for 100 km west to east along the coast.

Inland are steep hills, covered by forest. There is little space for expansion.

The city has spread along the coastline of the Bosphorus and Sea of Marmara.

Key

Urban area in 2010

Figure 2 *The urban area of Istanbul in 2010*

Six Second Summary

- Istanbul's population has grown from one to 15 million since 1950.
- Most of this population growth has come from national migration.
- The city now stretches along the coast because it can't expand far inland.

Over to you

Describe and *explain* the size and shape of Istanbul with the help of Figure 2.

When you *describe*, say what you can *see* on the map, using the labels and scale on the map to help you.

When you *explain*, say *why* the city has grown and *why* it has grown into its present shape.

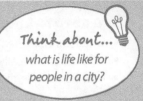

You need to know:

- what has happened to the historic core of Istanbul
- where people and business have gone
- how ways of life in the city are changing.

Your key question

What are the challenges and opportunities for cities today?

Think about...
what is life like for people in a city?

Case Study

Changes in Istanbul

Istanbul has grown outwards from its historic core. The old city centre is still the cultural heart of Istanbul and now attracts tourists. It is a bustling hotch-potch of markets and mosques, ferries and fishermen, tourists and trams (Figure 1).

As the old city has become congested, people and business have moved out. People have shifted to the suburbs (Figure 2). Business has moved to new high-rise, commercial centres in other parts of Istanbul.

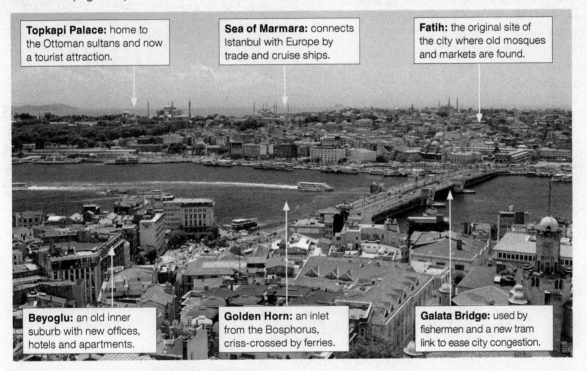

Topkapi Palace: home to the Ottoman sultans and now a tourist attraction.

Sea of Marmara: connects Istanbul with Europe by trade and cruise ships.

Fatih: the original site of the city where old mosques and markets are found.

Beyoglu: an old inner suburb with new offices, hotels and apartments.

Golden Horn: an inlet from the Bosphorus, criss-crossed by ferries.

Galata Bridge: used by fishermen and a new tram link to ease city congestion.

Figure 1 *Istanbul's historic core*

Six Second Summary

- Istanbul has grown outwards from its historic core.
- People have moved to the suburbs and business to new, commercial centres.
- The old centre is now a bustling hotch-potch of activities that gets congested.

Over to you

Draw a large spider diagram to summarise the ways of life in the *historic core of Istanbul*. Add your own details under each of the headings *markets, mosques, fishing, ferries, trams, tourism.*

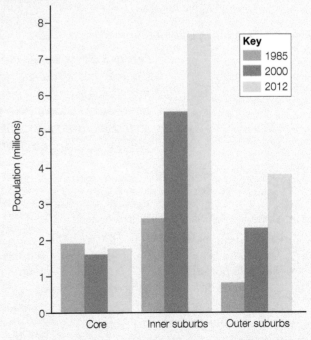

Figure 2 *Shift of population in Istanbul, 1985–2012*

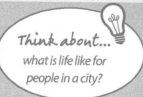

Case Study

You need to know:
- why Istanbul faces a housing challenge
- how people initially responded to the challenge
- how housing in the city has improved since then.

Your key question
What are the challenges and opportunities for cities today?

Think about...
what is life like for people in a city?

Istanbul's housing challenge

In the 1960s only about 20% of Turkey's population lived in cities. Today it is about 70%, which creates an urban housing challenge. In Istanbul, poor migrants have come up with their own solutions to this challenge (Figures 1, 2 and 3).

- They built squatter settlements around the city on vacant land. These were called **gecekondu**, meaning 'built overnight'. Over time, these have been improved or rebuilt to become part of the city.
- They transformed old homes in the city into apartment blocks, sometimes by adding new storeys to the building. They were not built to very high standards.

Figure 2 *Esenler – a former squatter settlement, once on the edge of the city, that has been demolished and redeveloped as a high-rise housing estate*

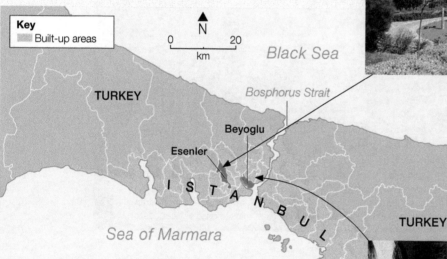

Figure 1 *Districts in Istanbul.*

Figure 3 *Beyoglu – an old area close to the city centre that had fallen into disrepair, where young professional people have moved in and improved the homes – a process called* **gentrification**

Six Second Summary

- Since the 1960s Turkey's urban population has grown from 20% to 70%.
- Migrants built squatter settlements or transformed old homes into apartments.
- Later, squatter settlements were redeveloped and old urban areas gentrified.

Over to you

Complete a table like this to compare two housing areas in Istanbul – Beyoglu and Esenler

District	Location in the city	What was housing like?	Who lived there?	How was it improved?
Beyoglu				
Esenler				

You need to know:

- why Istanbul has such a serious congestion problem
- how an integrated transport system could help
- about the Marmaray Rail Project in Istanbul.

Your key question

What are the challenges and opportunities for cities today?

Think about...
how can cities become more sustainable?

Istanbul's congestion problem

Istanbul is one of the most congested cities in the world.

Average traffic speed at peak hours is 8–10 km/hour.

About one-third of households own a car. By 2025 it could be two-thirds.

The Bosphorus is an obstacle to east/west traffic.

420 000 vehicles cross the Bosphorus every day, over just three bridges.

Over 25% of passenger journeys in Istanbul are made by car.

Figure 1 *Congestion in Istanbul*

An integrated transport solution

There are already many alternative forms of transport to cars in Istanbul, including:

- taxis and minibuses
- buses and trams
- trains
- ferries
- bicycles.

But, they don't always link with each other.

A sustainable solution to the congestion problem would be an **integrated transport system** where all forms of transport link together better.

An example of this is the Marmaray rail line, opened in 2013.

- The route links both sides of Istanbul with a rail tunnel under the Bosphorus.
- The line is expected to increase the proportion of passengers using rail from 5% to 30%.

Six Second Summary

- Istanbul is one of the most congested cities in the world.
- Over 25% of passenger journeys are by car and car ownership is growing.
- The Marmaray Rail Project could help to reduce congestion as part of an integrated transport system.

Over to you

a Explain why congestion is a problem in Istanbul. Give three reasons.
b How could the Marmaray Rail Project help to reduce the problem? Mention three ways.

Topic 6:
Dynamic Development

Your exam

Dynamic Development is part of Paper 2: People and Society. It is a 1 hr 15 min written exam and makes up 35% of your GCSE. The whole paper carries 70 marks (including 3 marks for SPaG).

There are two sections on the paper:

- Section A: questions on all the human geography topics, including *Dynamic Development*

- Section B: human geography fieldwork.

You will have to answer all questions on the paper.

Your revision checklist

Tick these boxes to build a record of your revision

Spec key question	Theme	1	2	3
Why are some countries richer than others?				
What is development and how can it be measured?	6.1 Defining development			
	6.2 The global development divide			
	6.3 Measuring development			
	6.4 Development changes lives			
What has led to uneven development?	6.5 How uneven development happened			
	6.6 Uneven development and climate change			
	6.7 Obstacles to development – trade and debt			
	6.8 Obstacles to development – political unrest			
Are LIDCs likely to stay poor?				
How has an LIDC developed so far?	6.9 Zambia – a low-income developing country			
	6.10 Zambia's zigzag path to development			
	6.11 Zambia's development goals			
	6.12 Invest in Zambia			
What global connections influence its development?	6.13 Zambia's reliance on copper			
	6.14 Trans-national companies in Zambia			
	6.15 Aid and debt in Africa			
What development strategy is most appropriate?	6.16 Top-down development in Zambia			
	6.17 Bottom-up development in Zambia			

You need to know:
- what development is
- how countries are classified by their level of development
- the different aspects of development.

Your key question
Why are some countries richer than others?

what is development and how can it be measured?

What is development?

Development means an improvement in living standards through better use of resources.

Geographers classify countries according to their level of development:

- **Advanced countries (ACs)** – countries that are wealthy and have a wide range of jobs and many services.
- **Emerging and developing countries (EDCs)** – countries that are in transition from being LIDCs to becoming ACs.
- **Low-income developing countries (LIDCs)** – countries that are poor and have a narrow range of jobs and few services.

Aspects of development

Development is about wealth, but it is also about other things:

- **Economic development** – an increase in the total goods and services a country produces.
- **Social development** – an improvement in human welfare to meet people's needs in a country.
- **Sustainable development** – economic, social and environmental development to meets people's needs now, as well as the needs of future generations (Figure 1).

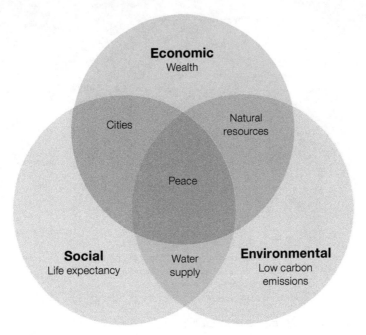

Figure 1 *Sustainable development*

Six Second Summary

- Development means an improvement in living standards through better use of resources.
- Countries can be classified into advanced countries (ACs), emerging and developing countries (EDCs) and low-income developing countries (LIDCs).
- Sustainable development includes economic, social and environmental development.

Over to you

Make a large copy of the Venn diagram in Figure 1. Think of at least one more aspect of development to put in each space on the diagram.

You need to know:
- how the world was once divided
- the ways in which the divisions are changing
- which are the world's fastest growing economies.

Your key question

Why are some countries richer than others?

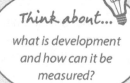

Think about...
what is development and how can it be measured?

How the world is divided

For a long time, geographers divided the world into 'developed' and 'developing' countries. The 'Brandt Line' divided the world into the 'rich North' and 'poor South'.

As the world develops, it gets harder to divide countries into groups. The International Monetary Fund (IMF) now classifies countries into three groups – ACs, EDCs and LIDCs (Figure 1).

BRICs and **MINTs** are two groups of countries with rapidly growing economies in Asia, South America and Africa. The economies of most countries in Europe and North America are growing more slowly.

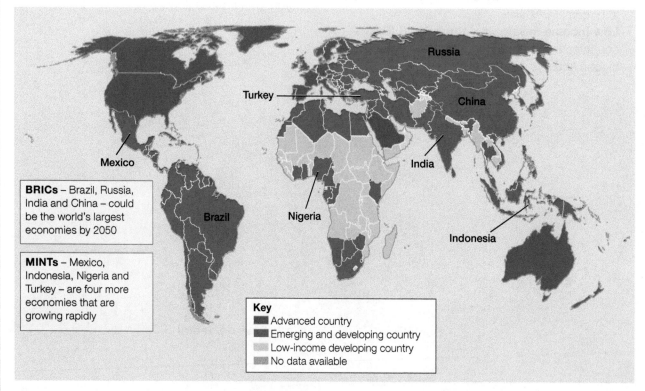

BRICs – Brazil, Russia, India and China – could be the world's largest economies by 2050

MINTs – Mexico, Indonesia, Nigeria and Turkey – are four more economies that are growing rapidly

Key
- Advanced country
- Emerging and developing country
- Low-income developing country
- No data available

Figure 1 *The world divided into ACs, EDCs and LIDCs*

 Six Second Summary

- The world was once divided into 'developed' and 'developing' countries.
- As the world develops it becomes harder to classify countries into groups.
- BRICs and MINTs are countries with rapidly growing economies.

Over to you

a Identify three countries in each of these groups on the map in Figure 1 – ACs, EDCs and LIDCs.
b Describe the distribution of each of the three groups of countries on the map.

You need to know:

- how development can be measured
- the criticisms of wealth as a measure of development
- what the Human Development Index measures.

Your key question

Why are some countries richer than others?

Think about...
what is development and how can it be measured?

Wealth as a measure of development

One measure of development is wealth. A country's wealth is measured by **gross national income per capita (GNI/capita)** – or average wealth per person. Taking into account the cost of living in the country, it is measured by GNI/capita at **purchasing power parity (PPP)**.

There are criticisms of using wealth alone as a measure of development;

- GNI/capita is only an average – many people are richer or poorer than average.
- Not all wealth is included, e.g. food grown by farmers to feed their families.
- Social development or sustainable development are not included.

HDI as a measure of development

Another way to measure development is the **Human Development Index** (Figure 1). It includes:

- wealth measured by GDP/capita at PPP
- health measured by **life expectancy**, the average age to which people are expected to live
- education measured by the **adult literacy rate**, the percentage of adults who are able to read

Scores for HDI range from the lowest (0) to highest (1) levels of development.

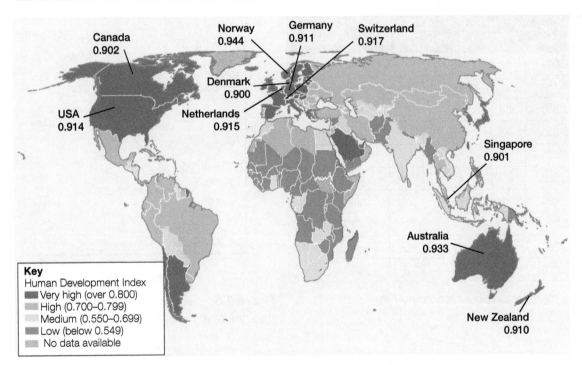

Canada 0.902
Norway 0.944
Germany 0.911
Switzerland 0.917
Denmark 0.900
USA 0.914
Netherlands 0.915
Singapore 0.901
Australia 0.933
New Zealand 0.910

Key
Human Development Index
- Very high (over 0.800)
- High (0.700–0.799)
- Medium (0.550–0.699)
- Low (below 0.549)
- No data available

Figure 1 *HDI by country, including the world's top 10 most developed countries*

Six Second Summary

- Wealth is measured by gross national income per capita at PPP.
- There are criticisms of using wealth alone to measure development.
- The Human Development Index includes wealth, health and education.

Over to you

Make flash cards to revise each of the different ways of measuring development – GNI/capita at PPP, Human Development Index, life expectancy, adult literacy rate.

Try to explain each one in your own words.

- what the global pattern of development is
- how development between different countries compares
- the relationship between different measures of development.

why are some countries richer than others?

Think about...

what is development and how can it be measured?

Comparing development between countries

Globally, there is **uneven development** between countries. Most ACs are in Europe, North America and Oceania; most EDCs are in Asia and South America, while most LIDCs are in Africa.

The different measures of development for each country are connected (Figure 1). Wealthy countries are likely to have more money to spend on health and education. Measures like life expectancy and adult literacy tend to increase with wealth (Figure 2).

Uneven development in Qatar

Qatar, the richest country in the world, has a lower life expectancy than some countries with less wealth. It is a small country in the Middle East, which has become extremely wealthy from its resources of oil and gas. It does not have a large workforce, so depends on migrant workers from countries like India. Most of these workers live in poor, overcrowded conditions on low pay.

Country	GNI/capita at PPP ($)	Rank	Life expectancy	Rank	Adult literacy (%)	Rank
Afghanistan	2 000	1	48	1	38	1
Brazil	14 750	6	73	5	91	5
China	11 850	5	74	6	95	6
India	5 350	3	65	4	74	3
Nigeria	5 360	4	54	3	61	2
Norway	66 520	9	81	9	100	10
Qatar	123 860	10	78	7	96	7
UK	35 760	7	81	9	99	8
USA	53 960	8	79	8	99	8
Zambia	3 076	2	52	2	80	4

Figure 1 *Development for ten countries, from Afghanistan to Zambia*

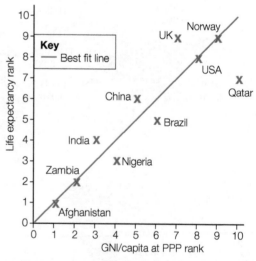

Figure 2 *Scatter graph to compare wealth and health in ten countries*

 Six Second Summary

- Globally, there is uneven development between countries.
- Wealthy countries often have a higher life expectancy and literacy rates.
- Qatar, the world's wealthiest country, does not have the highest life expectancy or adult literacy.

Over to you

You can learn a lot from scatter graphs, either by interpreting them or drawing them.

a **Describe** the relationship between wealth and life expectancy in the scatter graph in Figure 2. Then **explain** this relationship.

b Draw a similar scatter graph to show the relationship between wealth and adult literacy, using data from the table in Figure 1. **Describe** and **explain** the relationship you can see.

You need to know:

- the physical and human factors that can influence development
- the importance of history in countries' development
- how colonialism influenced development.

Your key question

Why are some countries richer than others?

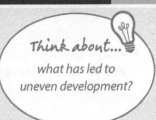

Think about...
what has led to uneven development?

Factors that influence development

The uneven development that we see around the world today did not always exist. Some of the physical and human factors that help countries to develop include:

- a large population
- warm climate
- flat, fertile land
- abundant natural resources.

Unfortunately, none of these factors fully explain why some countries develop. We also need to know about a country's history.

The importance of history

Historically, European countries explored and traded with other parts of the world. Later, they conquered and ruled some of these places. This process was called **colonialism** (Figure 1).

Colonialism helped Europe to develop because it enabled them to obtain **commodities** like sugar. But, it slowed down development in the **colonies** Europe ruled. The influence of colonialism is still seen around the world, even though the countries are now independent.

Figure 1 *A history of colonialism*

 Six Second Summary

- Population, climate, land and resources can all influence development.
- History can better explain why some countries developed more than others.
- Colonialism helped Europe to develop, but slowed development in other places.

 **Over to you**

Use the drawings in Figure 1 to help you to write a short story of colonialism. Write one sentence about each drawing. Include the following words in your story – *Europe, trade, slavery, colonies, commodities, independence.*

You need to know:

- what the global effects of climate change are
- why the consequences could be worse for LIDCs and EDCs.

Your key question

Why are some countries richer than others?

Think about...

what has led to uneven development?

Global effects of climate change

Climate change could make the problem of uneven development worse. The effects of climate change include:

- gradual rise in sea level
- stronger cyclones
- warmer days and nights
- more unpredictable rainfall and drought
- hotter and longer heatwaves (Figure 1).

Why the consequences are worse in LIDCs

The consequences of climate change are likely to be worse for LIDCs and EDCs because they lack the resources that are necessary to adapt. This could result in:

- increased hunger
- more conflict
- migration
- worse poverty.

ACs have produced carbon emissions for over 200 years; LIDCs emit small amounts. LIDCs are more likely to suffer from the impacts of climate change.

Melting glaciers will initially lead to flooding but, later, to water shortage.

Disease will increase as temperatures rise, so bacteria and insects will spread.

More weather disasters like typhoons will occur and rainfall will increase.

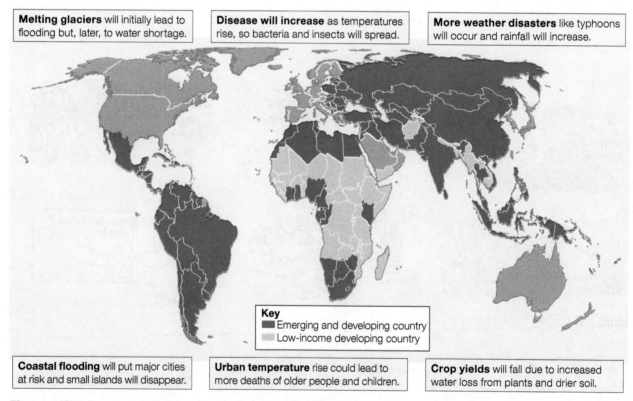

Key
 Emerging and developing country
Low-income developing country

Coastal flooding will put major cities at risk and small islands will disappear.

Urban temperature rise could lead to more deaths of older people and children.

Crop yields will fall due to increased water loss from plants and drier soil.

Figure 1 *The impact of climate change in LIDCs and EDCs*

Six Second Summary

- Climate change could make the problem of uneven development worse.
- The consequences of climate change are worse for LIDCs and EDCs.
- LICDs and EDCs lack the resources necessary to adapt to climate change.

Over to you

Briefly explain how climate change could have each of these consequences in LIDCs:

- increased hunger
- more conflict
- migration
- worse poverty

You need to know:

- what trade and debt are
- how trade can be an obstacle to development for LIDCs
- why debt is a more serious problem for LIDCs than for ACs.

Your key question

Why are some countries richer than others?

Think about... what has led to uneven development?

Trade as an obstacle

Trade is a way of obtaining things that a country needs and a way for it to earn money. You would expect that trade would help development. But, that is not always the case for LIDCs (Figure 1).

Most trade is between ACs. Europe, the USA and China dominate world trade.

ACs produce manufactured goods and services, while LIDCs rely on the export of natural commodities.

The price of natural commodities go up and down, while the price of goods and services mainly go up.

Most world trade is controlled by **trans-national companies** (TNCs), usually based in ACs.

Figure 1 *Reasons why trade can be an obstacle to development*

Debt as an obstacle

Debt is money owed by any country that has borrowed. Countries often have to cut spending to repay their debts. The impact of debt is worse for LIDCs because they have less money. They may not have enough to spend on basic needs, like health and education.

Some countries are in surplus, with more money than they need.

- Countries in surplus include Germany, China and just five African countries.
- Countries in debt include the USA, UK and 19 African countries.

Six Second Summary

- Trade is a way for a country to obtain what it needs and for it to earn money.
- World trade is dominated by ACs and can work against the interests of LIDCs.
- Debt is a more serious problem for LIDCs, with less money to spend on basic needs.

Over to you

a Weigh up the pros and cons of trade for LIDCs. Make two lists.

b Now, do the same for the pros and cons of borrowing money for LIDCs.

Why are trade and debt obstacles to development for LIDCs?

You need to know:

- what causes political unrest
- how political unrest can be an obstacle to development
- which countries have experienced the worst unrest.

Your key question

Why are some countries richer than others?

Think about... what has led to uneven development?

Political unrest as an obstacle

Political unrest happens in countries where there is widespread dissatisfaction with the government (Figure 1). This could be the result of:

- social inequality
- poor government or corruption
- high taxes
- lack of government spending
- rising prices of essential items like food
- conflict over resource ownership.

Political unrest is less likely in **democratic** countries where people can vote to change their government. It can start with street protests but can develop into full-scale **civil war**, setting back development by displacing people, disrupting services and the production of food.

South Sudan

South Sudan is the world's newest country and also one of the poorest. It gained independence from Sudan in 2011, ending Africa's longest-running civil war. One of the causes of conflict was oil. Sudan was rich in oil, most of it in South Sudan.

In 2013 a new civil war broke out in South Sudan. Thousands were killed and a million displaced. Production of oil almost stopped. Many of the population are cattle herders, who also fight each other in disputes over land.

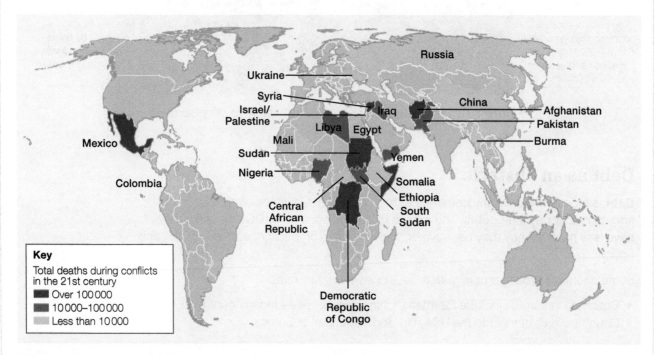

Figure 1 *Civil war and political unrest around the world in the 21st century*

Six Second Summary

- Political unrest starts with widespread dissatisfaction with the government.
- The worst political unrest in the 21st century has been in EDCs and LIDCs.
- Political unrest can set back development, displacing people and disrupting the economy.

Over to you

Compare Figure 1 above with Figure 1, 6.2, which shows the distribution of ACs, EDCs and LIDCs. Which types of country experience the worst political unrest? How can you explain that?

You need to know:

- where Zambia is
- what has happened to Zambia in the past
- what makes it a LIDC today.

Your key question

Are LIDCs likely to stay poor?

Think about...
how has an LIDC developed so far?

Zambia – the basics

Zambia is a country in central southern Africa. It is a **land-locked country**, surrounded by other countries and without its own coastline (Figures 1 and 2). It has the characteristics of a low-income developing country (Figure 3).

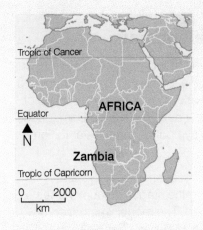

Figure 1 Zambia's location in Africa

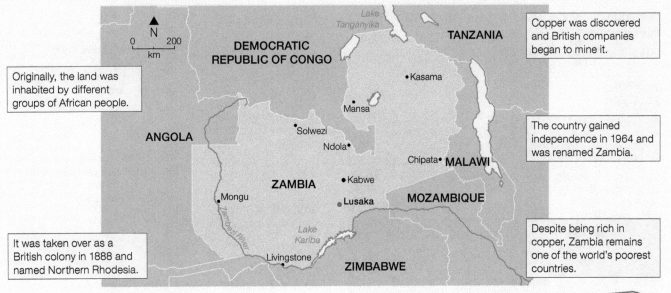

Copper was discovered and British companies began to mine it.

Originally, the land was inhabited by different groups of African people.

The country gained independence in 1964 and was renamed Zambia.

It was taken over as a British colony in 1888 and named Northern Rhodesia.

Despite being rich in copper, Zambia remains one of the world's poorest countries.

Figure 2 Map of Zambia

Six Second Summary

- Zambia is a land-locked country in central southern Africa and is a LIDC.
- The country was once a British colony, when copper was discovered and mined.
- Despite being rich in copper, it remains one of the world's poorest countries.

Over to you

List all the features in column 1 in Figure 3, and then cut them out. Do the same for all the key facts in column 2.

Then, without the book to help you, try to match each feature with the correct fact.

Population	14.5 million
Area	752 614 km²
Population growth rate	2.9%
Birth rate	43 per 1000
Death rate	13 per 1000
Average life expectancy	52
Literacy rate	80%
GNI/capita	$3070
Human Development Index	0.43 (ranked 164/187 in the world)
Urban population	36%
Economic growth rate	6.5% per year
Exports	copper (64%), cobalt, tobacco, flowers, cotton
Imports	machinery, transport equipment, oil, fertiliser, food, clothing

Figure 3 Zambia fact file

Case Study

You need to know:

- how Zambia has developed since 1964
- the extent to which Zambia's development has been in a zigzag pattern
- the factors which have helped or hindered its development.

Your key question

Are LIDCs likely to stay poor?

Think about...
how has an LIDC developed so far?

Zambia's development

When Zambia achieved independence in 1964, it was expected to follow in the footsteps of more advanced countries towards development. The construction of a large hydro-electricity dam, the Kariba Dam, on the Zambezi River was a symbol of Zambia's ambition (Figure 1).

The **Rostow model** of economic development is a straight line, showing the stages a country goes through as it developed. The model was based on the experience of ACs. However, Zambia's path to development since 1964 has been more of a zigzag than a straight line. Figure 2 shows that the economy has gone through a series of ups and downs.

1964 Zambia gains independence. Most power and wealth is still in European hands.

1970 The global price of copper falls. Zambia has to borrow money to develop.

1975 The Kariba Dam starts to generate power, used by the copper industry.

1980 HIV/AIDS spreads across Africa. Life expectancy in Zambia falls.

1990 Zambia's debt is very high. There are riots as food gets more expensive.

2000 The global price of copper starts to rise again, increasing Zambia's earnings.

2006 The IMF cancels Zambia's debts so it can spend more on health and education.

2010 Zambia begins to develop industries like tourism, farming and hydro-power.

Figure 2 *Zambia's development timeline*

Figure 1 *HEP production at the Kariba Dam on the Zambezi River*

 Six Second Summary

- In 1964 Zambia was expected to follow the footsteps of ACs to development.
- In fact, Zambia's path to development has been more of a zig-zag than a straight line.
- Many different factors helped and hindered Zambia's development.

 **Over to you**

Draw a zig-zag line. On one side of the line list the factors that have helped Zambia to develop and, on the other side, list the factors that have hindered it, giving reasons. For example, when the global price of copper fell it hindered development because Zambia earned less money.

You need to know:

- what the Millennium Development Goals were
- how much progress Zambia made in meeting the MDGs.

Your key question

Are LIDCs likely to stay poor?

Think about...

how has an LIDC developed so far?

Case Study

Development goals

In 2000, world leaders from 198 countries signed an agreement, committing their governments to eight **Millennium Development Goals** (MDGs), with the aim of cutting world poverty in half by 2015. Globally, progress towards meeting the goals has been mixed.

Zambia's progress towards meeting the MDGs by 2015 has also been mixed (Figure 1). It has met some targets, but not others. Urban areas, like Lusaka, saw much bigger improvements than rural areas.

MDGs in 2000

- Halve extreme poverty and hunger.
- Achieve primary education everywhere.
- Promote gender equality and empower women.
- Reduce **child mortality**.
- Improve **maternal health** (mothers' health).
- Combat HIV/AIDS and other diseases.
- Ensure environmental sustainability.
- Develop a global partnership for development.

Extreme poverty

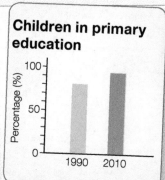

Children in primary education

Gender equality

Zambia was expected to achieve equal primary school enrolment for boys and girls in 2015. More has to be done to achieve equal enrolment in secondary schools and universities.

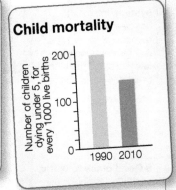

Child mortality

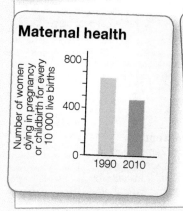

Maternal health

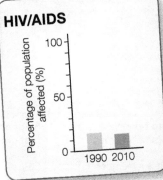

HIV/AIDS

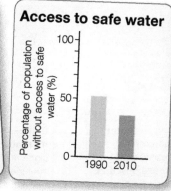

Access to safe water

Global partnership

Zambia has obtained international debt relief. It has also attracted foreign investment, particularly from China into mining. Zambia's trade has grown, with more products now exported.

Figure 1 *Zambia's progress towards meeting Millennium Development Goals*

 **Over to you**

Assess Zambia's progress towards meeting the eight MDGs, using the data in Figure 1.

a what progress towards each MDG has been made?
b what still has to be achieved?

You could summarise the information in a table like this

MDG	What Zambia achieved	What has still to be achieved
Halve extreme poverty		

Six Second Summary

- World leaders set the MDGs in 2000, to cut world poverty in half by 2015.
- Globally, progress towards meeting the MDGs has been mixed.
- Zambia has achieved some goals but not others.

Case Study

You need to know:

- what is happening to Zambia's economy
- why the government wants to attract foreign investment
- the factors that attract investment to Zambia.

Your key question

Are LIDCs likely to stay poor?

Think about...
how has an LIDC developed so far?

Zambia's growing economy

Zambia has one of the fastest-growing economies in Africa. On average, it grows by about 6% each year. Yet Zambia remains a very unequal country, with almost half the country living in poverty.

The Zambian government wants to achieve 'a better Zambia for all'. It aims to become an EDC by 2030. To achieve this, the government encourages **foreign investment** through large companies bringing their business to Zambia (Figure 1).

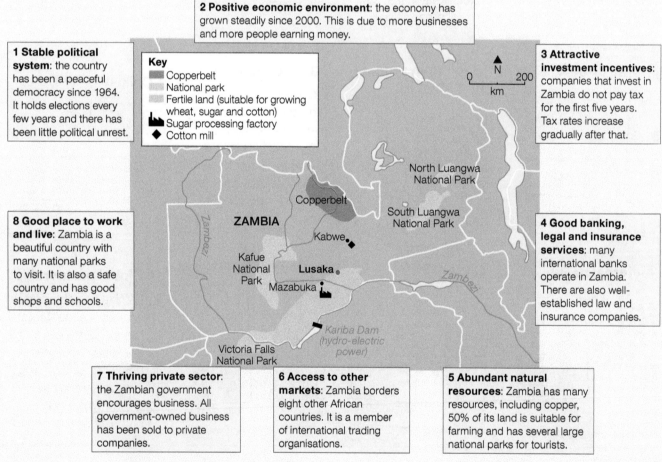

2 Positive economic environment: the economy has grown steadily since 2000. This is due to more businesses and more people earning money.

1 Stable political system: the country has been a peaceful democracy since 1964. It holds elections every few years and there has been little political unrest.

Key
- Copperbelt
- National park
- Fertile land (suitable for growing wheat, sugar and cotton)
- Sugar processing factory
- Cotton mill

3 Attractive investment incentives: companies that invest in Zambia do not pay tax for the first five years. Tax rates increase gradually after that.

8 Good place to work and live: Zambia is a beautiful country with many national parks to visit. It is also a safe country and has good shops and schools.

4 Good banking, legal and insurance services: many international banks operate in Zambia. There are also well-established law and insurance companies.

7 Thriving private sector: the Zambian government encourages business. All government-owned business has been sold to private companies.

6 Access to other markets: Zambia borders eight other African countries. It is a member of international trading organisations.

5 Abundant natural resources: Zambia has many resources, including copper, 50% of its land is suitable for farming and has several large national parks for tourists.

Figure 1 Why invest in Zambia?

Six Second Summary

- Zambia has one of the fastest-growing economies in Africa.
- The Zambian government wants to attract investment to become an EDC by 2030.
- There are political, economic and environmental reasons to invest in Zambia.

Over to you

Draw a spider diagram with 'Zambia' in the centre and eight reasons to invest in Zambia around it. Without using the book, try to explain each reason in your own words.

You need to know:

- what Zambia exports
- the importance of copper to Zambia's economy
- how Zambia's copper production goes up and down, and why.

Your key question

Are LIDCs likely to stay poor?

Think about... what global connections influence its development?

Case Study

Zambia and copper

Zambia relies on copper for 70% of its exports (Figure 1). This can be a problem because the global price of copper goes up and down. When the price goes up, so does production of copper but, when the price goes down, production falls (Figure 2).

The Zambian government wants to diversify the economy so that, in future, the country does not rely so much on copper. Over 500 Chinese companies now invest in Zambia in businesses ranging from mining to manufacturing, farming to tourism.

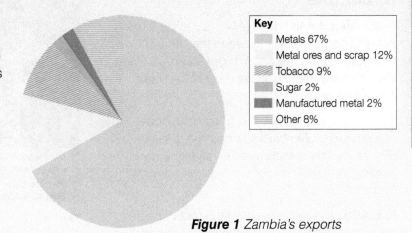

Key
- Metals 67%
- Metal ores and scrap 12%
- Tobacco 9%
- Sugar 2%
- Manufactured metal 2%
- Other 8%

Figure 1 *Zambia's exports*

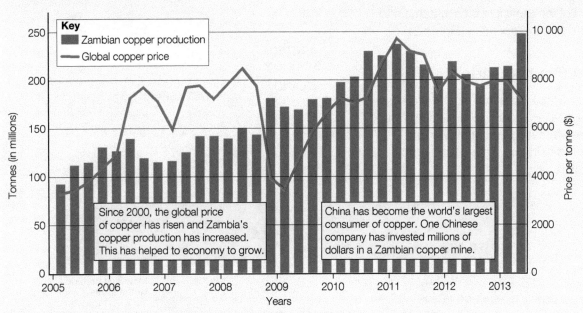

Since 2000, the global price of copper has risen and Zambia's copper production has increased. This has helped to economy to grow.

China has become the world's largest consumer of copper. One Chinese company has invested millions of dollars in a Zambian copper mine.

Figure 2 *Zambia's copper production and the global price for copper, 2005–2013*

Six Second Summary

- Zambia relies on copper for 70% of its exports.
- Zambian copper production goes up and down with the global price of copper.
- The Zambian government want to diversify the economy with the help of Chinese investment.

Over to you

Explain the connection between the global price of copper and Zambia's copper production in Figure 2.

a Why does production increase when the price goes up?

b Why does production decrease when the price goes down?

You need to know:

- about one trans-national company in Zambia
- how Associated British Foods avoids paying tax in Zambia
- the benefits and problems trans-national companies bring.

Your key question

Are LIDCs likely to stay poor?

Think about...

what global connections influence its development?

ABF – a trans-national company in Zambia

Associated British Foods (ABF) is a large trans-national company. It is based in the UK and operates around the world. It owns Zambia Sugar, the company that produces most of Zambia's sugar and also exports it.

Zambia Sugar's factory is in Mazabuka, the town at the heart of Zambia's sugar-growing region (Figure 1). The company is the main employer, helping to make it one of the most prosperous towns in Zambia.

But, ABF pays almost no tax in Zambia and this does not help the national economy. Instead, it transfers most of the profit it makes in Zambia to other countries with low tax rates (Figure 2).

Zambia's difficult situation

Zambia is in a difficult situation. It needs to raise income through tax in order to pay for services like health and education. But, it also wants to encourage TNCs to invest in the country by offering low tax rates.

Six Second Summary

- Associated British Foods is a large trans-national company, based in the UK.
- ABF avoids paying tax in Zambia by transferring profits to other countries.
- Zambia wants to encourage investment from TNCs but also needs to raise income through tax.

Over to you

Weigh up the benefits and problems of TNCs in an LIDC like Zambia. Make a list of all the benefits and problems of ABF in Zambia. Why is Zambia in a difficult situation?

Sugar workers earn money, helping their families, and pay taxes, helping Zambia.

Their wages are low compared with similar workers in richer countries.

Figure 1 *A cane-cutter working for Zambia Sugar*

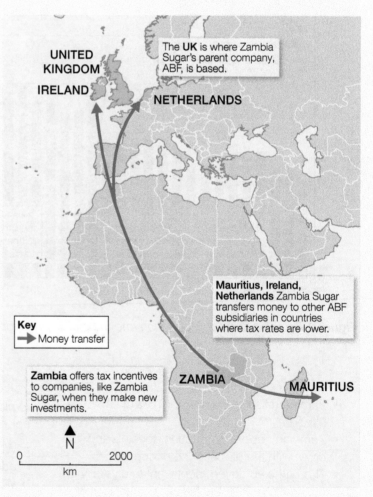

The **UK** is where Zambia Sugar's parent company, ABF, is based.

UNITED KINGDOM

IRELAND

NETHERLANDS

Mauritius, Ireland, Netherlands Zambia Sugar transfers money to other ABF subsidiaries in countries where tax rates are lower.

Key
→ Money transfer

Zambia offers tax incentives to companies, like Zambia Sugar, when they make new investments.

ZAMBIA

MAURITIUS

N

0 ——— 2000
km

Figure 2 *How Zambia Sugar avoids tax*

You need to know:
- what aid and debt relief are
- the types of aid and the differences between them
- the advantages and disadvantages of aid and debt relief.

Your key question
Are LIDCs likely to stay poor?

Think about...
what global connections influence its development?

Case Study

Aid

International aid (or just 'aid') is help given to a country. Most aid is given by ACs to LIDCs, but there are many different types (Figure 1).

There are both advantages and disadvantages of aid (Figure 2). For example, a lot of aid is given with conditions attached – this is known as **tied aid**. The country receiving aid may have to use the money to buy goods from the country that gives the aid.

Debt relief

A problem for LIDCs is international debt. The amount of debt they have to repay can be greater than the amount of aid they receive. In 2006, 39 **highly indebted poor countries (HIPCs)**, including Zambia, were given debt relief. As a result, they were able to increase spending on health and education.

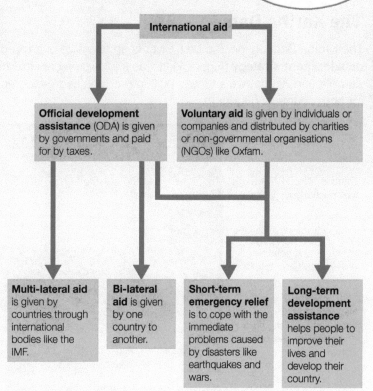

International aid

Official development assistance (ODA) is given by governments and paid for by taxes.

Voluntary aid is given by individuals or companies and distributed by charities or non-governmental organisations (NGOs) like Oxfam.

Multi-lateral aid is given by countries through international bodies like the IMF.

Bi-lateral aid is given by one country to another.

Short-term emergency relief is to cope with the immediate problems caused by disasters like earthquakes and wars.

Long-term development assistance helps people to improve their lives and develop their country.

Figure 1 *Types of aid*

Advantages

Aid is an attempt to rebalance global inequality.

Aid is repayment for the benefits ACs got from colonialism.

Everyone, wherever they live, should have the right to the essentials of life.

Disadvantages

Aid discourages people from trying to look after themselves.

Aid may be given to a corrupt government or used to pay for a country's wars.

Donors may decide what aid to give and it may not be what is most needed.

Figure 2 *Advantages and disadvantages of aid*

Six Second Summary

- Aid and debt relief are two ways in which ACs can help LIDCs.
- Aid can be given by governments, charities or large bodies like the IMF.
- The problem of international debt can be solved by debt relief.

Over to you

Copy the **bold** words on this page onto individual flash cards. Then, try to explain each one in your own words on the card. Check your ideas. If you are wrong, have another go on the other side of the card.

Case Study

You need to know:
- about a top-down development strategy in Zambia
- why the Kariba Dam was built
- what impacts the Kariba Dam has had.

Your key question
Are LIDCs likely to stay poor?

Think about...
what development strategy is most appropriate?

The Kariba Dam

The Kariba Dam on the Zambezi River is an example of a **top-down development strategy** (Figure 1). It was a joint project in the 1950s between Zambia and Zimbabwe and was built to produce hydro-electric power (HEP) for both countries (Figure 2).

Positive impacts

The dam generates large amounts of HEP for cities and the copper industry.

HEP is a renewable form of energy and does not produce carbon emissions.

New industries, like fishing and tourism, have developed around Lake Kariba.

Negative impacts

Many farmers were moved and resettled on less fertile land.

Natural flooding no longer occurs, leading to loss of farmland and ecosystems.

Communities on either side of the lake are cut off from each other.

Figure 1 *Impacts of the Kariba Dam*

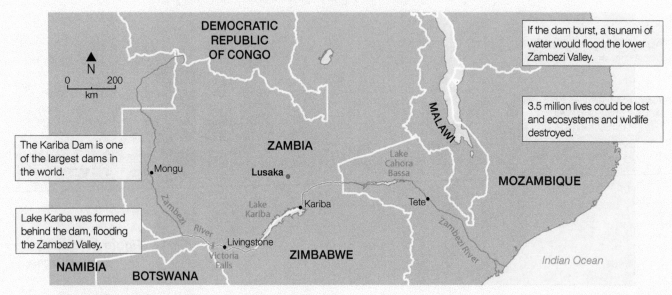

The Kariba Dam is one of the largest dams in the world.

Lake Kariba was formed behind the dam, flooding the Zambezi Valley.

If the dam burst, a tsunami of water would flood the lower Zambezi Valley.

3.5 million lives could be lost and ecosystems and wildlife destroyed.

Figure 2 *The Zambezi River and Lake Kariba*

 **Six Second Summary**

- The Kariba Dam was a top-down development strategy in Zambia.
- It was built to produce hydro-electric power for Zambia and Zimbabwe.
- It produces renewable energy but had negative impacts on people and environment.

Over to you

Draw a sketch map of Zambia. Label the Zambezi River, Lake Kariba, Lusaka and the neighbouring countries. Mark the Kariba Dam on your map.

Now, in your own words, annotate your map to explain, a) the purpose and, b) the impacts, of the dam.

Case Study

You need to know:

- about a bottom-up development strategy in Zambia
- why literacy is important for a country's development
- how literacy in Zambia compares with other African countries.

Your key question

Are LIDCs likely to stay poor?

Think about...
what development strategy is most appropriate?

Improving literacy in Zambia

The opposite of top-down is **bottom-up development**. Bottom-up development strategies are funded and carried out by non-governmental organisations (NGOs), together with local communities.

Room to Read is an NGO that works to improve literacy and gender equality in Zambia (Figure 1). There is a much higher drop-out rate from school among girls. Reasons for this include:

- girls are expected to take responsibility for domestic chores
- girls may have to go out to earn money to support their family at a young age
- parents do not value education for girls in the same way as they do for boys
- girls are sometimes pushed into early marriage or become pregnant.

Kofi Annan, former UN Director-General said:

'Literacy unlocks the door to learning throughout life, is essential for development and health and opens the way for democratic participation and active citizenship.'

Figure 1 *Room to Read*

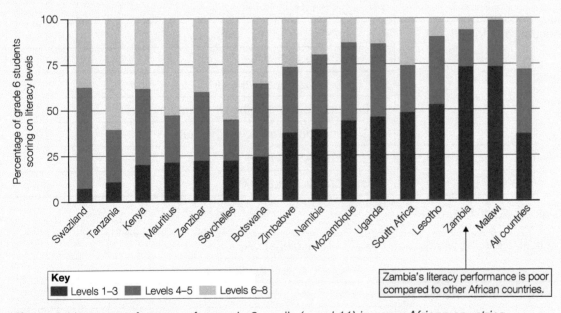

Zambia's literacy performance is poor compared to other African countries.

Key
■ Levels 1–3 ■ Levels 4–5 ▢ Levels 6–8

Figure 2 *Literacy performance for grade 6 pupils (aged 11) in some African countries*

Six Second Summary

- Room to Read is an NGO that works to improve literacy and gender equality.
- Room to Read is an example of a bottom-up development strategy in Zambia.
- Zambia has a poorer literacy performance than most other African countries.

Over to you

Read, and try to remember, the quote from Kofi Annan about the importance of literacy in Figure 1.

Now, try to explain why literacy is so important for: **a)** health and development **b)** democratic participation and active citizenship.

Topic 7:
UK in the 21st Century

Your exam

UK in the 21st Century is part of Paper 2: People and Society. It is a 1 hr 15 min written exam and makes up 35% of your GCSE. The whole paper carries 70 marks (including 3 marks for SPaG).

There are two sections on the paper;

- Section A: questions on all the physical geography topics, including *UK in the 21st Century*

- Section B: human geography fieldwork.

You will have to answer all questions on the paper.

Tick these boxes to build a record of your revision

Your revision checklist

Spec key question	Theme	1	2	3
How is the UK changing in the 21st century?				
What does the UK look like in the 21st century?	7.1 Human geography of the UK			
	7.2 Physical geography of the UK			
How is the UK's population changing?	7.3 The UK's changing population			
	7.4 Our ageing population			
	7.5 Retirement dreams			
	7.6 London's booming population			
How is the UK's economy changing?	7.7 The UK's changing economy			
	7.8 Post-industrial UK			
	7.9 Economic hubs in the UK			
	7.10 London's place in the UK economy			
	7.11 Cambridge – an economic hub			
Fieldwork skills	7.12 Economic fieldwork – 1			
	7.13 Economic fieldwork – 2			
Is the UK losing its global significance?				
What is the UK's political role in the world?	7.14 The UK's global role			
	7.15 The UK in the Middle East			
How is the UK's cultural influence changing?	7.16 The influence of UK media			
	7.17 The great British takeaway			

You need to know:

- how many people live in the UK and how crowded it is
- the area covered by the main land uses in the UK
- why there is a housing shortage in the UK.

Your key question

How is the UK changing in the 21st century?

How crowded is the UK?

Figure 1 is a satellite image of the UK at night. The bright spots are cities. Maybe it is not as crowded as you think? Figure 2 shows how land is used in the UK.

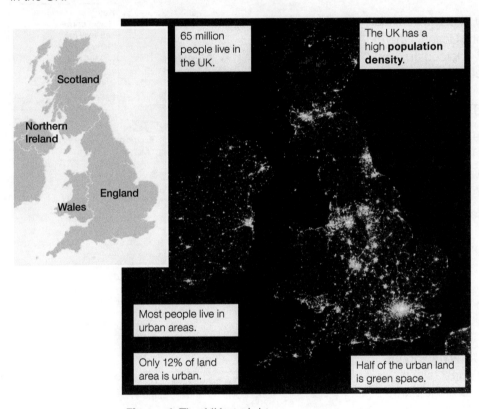

- 65 million people live in the UK.
- The UK has a high **population density**.
- Most people live in urban areas.
- Only 12% of land area is urban.
- Half of the urban land is green space.

Scotland
Northern Ireland
England
Wales

Figure 1 *The UK at night*

Land use in the UK

Land use	%
Urban: cities and towns	12
Arable land: farmland growing crops	20
Grassland: grazing land for animals	44
Woodland	13
Mountain and moorland	7
Water: lakes and rivers	1
Other land uses: e.g. roads and transport	3

Figure 2 *Land use in the UK*

Why the UK has a housing shortage

There is a lot of space where houses could be built. Yet, there is a **housing shortage**, especially in south-east England. Why is that?

- New housing needs planning permission and there is often local opposition to new homes.
- Land around many cities is protected as green belt with strict planning controls.
- The price of land keeps rising, so landowners do not sell in the hope that prices will rise further.

Six Second Summary

- 65 million people live in the UK, a small island with a high population density.
- Most people in the UK live in urban areas, which cover 12% of land area.
- The UK has a housing shortage despite having plenty of land to build on.

Over to you

Is the UK a crowded country? Argue, *either* that the UK **is** crowded, *or* that it **is not** crowded. Use any information on this page to help you.

Relief and rainfall in the UK

A relief map of the UK shows the shape of the land (Figure 1). Relief has an important effect on the weather and climate.

The **prevailing wind** in the UK blows from the south-west across the Atlantic Ocean. When moist air reaches the land it is forced up over mountains and produces **relief rainfall** (Figure 2).

Water stress in the UK

Water stress occurs where demand for water is greater than water supply. This happens mainly in the south-east of England, where there is high population density and low rainfall.

One solution to water stress would be to pipe water from areas of high supply/low demand in the north-west to areas of low supply/high demand in the south-east.

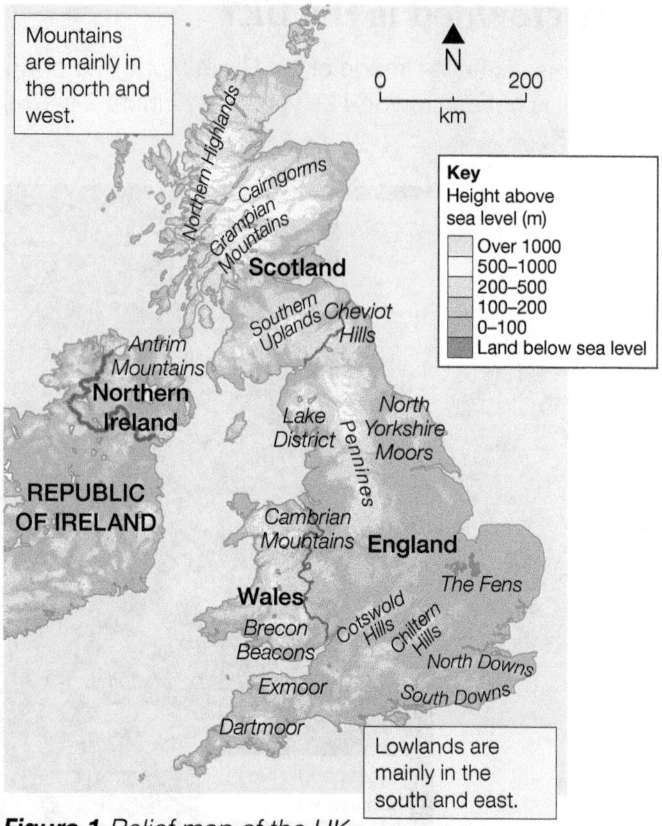

Six Second Summary

- The highest land in the UK, to the north and west, also has the highest rainfall.
- Relief rainfall happens when wind blows moist air over mountains.
- Water stress occurs where the demand for water is greater than water supply.

Over to you

Draw a cross-section of the UK from west to east. Then annotate your cross-section to explain how relief rain happens and why the west of the UK is wetter than the east. Include these words in your annotations – *prevailing wind, mountains, high rainfall, low rainfall.*

Mountains are mainly in the north and west.

0   N   200
km

Key
Height above sea level (m)

Over 1000
500–1000
200–500
100–200
0–100
Land below sea level

Northern Highlands
Cairngorms
Grampian Mountains
Scotland
Southern Uplands Cheviot Hills
Antrim Mountains
Northern Ireland
Lake District
North Yorkshire Moors
Pennines
REPUBLIC OF IRELAND
Cambrian Mountains **England**
The Fens
Wales
Brecon Beacons
Cotswold Hills
Chiltern Hills
North Downs
Exmoor
South Downs
Dartmoor

Lowlands are mainly in the south and east.

Figure 1 *Relief map of the UK*

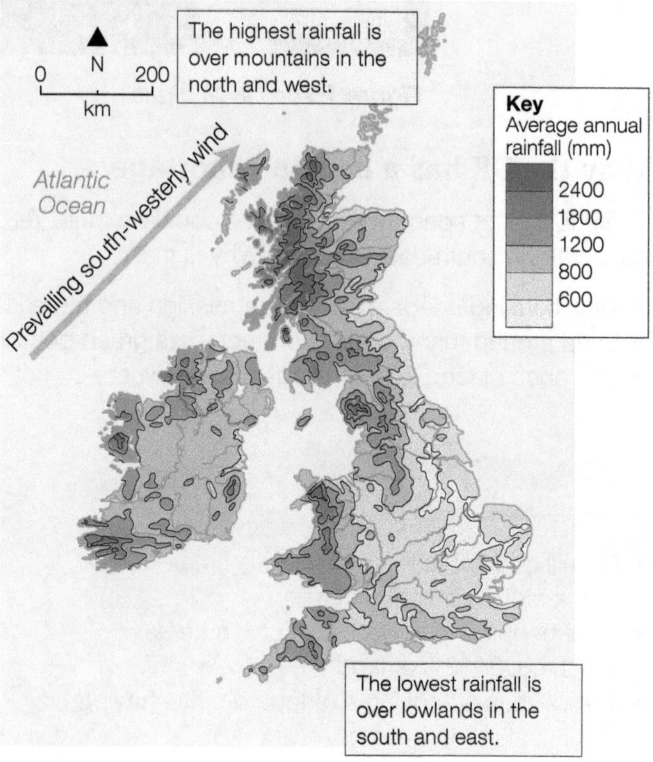

0   N   200
km

The highest rainfall is over mountains in the north and west.

Key
Average annual rainfall (mm)

2400
1800
1200
800
600

Atlantic Ocean

Prevailing south-westerly wind

The lowest rainfall is over lowlands in the south and east.

Figure 2 *Rainfall in the UK*

You need to know:

- the factors that contribute to UK population growth
- the factors that affect the UK's population structure
- how the UK fits the Demographic Transition Model.

Your key question

How is the UK changing in the 21st century?

Think about...

how is the UK's population changing?

UK population growth

The UK's population is about 65 million and is still rising. It is predicted to reach 70 million by 2030.

Two main factors contribute to the UK's population growth (Figure 1):

- natural increase – the difference between birth rate and death rate
- **net migration** – the difference between immigration and emigration.

Population structure

Population structure is the number of people in each age group. This is shown in the UK's **population pyramid** (Figure 2). The pyramid also gives clues to birth and death rates and how the UK's population will change.

The **Demographic Transition Model** describes the stages that a country's population is likely to go through. There are five stages. The UK is at stage 4, with low birth and death rates, and little natural change.

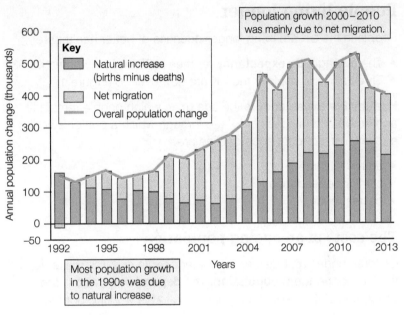

Population growth 2000–2010 was mainly due to net migration.

Key
- Natural increase (births minus deaths)
- Net migration
- Overall population change

Most population growth in the 1990s was due to natural increase.

Figure 1 *Natural increase and net migration to the UK, 1992–2013*

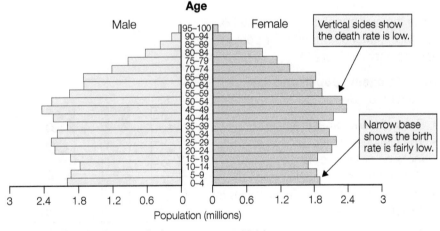

Age

Male / Female

Vertical sides show the death rate is low.

Narrow base shows the birth rate is fairly low.

Figure 2 *The UK's population structure, 2011*

Six Second Summary

- Natural increase and net migration contribute to the UK's population growth.
- The UK's population structure gives a clue to how its population will change.
- Birth and death rates in the UK are both quite low, so there is little natural change.

Over to you

Give four characteristics of the UK's population. For each one, explain in your own words, what effect it would have on population change in the UK.

You need to know:

- what life expectancy is in the UK
- what the dependency ratio is and how it is calculated
- what the costs of people living longer are.

Your key question

How is the UK changing in the 21st century?

Think about...
how is the UK's population changing?

People living longer

People in the UK are living longer because of better healthcare.

- The average **life expectancy** for men is 79 and for women it's 83.
- Three million people in the UK are now over 80 (Figure 1).

Healthy life expectancy is the age up to which people remain fit and active. The stages of old age through which a person's health and level of independence decline are:

- active retirement
- semi-independence
- dependence.

The costs of an ageing population

Children under 16, together with older people over 65, make up the UK's **dependent population**. The **dependency ratio** is the proportion of the dependent population to the working population.

$$\text{Dependency ratio} = \frac{\text{children + older people} \times 100}{\text{working population (16–64)}}$$

While the number of children in the UK has fallen, the number of older people has increased (Figure 2).

The UK's **ageing population** creates costs for the government and families:

- Pensions and other old age benefits.
- The National Health Service spends more on older people.
- Care for the elderly in nursing homes.
- Lost earnings for people who care for elderly relatives.
- More money spent on care means less is spent on other services.

Figure 1 *Old age in the UK*

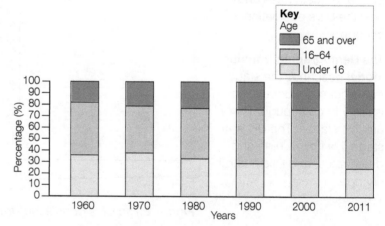
Figure 2 *Dependency in the UK. By 2050 there will be more over 65s than under 16s*

Six Second Summary

- Life expectancy in the UK is increasing, with different stages of old age.
- The dependency ratio is calculated from the proportion of children and older people in the population.
- Increased life expectancy creates more costs for the government and families.

Over to you

Make a list of the terms in **bold** on this page. Try to write your own definition for each one and then check them. Rewrite any definition you got wrong or copy out any you did not know. Test each other on the definitions.

Where older people live

Some parts of the UK have an older population than others (Figure 1). This is because:

- older people tend to move to the seaside or countryside when they retire
- young people often move to cities to find work
- the younger city populations have higher birth rates, so there are more children.

The ageing population of a seaside town

Rother, in East Sussex, has one of the highest proportions of older people in the UK (Figure 2). This creates challenges and opportunities. Older people may:

- have income from their pensions and savings
- change their housing needs with age
- need increasing levels of care with age
- need help with mobility.

- A higher proportion of older people in the UK live in coastal and rural areas.
- Rother, in East Sussex, has one of the highest proportions of older people in the UK.
- Areas with more older people face both challenges and opportunities.

Over to you

Create a factfile for Rother to highlight the causes and consequences of an ageing population. Include:

a its location in the UK
b the proportion of older people
c its population structure compared to the rest of the UK
d challenges and opportunities it faces with an ageing population

Key
Average age of population
- Under 35
- 35–40
- 40–46
- 46–52
- 52+

Urban areas have fewer older people.

Coastal and rural areas have more older people.

North Norfolk

West Somerset

Christchurch

Rother

Figure 1 *Distribution of the UK's ageing population*

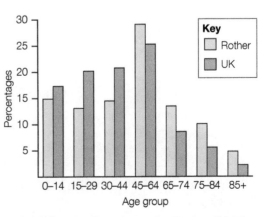

Figure 2 *Age comparison for Rother District and the rest of the UK*

You need to know:
- what is London's current population
- how its population has changed
- the ethnic composition of London's population.

Your key question

How is the UK changing in the 21st century?

Think about...

how is the UK's population changing?

London's ups and downs

In 2015 London's population reached 8.6 million, as high as it has ever been (Figure 1). It is expected to reach 10 million by 2030.

- Most of London's growth is due to natural increase rather than net migration.
- Many people come to London for work, so a high proportion are aged between 20 and 40.
- The young population leads to a high birth rate, so natural increase is high.
- Many immigrants arrive but people also leave, so net migration is low.

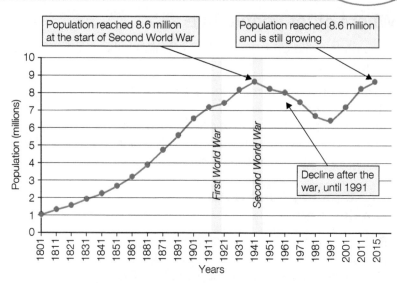

Figure 1 *London's population growth, 1801–2015*

London's ethnic majority

The majority of London's population are not white British (Figure 2). Many of this 'ethnic majority' were born in the UK to immigrant parents or grandparents.

London has greater **ethnic diversity** than any other UK city. In 2011, 38% of its population was born abroad, including Commonwealth and European countries.

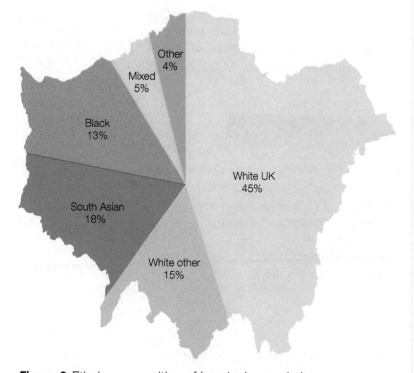

Figure 2 *Ethnic composition of London's population*

Six Second Summary

- London's population reached 8.6 million in 2015, as high as it has ever been.
- It is predicted to keep rising to 10 million by 2030.
- London has more ethnic diversity than any other UK city.

Over to you

Identify the dates on the graph in Figure 1 when London's population was *1, 2, 4, 8* and *8.6 million*. Then, without the book, draw your own graph of London's population growth from 1801–2015.

Changing employment

The past 50 years have seen dramatic changes in the UK economy. People now work in different **employment sectors** than in the past (Figure 1). The UK has become a **post-industrial economy**.

Unemployment in the UK

More people are employed in the UK than ever before. But, there is still **unemployment**.

The highest levels of unemployment are found in regions that once relied on manufacturing (Figure 2).

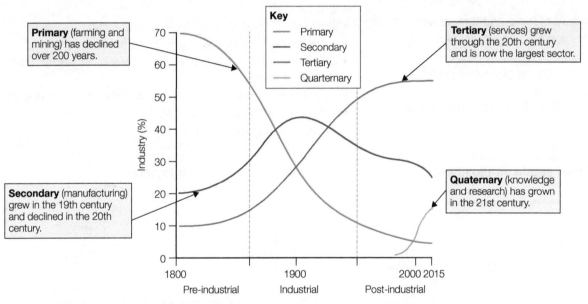

Primary (farming and mining) has declined over 200 years.

Secondary (manufacturing) grew in the 19th century and declined in the 20th century.

Tertiary (services) grew through the 20th century and is now the largest sector.

Quaternary (knowledge and research) has grown in the 21st century.

Figure 1 *Changing employment in the UK economy*

Six Second Summary

- The UK has a post-industrial economy where most people work in services.
- Primary and secondary industries have declined, while tertiary and quaternary industries have grown.
- Higher levels of unemployment are found in regions where manufacturing has declined.

Over to you

Give the % figures for employment in each economic sector in 1800, 1900 and 2015. Use your figures to describe employment in the UK's:

a pre-industrial economy
b industrial economy
c post-industrial economy.

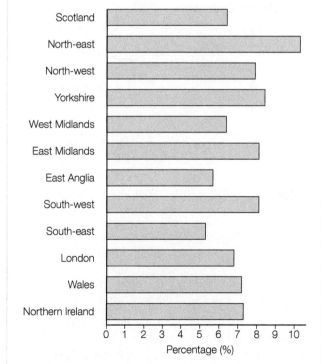

Figure 2 *Unemployment in the UK, 2014*

You need to know:
- how employment is changing in a post-industrial economy
- about the changing roles of men and women
- the ways in which we work more flexibly.

Your key question
How is the UK changing in the 21st century?

Think about...
how is the UK's economy changing?

Changes at work

Many more people work in the service sector (tertiary industry) in the post-industrial economy.

There have been other changes in employment in the UK (Figure 1), including;

- numbers of male and female workers
- unemployment levels for men and women
- the percentage of people in self-employment
- the number of people in different types of work.

More flexible working

In the 21st century the government wants the UK to compete in the global economy, which means we need to be more flexible and better qualified. Some of the new work patterns include:

- part-time work – to fit in family responsibilities or another job
- flexi-time – choose when to start and finish
- job sharing – two people share one full-time job
- sub-contracting – an outside company or self-employed person is used
- zero-hours contract – people are available for work any time
- teleworking/homeworking – work from home with a computer or phone.

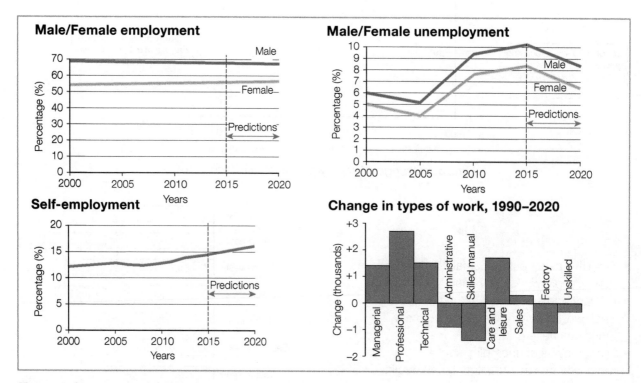

Figure 1 *Changes in employment in the UK, 2000–2020*

Six Second Summary

- Employment rates are higher for men than women, but the gap is narrowing.
- Self-employment is growing and the types of work we do are changing.
- People in the 21st century work more flexibly to compete in a global economy.

Over to you

a Write one sentence about each graph in Figure 1 to summarise the changes in employment in the UK.
b If you had to choose one graph to highlight the most important change, which one would it be, and why?

You need to know:

- what an economic hub is
- the reasons that some cities become economic hubs
- where the main economic hubs in the UK are.

Your key question

How is the UK changing in the 21st century?

Think about...

how is the UK's economy changing?

Economic hubs

The core UK **economic hubs** are cities where economic growth is strongest. Economists distinguish *high growth cities* (those with the fastest growth since 2008, e.g. Manchester) from *dynamic growth cities* (those with the greatest potential for future growth, e.g. Cambridge). London comes top in both categories (Figure 1).

High growth criteria

- Economic growth, including the number of businesses and jobs.
- Demographic growth, including a young, educated workforce.
- Place growth, including the number of homes and offices.

Figure 1 *Canary Wharf in London is an economic hub*

Dynamic growth criteria

- Knowledge-intensive business, with most potential for growth.
- Highly skilled workforce, educated to degree level or above.
- New business formation, with potential to grow into larger businesses.
- Good transport connections, including rail, road and air.

Growth corridors

Growth corridors link some of the main economic hubs, particularly London (Figure 2). They extend beyond traditional city boundaries and are influenced by major transport routes, such as the M11 from London to Cambridge.

Six Second Summary

- Economic hubs are cities where economic growth is strongest.
- Economists distinguish between high growth and dynamic growth cities.
- Growth corridors link some of the main economic hubs, particularly London.

Over to you

Explain why London–Cambridge is a growth corridor. Give at least three reasons.

Figure 2 *Growth corridors in England*

Your key question

How is the UK changing in the 21st century?

Think about...

how is the UK's economy changing?

London and the UK economy

The economic divide between London and the rest of the UK has widened in the 21st century. London now has 13% of the UK's population but produces 22% of the country's wealth (Figure 1).

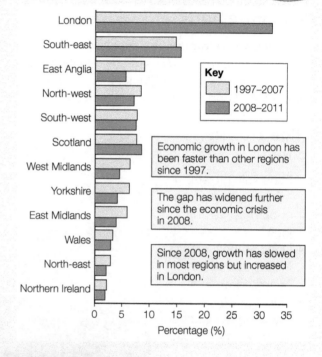

Key
- 1997–2007
- 2008–2011

Economic growth in London has been faster than other regions since 1997.

The gap has widened further since the economic crisis in 2008.

Since 2008, growth has slowed in most regions but increased in London.

Figure 1 *Share of economic growth in the UK regions*

The hi-tech industry in London

Old Street roundabout has become a focal point for **hi-tech industries** in London.

Public transport in London is excellent, so few people need cars.

Many new **start-up companies** are based here and attract each other.

Similar companies support each other and staff move between companies.

Other large technology companies (e.g. Facebook, Google) have invested nearby.

Young people with qualifications are attracted to London for jobs.

Figure 2 *Old Street Roundabout in London, also known as 'Silicon Roundabout'*

Six Second Summary

- Economic growth in London since 1997 has been faster than other UK regions.
- London now has 13% of the UK's population but produces 22% of the wealth.
- Old Street Roundabout has become a focal point for hi-tech industries.

Over to you

What would attract a hi-tech company, like Google, to invest in London, rather than another UK region? Make a list of at least four factors it would consider. Put them in order of importance.

You need to know:

- why Cambridge is an economic hub
- what advantages it has as a location for new industries
- how one bio-tech company grew there.

Your key question

How is the UK changing in the 21st century?

Think about...

how is the UK's economy changing?

Case Study

New industries in Cambridge

Cambridge is an economic hub in south-east England (Figures 1 and 2).

- The city has been home to one of the world's top universities for 800 years.
- In the 21st century it has emerged as a centre for new hi-tech industries.
- There are now over 1500 bio-tech and IT companies based there.

Abcam – a bio-tech company

Abcam is a successful bio-tech company based in Cambridge, started by graduates from the university. It produces antibodies used in the treatment of diseases. The company is now worth £1 billion and employs 200 staff with PhDs.

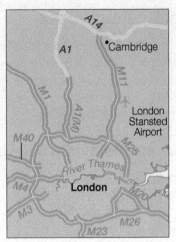

Figure 1 *The London–Cambridge growth corridor*

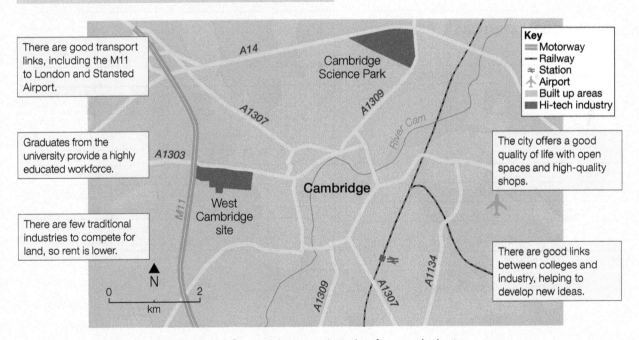

There are good transport links, including the M11 to London and Stansted Airport.

Graduates from the university provide a highly educated workforce.

There are few traditional industries to compete for land, so rent is lower.

The city offers a good quality of life with open spaces and high-quality shops.

There are good links between colleges and industry, helping to develop new ideas.

Key
- Motorway
- Railway
- Station
- Airport
- Built up areas
- Hi-tech industry

Figure 2 *Advantages of Cambridge as a location for new industry*

Six Second Summary

- Cambridge has emerged as a centre for hi-tech industries in the 21st century.
- The city is linked to London and Stansted Airport by the M11.
- The bio-tech company, Abcam, started there and is now worth £1 billion.

Over to you

List the advantages of Cambridge for new hi-tech industries under two headings:

- Cambridge's location
- Cambridge's characteristics.

Fieldwork

You need to know:

- how to plan an economic fieldwork enquiry
- the sort of questions you could investigate through fieldwork
- the methods you could use to carry out your enquiry.

Why do economic fieldwork?

The UK economy is changing, making it an interesting focus for fieldwork wherever you live. You could do fieldwork about the economy almost anywhere in the UK, even in a rural area. But, there are more opportunities in urban areas because that is where most of the jobs are.

Planning an economic fieldwork enquiry

- Decide on the topic you are going to investigate, e.g. changing economic activities in your area.
- Think of a question you could investigate, e.g. *how are economic activities in this area changing?*, or a hypothesis you could test.
- Choose suitable fieldwork methods that help you to answer the question or hypothesis (see panel). You will use them to collect **primary data**.
- Think about what **secondary data** you will need to use, such as old maps, employment data or company web sites.

Economic fieldwork methods.

- **Employment mapping** – map the places where people are working.
- **Changing workplaces** – use old maps and photos to compare jobs in the past with jobs in the same area now.
- **Employment questionnaire** – ask people about the work they do (Figure 1).
- **Job classification** – classify work into different types, such as primary, secondary, tertiary or quaternary activities.
- **Environmental impact assessment** – assess the positive and negative impacts of workplaces on the environment.

EMPLOYMENT QUESTIONNAIRE

Location: _____

Male	Female

Workplace				
Office	Shop	Factory	Public service	At home

Age groups			
Under 25	25–40	40–55	55+

Type of work			
Full-time employment	Self-employment	Part-time employment	Voluntary work

Job title: _____

Figure 1 *Employment questionnaire*

 Six Second Summary

- Economic fieldwork enquiries should begin with a question or hypothesis.
- A range of fieldwork methods can be used in economic fieldwork.
- It may be necessary to use secondary data as well as primary data.

 Over to you

Plan an economic fieldwork enquiry you could do using a questionnaire.

a Think of a suitable question or hypothesis for your enquiry.
b Say how the questionnaire would help you to carry out your enquiry.
c What other primary or secondary data would you need?

You need to know:

- how to carry out a decision-making exercise
- the factors to consider when choosing a business location
- the fieldwork methods to help make your decision.

A fieldwork decision-making exercise

Economic fieldwork can take the form of a decision-making exercise.

For example, if you were choosing the best location for a new business in Cambridge (Figure 1) you would have to consider some of these factors:

- land availability
- suitable buildings
- the cost of land or rent
- transport for workers, customers and/or goods
- who will work there
- who will buy the goods or services
- competition or co-operation with other businesses
- the surrounding environment.

To investigate these factors, you can use a range of fieldwork activities, such as:

- interviews
- transport surveys
- land use surveys
- pedestrian counts.

Figure 1 *Three possible business locations in Cambridge*

 Six Second Summary

- Fieldwork can take the form of a decision-making exercise, like choosing the best location for a business.
- A range of factors, such as land, buildings, rent and transport, need to be considered.
- Fieldwork could help to investigate these factors in order to make a decision.

 Over to you

Plan a decision-making exercise to choose the best location for a new café in Cambridge.

a What would be the most important factors to consider? Choose three.
b How would you investigate each one. Choose one fieldwork activity you could use to investigate each factor.

You need to know:

- the extent of the British Empire on a world map
- why the Empire was important and what replaced it
- which international organisations the UK is part of now.

Your key question

Is the UK losing its global significance?

Think about...
what is the UK's political role in the world?

Empire and Commonwealth

The **British Empire** once covered about one-third of the world's land surface (Figure 1). It was known as 'The Empire on which the Sun never sets'.

Many of the countries that were part of the Empire are now part of the **Commonwealth**, a voluntary association of 53 countries.

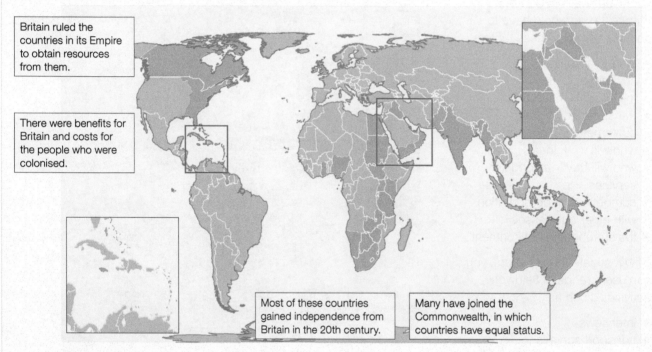

Britain ruled the countries in its Empire to obtain resources from them.

There were benefits for Britain and costs for the people who were colonised.

Most of these countries gained independence from Britain in the 20th century.

Many have joined the Commonwealth, in which countries have equal status.

Figure 1 *Countries that were once part of the British Empire*

The UK's influence today

The UK maintains its global influence today through its membership of international organisations, including;

- The **United Nations** (**UN**), with 193 member countries. The UK is one of five members of the UN Security Council, along with USA, Russia, China and France.
- The **North Atlantic Treaty Organization** (**NATO**), a military alliance of 28 countries in North America and Europe.
- The **European Union** (**EU**), a political and economic union of 28 countries, which the UK is due to leave in 2019.

Six Second Summary

- The British Empire once covered about one-third of the world's land surface.
- Most countries gained independence in the 20th century and became part of the Commonwealth.
- The UK is a member of the UN, NATO and (until 2019) the EU.

Over to you

Identify ten countries on the map in Figure 1 that were in the British Empire. Check in an atlas. Find out if these countries are now part of the Commonwealth.

You need to know:

- about the UK's past and present role in the Middle East
- where conflicts occur in the Middle East
- the importance of the UK's trade with the Middle East.

Your key question

Is the UK losing its global significance?

Think about...
what is the UK's political role in the world?

Conflict in the Middle East

The UK had a dominant **political role** in the Middle East during the days of the British Empire. Since countries gained independence in the 20th century, the UK's influence has declined. But, it still has a political interest in what happens in the region (Figure 1) as:

- the UK's trade with countries in the Middle East is growing
- Islamic terrorism, connected with the Middle East, threatens security in the UK.

UK and Middle East trade

Trade is the key factor that affects UK policy in the Middle East. The UK exports goods like aircraft and weapons, and imports oil and gas. The UK government's priority is to maintain friendly relations to increase trade.

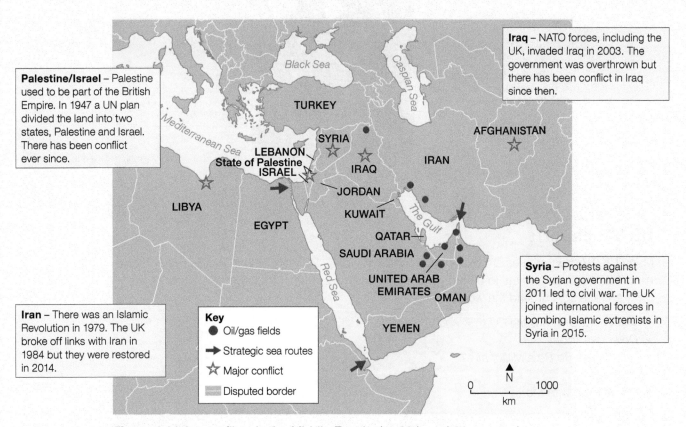

Palestine/Israel – Palestine used to be part of the British Empire. In 1947 a UN plan divided the land into two states, Palestine and Israel. There has been conflict ever since.

Iraq – NATO forces, including the UK, invaded Iraq in 2003. The government was overthrown but there has been conflict in Iraq since then.

Syria – Protests against the Syrian government in 2011 led to civil war. The UK joined international forces in bombing Islamic extremists in Syria in 2015.

Iran – There was an Islamic Revolution in 1979. The UK broke off links with Iran in 1984 but they were restored in 2014.

Key
- ● Oil/gas fields
- → Strategic sea routes
- ☆ Major conflict
- ▨ Disputed border

Figure 1 *Major conflicts in the Middle East in the 20th and 21st centuries*

Six Second Summary

- Parts of the Middle East were once part of the British Empire.
- The UK has been involved in conflicts in the Middle East, both past and present.
- The UK wants to maintain friendly relations in the Middle East to increase trade.

Over to you

Study Figure 1. Explain the influence that each of the following features could have on UK policy in the Middle East:

a oil/gas fields
b strategic sea routes
c major conflicts.

You need to know:

- how successful the UK media industry is
- what contribution it makes to the UK economy
- which TV programmes are exported.

Your key question

Is the UK losing its
global influence?

Think about...

*how is the UK's
cultural influence
changing?*

The UK film industry

The UK has one of the most critically acclaimed **media** industries in the world. Film-making has risen to new levels in the 21st century with some of the biggest, world-wide box office successes, such as *Skyfall* (Figure 1).

Creative industries in the UK, including film and TV, are worth over £70 billion a year to the UK economy and create 1.7 million jobs.

James Bond is one of the best-loved British film characters, dating back 50 years.

The film earned over £100 million at the UK box office.

The Bond film, *Skyfall*, became the most popular film ever in the UK in 2012.

UK films earned £5.3 billion worldwide in 2012, 15% of the world market.

Figure 1 *Skyfall, the 2012 James Bond film made in the UK*

UK TV exports

Many UK TV programmes are exported around the world. They are sold either as ready-made programmes or as formats to be adapted to the local culture in other countries. Some of the programmes sold around the world are:

- *The Great British Bake Off*
- *Downton Abbey*
- *Who Wants To Be a Millionaire?*
- *Top Gear*
- *Come Dine with Me*
- *Peppa Pig.*

Six Second Summary

- The UK has one of the most critically acclaimed media industries in the world.
- Creative industries contribute over £70 billion a year to the UK economy.
- UK TV programmes, like *The Great British Bake Off*, are exported around the world.

Over to you

Match the following figures with key facts on this page. First, cover up the page to see if you can work them out. Then, check your answers and correct any you got wrong.

- 1.7 million
- 15%
- £5.3 billion
- £100 million
- £70 billion

You need to know:

- what the most popular UK takeaway meals are
- why people eat more takeaway meals these days
- how new food can become part of British cuisine.

Your key question

Is the UK losing its global significance?

Think about...

how is the UK's cultural influence changing?

Eating habits in the UK

Our eating habits in the UK are changing. We buy more takeaway meals than we used to (Figure 1). There are a number of reasons for our change in eating habits:

- Average incomes have increased more than the cost of takeaway meals.
- We lead busier lives and have less time to cook.
- We travel more and experience a greater variety of food from around the world.
- More people from other parts of the world live in the UK and some of them open takeaway restaurants.

Chicken tikka masala

Chicken tikka masala has replaced fish and chips as the UK's favourite takeaway meal (Figure 2). It is not even a traditional Indian dish, but was probably invented in the UK to suit British tastes.

It illustrates the way in which food from other cultures can be absorbed into and help to enrich British **cultural life**. There is more evidence of this in TV cooking programmes like *Masterchef*.

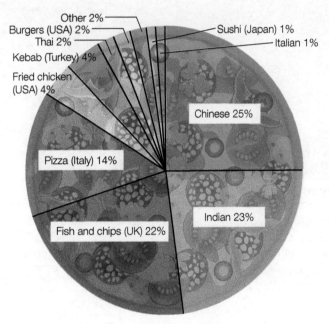

Other 2%
Burgers (USA) 2%
Thai 2%
Kebab (Turkey) 4%
Fried chicken (USA) 4%
Sushi (Japan) 1%
Italian 1%
Chinese 25%
Pizza (Italy) 14%
Indian 23%
Fish and chips (UK) 22%

Figure 1 The UK's most popular takeaway meals

Figure 2 Chicken tikka masala – the UK's favourite takeaway meal

 Six Second Summary

- The most popular type of takeaway meal in the UK is Chinese, followed by Indian.
- We eat more takeaway meals than we used to, because of increased incomes, busier lifestyle, travel and a multicultural society.
- Foods from other cultures are absorbed into and enrich British cultural life.

Over to you

List the four reasons we eat more takeaway meals in the UK these days, in order of importance. (There is no correct answer, but thinking about the four reasons should help you to remember them!)

Topic 8:
Resource Reliance

Your exam

Resource Reliance is part of Paper 2: People and Society. It is a 1 hr 15 min written exam and makes up 35% of your GCSE. The whole paper carries 70 marks (including 3 marks for SPaG).

There are two sections on the paper:

- Section A: questions on all the human geography topics, including *Resource Reliance*

- Section B: human geography fieldwork.

Your revision checklist

Tick these boxes to build a record of your revision

Spec key question	Theme	1	2	3
Will we run out of natural resources?				
How has increasing demand for resources affected our planet?	8.1 More resources please			
	8.2 Farming and fishing for food			
	8.3 Using fossil fuels for energy			
	8.4 Providing enough water			
Can we feed nine billion people by 2050?				
What does it mean to be food secure?	8.5 Food Security			
	8.6 Measuring food security			
	8.7 Two visions of the future			
How can countries ensure their food security?	8.8 Food security in Tanzania			
	8.9 Goat Aid in Babati, Tanzania			
	8.10 Tanzania's bid to grow all its own wheat			
	8.11 Tanzania's current bid for food security			
How sustainable are these strategies?	8.12 Attempts to achieve food security – 1 (through ethical consumption)			
	8.13 Attempts to achieve food security – 2 (through intensive and organic farming)			
	8.14 Attempts to achieve food security – 3 (through technology)			
	8.15 Small-scale approaches to food security			

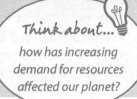

You need to know:

• the reasons why demand for Earth's resources is outstripping supply.

Your key question

Will we run out of natural resources?

Think about...

how has increasing demand for resources affected our planet?

Resource shortages

The world is seeing shortages of resources like food, water and energy. This is because the **supply** of resources is not keeping up with **demand**. There are three reasons for this:

1 Population growth

Earth's population has increased rapidly since 1950 and is expected to reach 9 billion people by 2050 (Figure 1). More people means more demand for resources.

2 Economic development

People in ACs use more resources because they have things like central heating, cars, lots of electrical products, and water in their homes. They also eat more food, particularly meat. As LIDCs and EDCs develop, their people want lifestyles similar to people in ACs. Development leads to more industry (increasing demand for energy) and agriculture (increasing demand for water).

3 Finite and threatened supply

Finite supply means there is a limited supply. Water, oil, gas and other resources are finite. There is also a potential limit to the amount of food that can be grown.

Supplies of food are threatened because more **biofuels** (crops that can be used for fuel) are being grown reducing the land we can grow food on. Climate change is reducing the amount of freshwater on Earth (see 2.8).

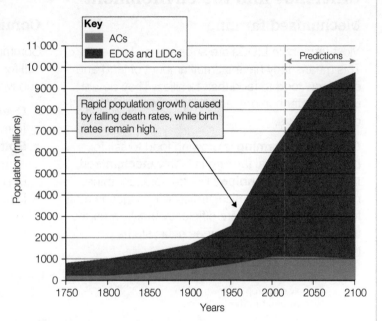

Figure 1 *World population growth*

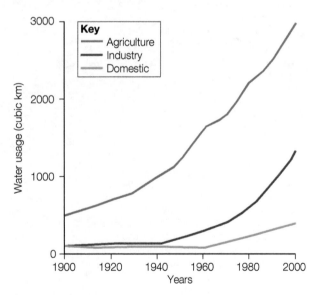

Figure 2 *Global use of water in different sectors*

Six Second Summary

• Population growth and economic development is increasing demand for resources.
• Resources are finite and supply is threatened.

Over to you

Use the word RESOURCES to create an acrostic outlining why demand is outstripping supply.

You need to know:
- what mechanised farming and commercial fishing are
- how mechanised farming and commercial fishing change the environment and ecosystems.

Your key question
Will we run out of natural resources?

Think about...
how has increasing demand for resources affected our planet?

Efficiency and the environment

Mechanised farming

Most farmers in LIDCs are subsistence farmers. This means they have a small amount of land and only grow food to feed their families. They do not use much technology and tend to grow a variety of different crops.

Commercial farming is growing food to sell for profit. Commercial farming is highly **mechanised.** It uses lots of **technology** like tractors, combine harvesters, and chemical fertiliser. This means more food can be grown more efficiently but it damages the environment and changes ecosystems (Figure 1).

Commercial fishing

Commercial fishing catches huge amounts of fish to sell for profit. Commercial fishing methods modify ecosystems and the environment:

- **Over-fishing**: is when too many fish are removed from the ecosystem.
- **Bottom trawling**: huge nets are dragged along the sea bed scooping up and destroying everything in their path.
- **Dynamite fishing**: sticks of dynamite are thrown into the sea which kills everything around the explosion.

Only one crop is grown which **reduces biodiversity**. The ecosystem is modified because it has less variety of plants, insects and animals.

More land is exposed to the wind and rain. This **increases soil erosion** and damages the environment.

Lots of herbicides and pesticides are used to kill weeds and insects. The ecosystem is modified because they **reduce biodiversity**, pollute the soil and water sources, and get into the food chain.

The land is over-farmed which modifies the environment by **destroying soil nutrients**.

Figure 1 *How mechanised commercial farming affects the environment*

Six Second Summary

- Mechanised farming and commercial fishing are concerned with producing food to sell for profit.
- They can both destroy ecosystems and severely damage the environment.

Over to you

For each commercial fishing method write an explanation of how they modify the ecosystem.

You need to know:
- how energy is provided by deforestation and mining
- how the environment and ecosystems are modified by deforestation and mining.

Your key question
Will we run out of natural resources?

Think about...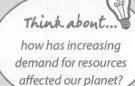
how has increasing demand for resources affected our planet?

Deforestation and energy supplies

2 billion people rely on wood as their main source of energy. Wood is obtained by chopping down trees. Often this involves **deforestation** (clearing large areas of trees). This modifies (changes) **ecosystems** because the plants, animals, and insects living in the forest lose their habitats.

Mining for fossil fuels like coal can involve deforestation. Often tropical rainforests contain large amounts of fossil fuels. Open-cast mining completely clears the forest to get at the coal under the surface.

Mining clears vast areas of forest.

Habitats of plants, insects, and animals are destroyed.

Figure 1 *Mining for iron in Brazil*

Mining and Pollution

Mining creates different kinds of pollution which changes ecosystems by killing plants, animals and insects.

Soil Pollution: chemicals leak into the soil killing vegetation which reduces the diversity of plants, animals and insects.

River pollution: chemicals are washed into local rivers killing fish and plant species (Figure 2).

Groundwater pollution: chemicals from mines can leach into groundwater supplies. This affects plants in the ecosystem.

Ocean pollution: oil wells in oceans sometimes leak millions of barrels of oil, which kill fish, dolphins, sea turtles and other wildlife.

Air pollution: dust containing dangerous chemicals is released into the atmosphere around mines. This pollutes the air, and then the soil and water supplies.

Figure 2 *A polluted river near a mine*

Six Second Summary

- Deforestation to obtain wood and create mines destroys the local ecosystem.
- Mining creates different kinds of pollution which affects the environment and ecosystems.

Over to you

Using the letters S, G, R, O, A, think of a mnemonic to remember the different types of pollution caused by mining. (Hint: a famous shop/ancient Greek city).

You need to know:

- how reservoirs and water transfer schemes meet water demand.
- how the environment and ecosystems are changed by reservoirs and water transfer schemes.

Your key question

Will we run out of natural resources?

Think about...

how has increasing demand for resources affected our planet?

Reservoirs

A reservoir is a large natural or artificial lake used as a store of water. When reservoirs are built, large areas of land are flooded to create the water store. This destroys the habitats of plants and animals that previously lived on the land.

Often reservoirs are created by building a dam across a river, flooding the land behind the dam. This affects ecosystems both upstream and downstream of the dam.

Upstream impacts

- Flooding the land destroys existing ecosystems.
- Floodwater might cover towns and industry which pollutes the water.
- Deep water behind the dam can become a 'dead zone' with not enough oxygen for species to survive.
- The dam blocks fish migration routes.

Downstream impacts

- The dam releases oxygen starved water, killing fish downstream
- Diversity of fish and other river species is reduced.
- The dam traps sediment so less sediment is deposited when the river floods downstream. This changes floodplain ecosystems.

Figure 1 *The effects of building a dam on ecosystems upstream and downstream*

Water transfer schemes

Water needs can be met by transferring water from one area to another in artificial channels or pipes. This can affect ecosystems because:

- species can be transferred from one ecosystem to another along with the water
- natural floods in the donor areas are reduced.

Six Second Summary

- Reservoirs store water for when it is needed.
- Creating reservoirs alters ecosystems upstream and downstream of the dam.
- Transferring water changes ecosystems at the donor and receiving ends.

Over to you

Learn two impacts that reservoirs have on ecosystems upstream of a dam, and two impacts downstream of a dam.

- How to define food security
- the physical and human factors that affect food security.

Can we feed nine billion people by 2050?

Think about...

what does it mean to be food secure?

Food security

Food security is defined as 'when all people at all times have access to sufficient, safe, nutritious food to maintain a healthy and active life'.

There are three parts to food security: availability, access, utilisation (Figure 1).

Physical factors influencing food security

Physical factors affecting food security are to do with the natural environment (Figure 2).

Human factors influencing food security

Human factors are to do with society and human activity.

- **Poverty**: people might not be able to afford food.
- **Distribution and Infrastructure**: food is sometimes available, but poor roads and distribution mean that people who need it cannot access it.
- **War and conflict**: wars disrupt farming and food distribution. People sometimes flee their homes and move to places without adequate food.
- **Land ownership**: poor farmers often compete for land with large TNCs, who grow food that is exported (sent out of the local area).
- **Waste**: food is wasted because of poor transport and storage.
- **Climate change**: global warming caused by human activity is causing water shortages in some parts of the world.

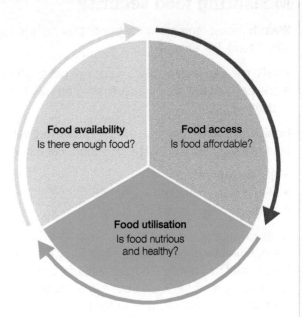

Food availability
Is there enough food?

Food access
Is food affordable?

Food utilisation
Is food nutrious and healthy?

Figure 1 Aspects of food security

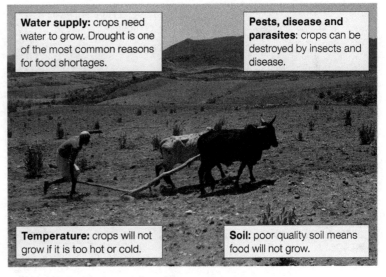

Water supply: crops need water to grow. Drought is one of the most common reasons for food shortages.

Pests, disease and parasites: crops can be destroyed by insects and disease.

Temperature: crops will not grow if it is too hot or cold.

Soil: poor quality soil means food will not grow.

Figure 2 Physical factors affecting food security

 Six Second Summary

- Food security refers to whether there is enough food – whether it is affordable, and whether it is nutritious.
- There are a range of physical and human factors that influence food security.

Over to you

For each of the physical and human factors affecting food security draw a cartoon to represent that factor.

You need to know:

- different ways of measuring food security
- what the Global Hunger Index is.

Your key question

Can we feed nine billion people by 2050?

Think about...

what does it mean to be food secure?

Measuring food security

Wealth measurements indicate whether people can afford food. For example:

- GNI per capita at purchasing power parity (PPP)
- the percentage of population living on less than a dollar a day

Health measurements tell us if people have been able to access and afford healthy food. For example:

- life expectancy
- death rate of children under five
- average daily calorie consumption

A disadvantage of these measurements is that they are not directly about food security. They look at factors that might indicate food security. Low life expectancy might also be because of factors like smoking rather than access to food.

The Global Hunger Index

The **Global Hunger Index** combines four indicators mainly focusing on children because they are especially vulnerable to food shortages. The higher the score, the more hunger (Figure1).

The four indicators used are:

Undernourishment: the percentage of the population who are undernourished.

Child wasting: the proportion of children under 5 who have low weight for their height.

Child stunting: the proportion of children under 5 who are short for their age.

Child mortality: the death rate of children under 5.

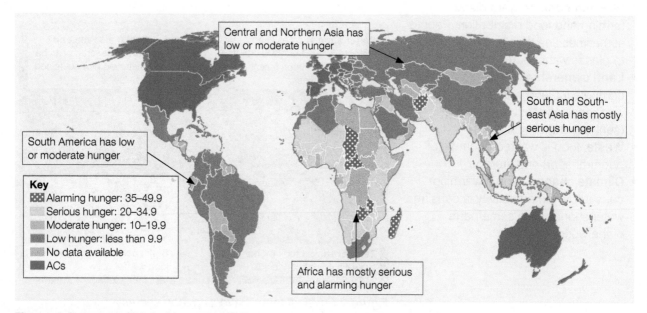

Figure 1 *Patterns of global hunger, 2015*

- Wealth and health indicators can be used to measure food security.
- The Global Hunger Index uses four indicators to score countries out of 100.

Over to you

Learn the four indicators used in the Global Hunger Index.

You need to know:
- Malthusian and Boserupian theories about the relationship between population growth and food supply
- the differences between these theories.

Your key question

Can we feed nine billion people by 2050?

Think about...

what does it mean to be food secure?

Food for a growing population

The world's population is currently 7.6 billion people and is predicted to reach 9 billion by 2050. There are two different theories about whether this will lead to a food crisis.

Malthus's theory

In 1798 Thomas Malthus argued that:

- population increases at a **geometric** rate (1, 2, 4, 8, 16, 32...)
- food supply only increases at an **arithmetic** rate (1, 2, 3, 4, 5, 6 ...).

The different rates of increase mean famine and starvation will occur (Figure 1).

Malthus argued there would be two types of check on population growth that would bring it back in line with food supply:

Positive checks: These are not 'good'. They are things like disease and famine that reduce the total population size.

Preventative checks: These are things that people do (delay marriage, have smaller families) that prevent the population size exceeding food supply.

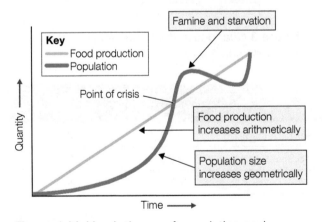

Figure 1 *Malthus's theory of population and food supply*

Boserup's theory

In 1965 Esther Boserup argued that when population size approaches the limits of food supply, it creates an incentive for people to invent new technology to increase food supply. New technology includes things like:

- irrigation to divert water onto previously unused land
- new types of seeds
- fertilisers or tractors.

These new technologies allow more food to be grown and population growth can continue (Figure 2).

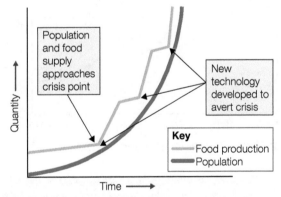

Figure 2 *Boserup's theory of population and food supply*

 Six Second Summary

- Malthus thought population would inevitably exceed food supply.
- Boserup argued people would invent technology to increase food supply when needed.

Over to you

Use text messages to debate with a friend whether Malthus or Boserup is correct about the relationship between population growth and food supply.

You need to know:

- statistics about food consumption and availability in Tanzania
- how this has changed over time.

Your key question

Can we feed nine billion people by 2050?

Think about...

how can countries ensure their food security?

Case Study

Introducing Tanzania

Tanzania is a very poor LIDC in East Africa. It has a population of 51 million people and most people live in rural areas.

Hunger in Tanzania

In 2015 Tanzania scored 28.7 in the Global Hunger Index (Figure 2). It was ranked 89th out of 116 countries and had a hunger rating of 'serious'.

Figure 4 shows that Tanzania's GHI score has improved but the percentage of people undernourished has got worse since 1990 (Figures 3 and 4). The improvements in the GHI score are because of improvements in child health rather than the availability of food.

Figure 1 *The location of Tanzania*

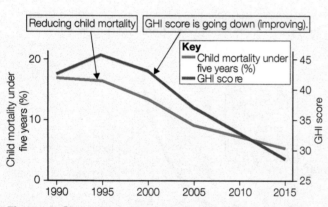

Figure 2 *GHI in Tanzania, and under-5 mortality (%)*

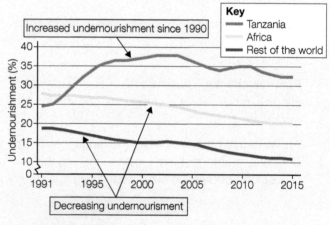

Figure 3 *Changes in the percentage of people who are undernourished*

Year	Undernourished population (%)	Wasting in children under 5 (%)	Stunting in children under 5 (%)	Under 5 mortality rate (%)	GHI score
1990	24.2	7.9	49.7	16.7	42.2
2000	36.8	5.6	48.3	13.2	42.5
2015	32.1	3.8	34.7	5.2	28.7

Figure 4 *Key hunger statistics in Tanzania 1990–2015*

 Six Second Summary

- Hunger is a serious problem in Tanzania.
- Tanzania's GHI score has improved since 1990 but the percentage of undernourished people has increased.

 Over to you

Write the statistics for the following on sticky notes. Stick these around your bedroom which should help you remember them.

- Tanzania's hunger ranking and rating
- GHI score in 2015 and 1990
- Undernourishment percentage in 2015 and 1990
- Under 5 mortality percentage in 2015 and 1990

You need to know:

- details about an attempt to improve food security at a local scale
- whether this has been successful or not.

Your key question

Can we feed nine billion people by 2050?

Think about...

how can countries ensure their food security?

Goat aid in Babati

Babati is an area in northern Tanzania where 90% of the people depend on agriculture for their livelihood.

- Between 1999 and 2006 a British charity called Farm Africa spent £200 000 on Toggenburg goats for the region to help improve food security.
- Toggenburg goats are dairy goats that produce three litres of milk a day compared to cows which produce one litre a day.
- They bring many social, economic, and environmental benefits (Figure 1).

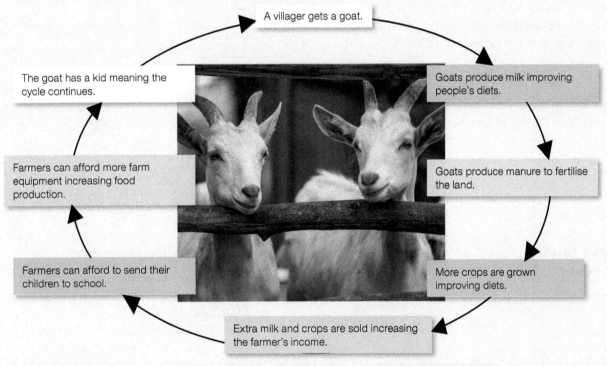

A villager gets a goat.

The goat has a kid meaning the cycle continues.

Goats produce milk improving people's diets.

Farmers can afford more farm equipment increasing food production.

Goats produce manure to fertilise the land.

Farmers can afford to send their children to school.

More crops are grown improving diets.

Extra milk and crops are sold increasing the farmer's income.

Figure 1 *Goats bring many social (red), economic (blue) and environmental (green) benefits*

Criticisms

- Goats require lots of water.
- Farmers might have to pay expensive vet bills.
- Small-scale projects only help a small number of people.

Has it been successful?

Goat aid gives long-term benefits, which continue after the aid project finishes. Statistics show that farmers who receive goats make three times more profit than farmers who do not receive goats.

 Six Second Summary

- Goat aid is an example of an attempt to achieve food security at a local scale.
- It brings social, economic, and environmental benefits.
- Income statistics show it is successful.

Over to you

Learn one statistic, three benefits, and one criticism of goat aid.

Case Study

You need to know:

- key details about a past attempt to achieve food security in Tanzania at a national scale
- whether this was effective.

Your key question

Can we feed nine billion people by 2050?

Think about...

how can countries ensure their food security?

Tanzania–Canada Wheat Programme

In the late 1960s and early 1970s Tanzania suffered from food shortages. The government asked Canada to help it develop its wheat production.

Between 1968 and 1993 Canada provided $95m of aid as Tanzania turned the Hanang Plains into huge wheat farms. Aid included seeds, training, chemical fertilisers and machinery such as tractors. At first the chemicals and equipment were free but eventually Tanzania had to pay for them. The land used to grow the wheat belonged to the Barabaig people who used it for grazing their cattle. They claim they were violently forced from their land.

Was the project effective?

There are different opinions about whether the project was successful. The Canadian and Tanzanian governments say it was successful. But with many disadvantages, many would argue it was failure (Figure 2).

Figure 1 *Wheat production at the Hanang Wheat Complex 1967–1993*

Figure 2 *Growing wheat involved using large amounts of machinery*

Benefits of wheat programme

- Produced 60% of Tanzania's wheat (Figure 1).
- 121 Tanzanians were trained in wheat production.
- 400 people worked on the farms.
- In the 1992 drought, Tanzania was the only southern African country not to rely on food aid.

Criticisms of wheat programme

- It would have been cheaper to import wheat.
- Most Tanzanians do not eat wheat – improving maize production would have been better.
- Lots of machinery fell into disrepair because Tanzanians could not afford the spare parts.
- Spare parts had to be bought from Canada which benefitted Canadian manufacturers not Tanzanians.
- 40 000 Barabaigs lost their land and livelihood.

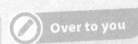 **Six Second Summary**

- The Tanzania–Canada wheat programme tried to grow huge quantities of wheat by using modern machinery and farming methods.
- At its peak it provided 60% of Tanzania's wheat.
- Much of the machinery broke and couldn't be repaired, and most Tanzanians could not afford the bread made from the wheat.

Over to you

Think of an exam question you might be asked about this topic. Write an answer to it.

You need to know:

- whether a current attempt to achieve food security at a national scale is effective.

Your key question

Can we feed nine billion people by 2050?

Think about...
how can countries ensure their food security?

Southern Agricultural Growth Corridor of Tanzania

The Southern Agricultural Growth Corridor of Tanzania (SAGCOT) is a large project aiming to improve food production along a large strip of land stretching across southern Tanzania (Figure 1). The project started in 2010.

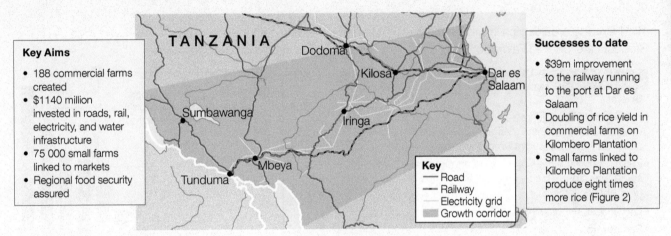

Key Aims

- 188 commercial farms created
- $1140 million invested in roads, rail, electricity, and water infrastructure
- 75 000 small farms linked to markets
- Regional food security assured

Key
- Road
- Railway
- Electricity grid
- Growth corridor

Successes to date

- $39m improvement to the railway running to the port at Dar es Salaam
- Doubling of rice yield in commercial farms on Kilombero Plantation
- Small farms linked to Kilombero Plantation produce eight times more rice (Figure 2)

Figure 1 The SAGCOT's aims and successes

Hub and out-grower model

The Hub and out-grower model is an important innovation to improve food production on small farms. Large, commercial farms act as hubs. They improve things like electricity supplies, transport links and irrigation. Small farms link to these hubs as 'out-growers'. They use the infrastructure and expertise to improve their own food production and connect to markets (Figure 2).

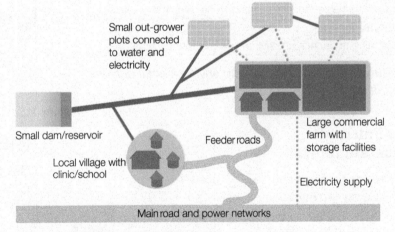

Small out-grower plots connected to water and electricity

Small dam/reservoir

Local village with clinic/school

Feeder roads

Large commercial farm with storage facilities

Electricity supply

Main road and power networks

Figure 2 Hub and out-grower model

Criticisms of SAGCOT

- Most money is invested in commercial farms.
- Nomadic tribes and some small landowners have lost land.
- Investment is promised but not yet given.
- It is a top-down project that does not consult with small landowners.

Is SAGCOT effective?

It is too early to make judgements. The hub and out-grower model is innovative and there are some early successes. However, some argue that this will benefit TNCs producing food for export more than small landowners.

Six Second Summary

- SAGCOT aims to develop a modern agricultural industry in Tanzania.
- Huge investment is planned.
- Partnerships between commercial farms and small landowners are developed through a hub and out-grower model.

Over to you

Study Figure 2. Close the book and draw the model. Keep practising until you can accurately sketch it.

You need to know:
- what ethical consumerism is
- whether fair trade and reducing food waste are socially, economically and environmentally sustainable approaches to food security.

Your key question
Can we feed nine billion people by 2050?

Think about... how sustainable are these strategies?

Making trade fairer

Ethical consumerism means buying products that have positive social, economic, or environmental impacts.

The Fairtrade organisation improves the pay that farmers in LIDCs get for their crops. Products are labelled Fairtrade if they meet minimum standards in their production.

Benefits of Fairtrade
Social
Farmers receive a guaranteed minimum price for their crops which is often above the market price. This helps farmers plan their futures knowing what their income might be.
Farming communities receive an annual bonus called a social premium. This is spent on things like building wells or schools.
Workers' rights are protected.
Economic
Farmers receive a guaranteed minimum price for their crops which is often above the market price.
Fairtrade helps farmers connect to international markets.
Environmental
Farming is done in an environmentally friendly way.

Figure 2 Social, economic and environmental benefits of Fairtrade

Key
- Others (e.g. free range eggs and poultry, sustainable fish)
- Vegetarian meat alternatives
- Fairtrade
- Rainforest Alliance
- Organic

(Figure 1 chart: y-axis Spend (million £) from 0 to 8000; x-axis Years 1999–2012)

Figure 1 Sales of ethical products in the UK

Is Fairtrade sustainable?

Fairtrade relies on people in ACs buying Fairtrade products, which is not guaranteed to continue.

Fairtrade also encourages farmers to produce primary products. It might be better to help them produce manufactured goods (e.g. chocolate bars instead of cocoa beans).

Reducing Food waste

Lots of food is thrown away because people in ACs want perfect-looking food. The Ugly Food Movement encourages people to buy ugly fruit and vegetables. This has social, economic and environmental benefits: Farmers in LIDCs earn more money (economic) because they sell more of their harvest. With more money they can afford a better and healthier diet (social). Eating all food produced means less energy is wasted (environmental).

Figure 3 An advert for ugly apples

Six Second Summary
- Fairtrade gives farmers a higher and guaranteed income.
- Eating ugly food reduces waste and improves the incomes of farmers.

Over to you
Become an expert. Teach your family about the advantages and disadvantages of buying Fairtrade products.

Intensive farming

Intensive farming produces lots of food by using lots of machinery and chemicals like fertiliser, herbicides, and pesticides. When producing animals it is called **factory farming**.

Agribusiness is taking over intensive food production, mainly in LIDCs. Big companies buy huge amounts of land and grow more food. But the main motive is profit, not food security.

Figure 1 A cropduster sprays a banana plantation with pesticide

Advantages of intensive farming

- Huge quantities of food are produced maximising the use of the land (social).
- Food is cheap to produce (economic).
- Food is sold cheaply in ACs making a healthy diet affordable (social).

Disadvantages of intensive farming

- Chemical sprays damage the health of farm workers (social).
- Farms tend to grow single crops reducing biodiversity (environmental).
- Fertilisers, pesticides, and herbicides pollute the environment (environmental).
- People eat chemicals if food is not washed properly (social).

Organic farming

Organic farming bans the use of chemicals in the production of food.

Advantages of organic farming

- Food produced without chemicals is potentially healthier (social).
- Biodiversity increases because a greater variety of crops are grown (environmental).

Disadvantages of organic farming

- Food is more expensive to buy making a healthy, balanced diet less affordable (social).
- More food is lost to pests and weeds meaning less is grown on the same amount of land (economic).

Food security and sustainability

In the short term, intensive agriculture is the best strategy to produce the quantities of food needed to feed the world's growing populations. However, environmental problems such as pollution and reducing biodiversity might make this an unsustainable approach.

Six Second Summary

- Intensive farming produces lots of cheap food but is environmentally damaging.
- Organic farming is better for the environment but does not produce as much food.

Over to you

Write a short speech to persuade someone that intensive farming or organic farming is the best approach to achieving food security.

You need to know:

- why genetically modified crops might be a technological solution to food security
- whether GM crops are a sustainable approach to food security.

Your key question

Can we feed nine billion people by 2050?

Think about...
how sustainable are these strategies?

Laboratory Food

Genetically modified (GM) crops are plants produced by inserting DNA from one species into a different species. For example, DNA from the Arctic flounder fish (which can survive at very low temperatures) has been inserted into strawberries. The result is a strawberry that can survive at very low temperatures.

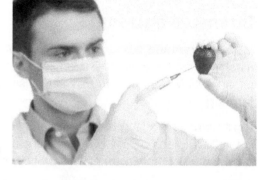

Figure 1 *GM crops are developed in laboratories*

GM crops		
	Advantage	**Disadvantage**
Social	Drought and frost resistant crops can be produced. This means food can be grown in more parts of the world. Food with additional health benefits (e.g. extra vitamins) can be grown.	GM crops might be unsafe to eat. GM crops are made by a small number of TNCs that control food supply.
Economic	Crops can be made resistant to herbicides so that weed killer kills just weeds and not crops. This saves money.	GM crops are made by a small number of TNCs who modify crops so they do not produce seeds. Farmers have to buy new seeds each year and get in debt.
Environmental	DNA that is harmful to pests and insects can be inserted into crops, reducing the need for pesticides.	Pollen from GM crops might contaminate non-GM crops, permanently changing natural species. Farmers will only grow GM crops, which reduces biodiversity.

Figure 2 *Social, economic and environmental impacts of GM crops*

Are GM crops sustainable?

Those in favour of GM crops point to the benefits and say they are our best hope of producing the quantity of food we will need in the future. Opponents point to the disadvantages, arguing the consequences will be disastrous in the long run (Figure 3).

Figure 3 *Protesters destroying a field of GM crops*

Six Second Summary

- GM crops are crops modified with DNA from different species.
- Experts can't agree if their potential advantages outweigh their disadvantages.

Over to you

Write each advantage and disadvantage of GM crops on separate sticky notes. Arrange advantages and disadvantages in order from strongest to weakest. Write a paragraph justifying your order.

You need to know:
- why urban gardens and permaculture might be a bottom-up solution to food security
- whether they are a sustainable approaches to food security.

Your key question
Can we feed nine billion people by 2050?

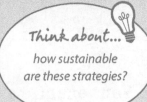
Think about...
how sustainable are these strategies?

Urban Gardens

Urban gardens are an example of a **bottom-up approach** to food security. They can be created in back gardens, allotments, shared community spaces, and even on factory rooftops (Figure 1). They provide an alternative to intensive agriculture.

Urban gardens are sustainable but whether they can provide the quantity of food needed is more questionable.

Figure 1 *Factory workers exercising on a rooftop farm*

Urban gardens		
	Advantage	**Disadvantage**
Social	The food is healthy and nutritious.	Food production is not centrally planned, so might not meet needs.
Economic	Food is grown cheaply. Extra food can be sold for profit.	If crops fail, people have wasted money and may struggle to buy food.
Environmental	Urban waste can be used as fertiliser. Urban gardens remove CO_2 from the atmosphere.	Diseases can spread in urban livestock.

Figure 2 *Social, economic and environmental impacts of urban gardens*

Permaculture

Permaculture means 'permanent' 'agriculture'. It is a bottom-up approach to food security that tries to copy what happens naturally.

Permaculture is environmentally sustainable. As with urban gardens, food is produced on a small scale so lots of permaculture farms are needed to be socially sustainable. It can also be expensive to establish permaculture gardens.

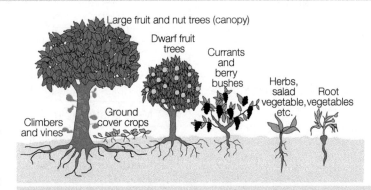

- Different food types grown together by stacking.
- Soil nutrients are not exhausted, so increased biodiversity (**environmental sustainability**).
- Year-round supply of food (**social sustainability**).

Figure 3 *Stacking can grow more food in the same space*

Six Second Summary

- Urban gardens involve turning disused urban spaces into places of food production.
- Permaculture copies nature to provide environmentally sustainable food.

Over to you

Look in your local community at all the spaces that could be used to grow food. Do you think relying on this approach is a sensible approach to food security? Write down your thoughts and use them to think critically about urban gardens.

Decision-making Exercises

Your exam

Paper 3: *Geographical Exploration* is different from Papers 1 and 2. It is a 1hr 30min exam and makes up 30% of your GCSE. The whole paper carries 60 marks. You will be given a Resource Booklet to go with the exam paper that provides data you will need to use. You are given more time for Paper 3 but you will need the additional time to read the Resource Booklet.

There is only one section on the paper and it takes the form of a decision-making exercise (DME). It brings together the physical and human geography that you

have done and requires you to use your geographical knowledge, understanding and skills to complete the DME.

There is no revision checklist for Paper 3. It is not based on any specific place or example you have studied. However, it will depend on the revision you have done for the physical and human topics you have studied for Papers 1 and 2.

The best preparation for Paper 3 is to practice doing DMEs. There are four in the book to choose from.

Decision-making exercises

Key question	Theme	Links with topics
How should the USA prepare for the next natural disaster?	9.1 Hazards in the USA	• Global Hazards
	9.2 From hazard to disaster	• Urban Futures
	9.3 Drought – a hidden disaster	• Dynamic Development
	9.4 Waiting for the 'Big One'	• Changing Climate
	9.5 Be prepared!	
Where should the UK get its energy from in future?	10.1 A wind farm controversy	• UK in the 21st Century
	10.2 Wind power in the UK	• Distinctive Landscapes
	10.3 UK energy sources	• Resource Reliance
	10.4 Shale gas – a non-renewable option	• Changing Climate
	10.5 Tidal power – a renewable option	• Sustaining Ecosystems
How could living in London be more sustainable?	11.1 London's ecological footprint	• Urban Futures
	11.2 More sustainable cities	• Sustaining Ecosystems
	11.3 Improving London's transport	• Resource Reliance
	11.4 Using London's green spaces	• UK in the 21st Century
	11.5 Sustainable urban living	• Changing Climate
Which way should China develop now?	12.1 China's economic development	• Dynamic Development
	12.2 China's carbon emissions	• Changing Climate
	12.3 Environmental problems in China	• Urban Futures
	12.4 China's water crisis	• Resource Reliance
	12.5 Sustainable development	• Sustaining Ecosystems

- what natural hazards the USA experiences
- about tornadoes as an example of a natural hazard
- the frequency and impacts of different hazards.

How should the USA prepare for the next natural disaster?

USA – a hazardous country

The USA experiences a range of natural hazards – both weather hazards, like tornadoes (Figure 1), and tectonic hazards, like earthquakes.

The frequency and impacts of hazards vary (Figures 2, 3, 4). While storms, including tornadoes, are frequent, dramatic and deadly, other hazards like heatwaves are less frequent or dramatic but just as deadly.

The USA suffers from more tornadoes than any other country.

On average, there are 1000 tornadoes in the USA each year.

They can be deadly and cause huge amounts of damage.

They mainly affect the mid-west of the USA.

Figure 1 *A tornado hits the mid-west of the USA*

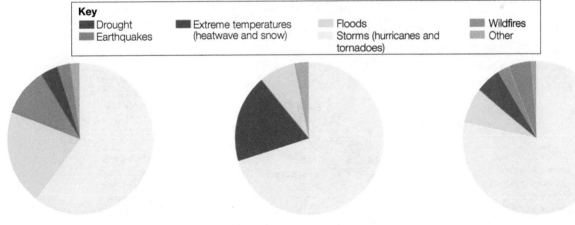

Key
- Drought
- Earthquakes
- Extreme temperatures (heatwave and snow)
- Floods
- Storms (hurricanes and tornadoes)
- Wildfires
- Other

Figure 2 *Frequency of hazards in the USA, 2005–2014*

Figure 3 *Deaths caused by hazards in the USA, 2005–2014*

Figure 4 *Economic costs of hazards in the USA, 2005–2014*

- The USA experiences a range of natural weather and tectonic hazards.
- One of the most frequent, deadly and damaging hazards are tornadoes.
- Hazards vary in both their frequency and impacts on lives and the economy.

Turn the information in Figures 2, 3 and 4 into a table with three columns, like the one below. List the frequency, deaths and economic costs of each hazard in rank order. For example, storms (including tornadoes) will be at the top of each list.

Frequency	Deaths	Economic costs
Storms	Storms	Storms

You will find out:

- what turns a hazard into a disaster
- about the impact of Hurricane Sandy in 2012
- which countries are best prepared for natural hazards.

Your key question

How should the USA prepare for the next natural disaster?

Hazard or disaster?

Hazards turn into disasters when they affect people. The USA, as an **advanced country (AC)**, has done a lot to reduce the risks posed by natural hazards to human life. But, the economic cost of disasters in the USA is higher because of the value of property and infrastructure (Figure 1).

The impact of Hurricane Sandy

When Hurricane Sandy hit the USA in 2012, 73 people died and it caused $65 billion worth of damage, most of it in New York, the USA's largest city.

It was one of the most costly natural disasters ever in the USA (Figure 2). But, its impact varied across the countries it hit. The death toll from disasters in **low-income developing countries (LIDC)** is often higher, but the economic cost is lower.

USA (2014 data)	
Population	324 million
Population density	34.6 people/km²
GDP	$16 800 billion ($16.8 trillion)
GDP/capita	$53.042
Urban population	81%
Number of natural disasters (2005–2014)	22
Deaths from natural disasters (2005–2014)	427
Percentage of GDP spent on disaster relief	0.03%

Figure 1 *USA economic factfile*

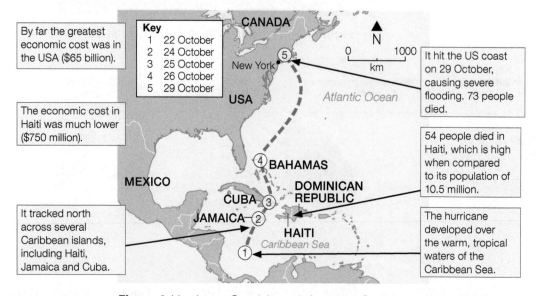

By far the greatest economic cost was in the USA ($65 billion).

Key
1   22 October
2   24 October
3   25 October
4   26 October
5   29 October

It hit the US coast on 29 October, causing severe flooding. 73 people died.

The economic cost in Haiti was much lower ($750 million).

54 people died in Haiti, which is high when compared to its population of 10.5 million.

It tracked north across several Caribbean islands, including Haiti, Jamaica and Cuba.

The hurricane developed over the warm, tropical waters of the Caribbean Sea.

Figure 2 *Hurricane Sandy's path from the Caribbean to the USA*

- Hazards turn into disasters when they affect people.
- Hurricane Sandy in 2012 was one of the most costly disasters ever to hit the USA.
- The economic cost of disasters in the USA is higher, but the risk to human life is lower.

Over to you

Explain the different impacts of Hurricane Sandy in the USA and Haiti.

a Why was the death toll so high in Haiti?
b Why was the economic cost so high in the USA?
c Which country would you say is best prepared for natural disasters? Explain.

You will find out:

- how the USA was hit by drought from 2012
- the history of drought in the USA
- what the government response was to drought.

Your key question

How should the USA prepare for the next natural disaster?

Drought in the USA

The drought that affected the USA from 2012 was the most costly natural disaster in US history. The worst hit state was California, where the drought continued until 2015 (Figure 1). Few people outside the USA know about it because no one died. The USA has experienced previous droughts in the 20th century (Figure 2).

Responses to the drought

In 2015 the US government announced financial help for those affected by the drought, especially farmers (80% of water used in California is for farming). The money was used for:

- efforts to conserve water on farmland by reducing wind erosion
- animal feed and access to water for livestock at risk of starvation
- rural communities at risk of running out of drinking water
- food banks for families in financial hardship because of the drought.

In addition, California imposed restrictions on some water consumption, especially the watering of lawns.

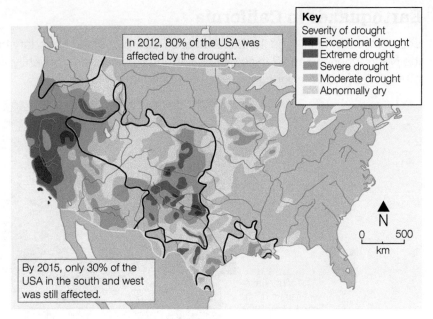

Figure 1 Areas of the USA affected by drought in 2015

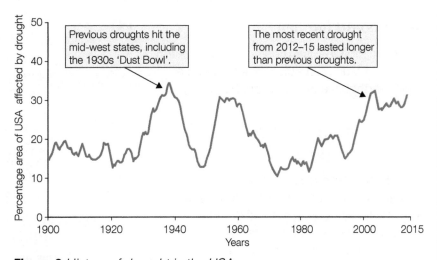

Figure 2 History of drought in the USA

Six Second Summary

- The 2012–2015 drought in the USA was the most costly disaster in its history.
- Most of the USA was affected, but the worst hit areas were the south and west.
- There have been previous droughts in the USA, but this one lasted longer.

Over to you

Think about how different people and businesses could be affected by drought. Then, try to explain these two facts about the 2012–2015 drought:

- It was the most costly natural disaster in US history.
- No one died.

You will find out:

- why California is at risk from earthquakes
- when earthquakes happened there in the past
- what damage a major earthquake could cause.

Your key question

How should the USA prepare for the next natural disaster?

Earthquakes in California

Southern California lies on the San Andreas Fault, part of the boundary between the North American and Pacific plates. Earthquakes happen frequently along parts of the fault. A major earthquake happened in 1994 (Figure 1).

The Northridge earthquake killed 33 people.

It caused $40 billion worth of damage.

The earthquake measured 6.7 on the Richter Scale.

The San Andreas Fault is due for a major earthquake in the next 30 years.

When the next earthquake happens, it is predicted to be 10 times more powerful (7.8 on the Richter Scale).

Figure 1 *Damage caused by the Northridge earthquake in 1994*

What could happen

The next 'Big One' is expected at the southern end of the fault where there has not been a major earthquake for 150 years (Figure 2).

Six Second Summary

- Southern California lies on the San Andreas Fault, part of a plate boundary.
- A 1994 earthquake measured 6.7, but the next one could be 10 times worse.
- A major earthquake is predicted to happen within the next 30 years.

Over to you

Draw a sketch map of Southern California to show the San Andreas Fault and the cities near it. Highlight where major earthquakes have happened and give dates.

Now, use your map to explain why you would be worried if you lived in Los Angeles.

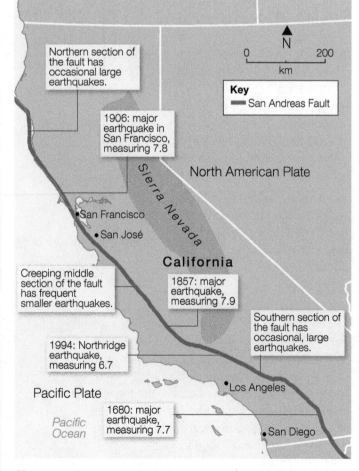

Figure 2 *Historic earthquakes on the San Andreas Fault*

You will find out:

- how a hazard map is created
- what the pattern of hazard risk is in the USA
- how we can be better prepared for natural hazards.

Your key question

How should the USA prepare for the next natural disaster?

Mapping hazard risk

Geographers have used information about natural hazards in the USA to create a map that shows the level of risk around the country (Figure 1).

The factors used to create the map include:

- the number of types of hazard in each area
- the frequency with which each type of hazard occurs
- the likely impact of hazards in lives lost and economic cost.

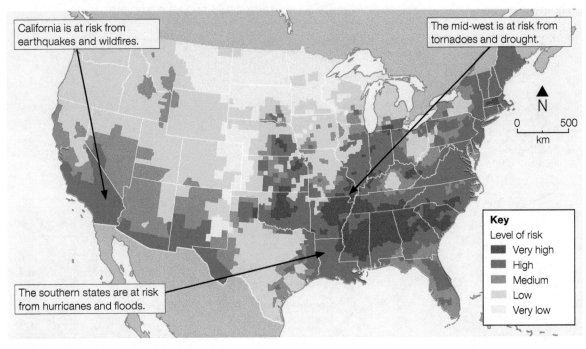

Figure 1 *Hazard risk map for the USA*

Preparing for natural hazards

It is impossible to prevent natural hazards from occurring but it is possible to prepare in order to minimise the risk. We can do this by:

- **prediction** – using knowledge and experience of previous events to forecast the likelihood of future events, e.g. earthquake monitoring
- **protection** – putting in place structures or infrastructure that will protect people and reduce the likelihood of injuries or deaths, e.g. flood barriers
- **planning** – putting in place plans for how to deal with the hazard when it happens and, if possible, keep people out of danger, e.g. evacuation.

Six Second Summary

- Risk depends on the range, frequency and impacts of hazards.
- The most hazardous parts of the USA are the mid-west and southern states.
- We can prepare for natural hazards by prediction, protection and planning.

Over to you

Wildfires are one of the natural hazards in the USA. Say how you would prepare for wildfires using the ideas of prediction, protection and planning.

You will find out:

- about one of the largest onshore wind farms in England
- the factors to consider when choosing a wind farm site.

Your key question

Where should the UK get its energy from in future?

Scout Moor Wind Farm

Scout Moor Wind Farm is one of the largest onshore **wind farms** in England. You will find most of it in squares 8218, 8318, 8317 and 8417 on the OS map in Figure 1.

The wind farm is on open moorland north of Rochdale in Greater Manchester. There are 26 wind turbines that generate energy for about 40 000 homes.

Choosing a wind farm site

The best site for a wind farm is one that is:

- on flat land, a hilltop or open moorland where it is windy
- away from buildings or trees which block the wind
- at least 1 km away from settlements where noise could disturb residents
- outside areas of natural beauty where a wind farm could spoil the landscape.

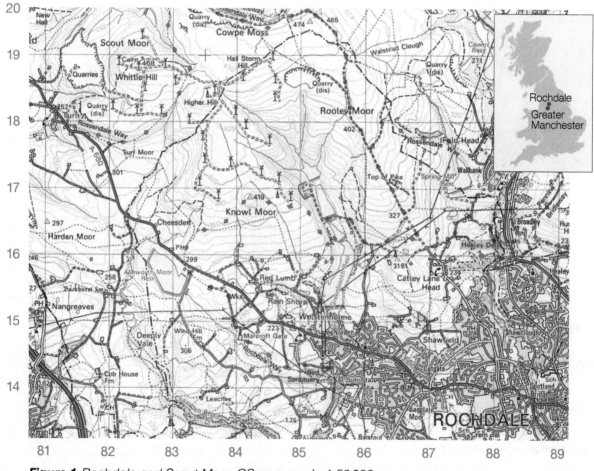

Figure 1 *Rochdale and Scout Moor, OS map, scale 1:50 000*

 Six Second Summary

- Scout Moor Wind Farm is one of the largest onshore wind farms in England.
- It is on open moorland, north of Rochdale in Greater Manchester.
- There are 26 wind turbines generating energy for 40 000 homes.

Over to you

Find Scout Moor Wind Farm on the map in Figure 1. Give at least three reasons why this is a good site for a wind farm. Are there any reasons why it is not a good site?

In 2018 the government had to decide whether to allow the wind farm to expand. You can find out what they decided by searching the internet for *Scout Moor Wind Farm decision*.

You will find out:
- how much energy we obtain from wind
- the differences between onshore and offshore wind
- the advantages and disadvantages of wind power.

Your key question
Where should the UK get its energy from in future?

Wind – a growing source of power

The number of wind farms in the UK is growing and so is the amount of wind energy we generate (Figure 1). The UK aims to meet the target of generating 30% of its electricity from **renewable sources** by 2030, including wind.

Onshore or offshore wind?

Most of the wind farms in the UK are **onshore**, but a growing number are now located **offshore** (Figure 2). The UK has a long coastline surrounded by shallow seas, with the potential to build many more offshore wind farms.

Year	Electricity generation (MW)	Percentage of total electricity generated
2008	2 974	1.5
2009	4 051	2.0
2010	5 204	2.3
2011	6 540	3.8
2012	8 871	5.5
2013	10 976	7.2
2014	12 440	9.3
2015	13 312	10.4

Figure 1 *UK wind generation, 2008–2015*

Advantages

- It is a renewable source of energy.
- It is relatively cheap, compared to other sources of energy.
- There is more wind in winter when demand is greater.

Onshore wind

- Land around each turbine can still be used for farming.

Offshore wind

- Does not use any land at all.

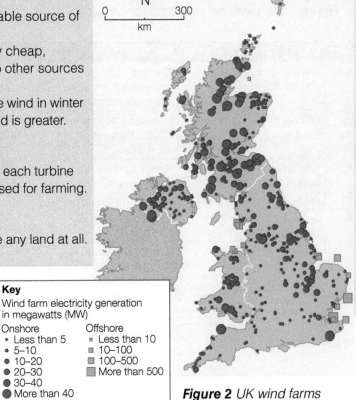

Key
Wind farm electricity generation in megawatts (MW)

Onshore
- Less than 5
- 5–10
- 10–20
- 20–30
- 30–40
- More than 40

Offshore
- Less than 10
- 10–100
- 100–500
- More than 500

Figure 2 *UK wind farms*

Disadvantages

- It is unreliable because wind does not always blow.
- Some say that wind turbines spoil the view.
- The moving turbine blades can cause injury to birds.

Onshore wind

- Wind turbines create noise.
- There are a limited number of sites with high, steady wind speeds.

Offshore wind

- It is more difficult and expensive to erect turbines on the seabed.

Six Second Summary

- A growing proportion of the UK's energy comes from wind power.
- There are onshore and offshore wind farms – a growing number of them are offshore.
- There are pros and cons for both onshore and offshore wind power.

Over to you

List the advantages and disadvantages of onshore and offshore wind farms. Which type of wind power should we use in the future?

UK electricity generation

The UK generates electricity in a number of ways (Figure 1).

- Over three-quarters comes from **non-renewable** sources of energy, including **fossil fuels**, like coal, oil and gas.
- Almost one-quarter comes from renewable sources like wind and solar power. Each source of energy has different impacts (Figure 2).

Renewable – there are about 1000 wind farms around the UK. Solar power is also widespread and there are plans for more tidal and wave power.

Nuclear – the UK has 19 nuclear power stations, located at coastal sites. There are plans to replace the old power stations with new ones.

Coal – the main source of energy in the UK for 200 years. Most of it is now imported. There are only ten coal power stations in the UK still working.

Gas – mainly imported by pipeline or shipped as liquefied natural gas (LNG). It arrives at nine terminals around the UK coast.

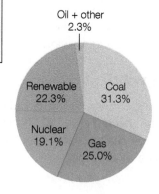

Oil + other 2.3%
Renewable 22.3%
Coal 31.3%
Nuclear 19.1%
Gas 25.0%

Figure 1 *Electricity generation in the UK, 2015*

Impact on...	Coal	Gas	Nuclear	Renewable, e.g. wind
Climate change	It emits more CO_2 than other fossil fuels.	It emits less CO_2 than coal or oil.	There are low CO_2 emissions from power station construction.	There are very low CO_2 emissions from construction.
Natural ecosystems	Burning coal produces acid rain, which affects trees and plants.	Drilling for gas affects sea life.	It makes little impact, but the process uses a lot of water.	Turbines can injure birds and bats.
Landscape	Power stations are large and dirty.	Gas storage terminals are large.	Power stations are large but isolated.	Wind farms are visible from far away.
Resources	The UK imports coal but still has plenty of its own.	North Sea gas is running out but shale gas could replace it.	The UK imports uranium and it may only last 50 years.	It will never run out.
Health and safety	Coal-mining is dangerous and emissions affect health.	Drilling for gas is dangerous.	Accidents are rare but very serious. Waste is also dangerous.	There is no risk to people.
Reliability	It is a very reliable form of energy.	It is reliable for now but not if we have to import.	It is a very reliable form of energy.	Wind is unpredictable.

Figure 2 *Sources of energy in the UK compared*

You will find out:

- where the UK obtains its gas from
- how to obtain shale gas by fracking
- why fracking is controversial.

Your key question

Where should the UK get its energy from in future?

The potential of shale gas

For the past 50 years the UK has relied on North Sea gas, particularly for heating our homes. It is now running out, so we need to import more gas.

The UK has another source of gas called **shale gas**. It is found in shale, a sedimentary rock that underlies large areas of the UK. It is estimated that there is enough to supply the UK for the next ten years.

The technique used to extract shale gas is **fracking** (hydraulic fracturing) (Figure 1). This is a controversial technique that has led to protests (Figure 2).

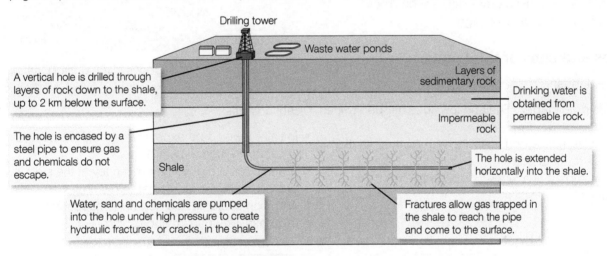

Figure 1 *How fracking works*

Figure 2 *Protests against fracking in the UK*

Six Second Summary

- North Sea gas is running out and shale gas provides an alternative source of gas.
- Shale gas is obtained from the ground by fracking (hydraulic fracturing).
- There have been protests in the UK against fracking because people don't want to live near drill sites.

Over to you

Explain fracking in your own words, using the diagram in Figure 1 to help you. Cover the labels so you don't copy them. Or, copy the diagram and write your own labels.

You will find out:

- the potential for tidal power in the UK
- the advantages and disadvantage of tidal power.

Your key question

Where should the UK get its energy from in future?

Plans for a tidal lagoon

Because the UK is an island, **tidal power** is another potential source of energy. The Swansea Bay Tidal Lagoon was the first of four proposed tidal lagoons in the Bristol Channel, which has the largest tidal range in the UK (Figure 1).

However, in 2018, the government rejected the plan for Swansea Bay Tidal Lagoon. They thought the cost was too high.

Pros and cons of tidal power

Advantages:

- It is predictable. High and low tides happen twice a day.
- The UK has a long coastline with many potential sites for tidal power.
- The impact of a lagoon on natural ecosystems is minimal.

Figure 1 Four proposed tidal lagoons in the Bristol Channel

Disadvantages:

- Initially, it would be expensive, though costs would fall as more lagoons are built.
- It would require government money at the start in order to compete with other forms of power.
- A lagoon could have a negative impact on local business, like tourism and fishing.

Low tide

Gates in the wall are closed as the tide falls. At low tide the gates open and water rushes out through the turbines to empty the lagoon.

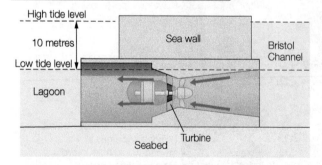

High tide

Gates in the wall are closed as the tide rises. At high tide the gates open and water rushes in through the turbines to fill the lagoon.

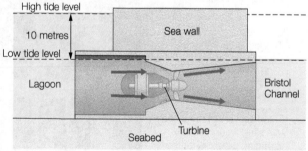

Figure 2 How a tidal power scheme works

Six Second Summary

- Tidal power is a potential source of energy for the UK as it is an island.
- The Swansea Bay Tidal Lagoon had the potential to provide power for 150 000 homes.
- There are pros and cons of tidal power.

Over to you

Compare one renewable source of energy (e.g. tidal power) with a non-renewable source (e.g. shale gas). You could choose two different examples from this chapter. Summarise the pros and cons of both sources of energy, and then decide which one the government should support.

You will find out:
- how cities work as a system
- what an ecological footprint is
- the size of London's ecological footprint.

Your key question
How could living in London be more sustainable?

Linear and circular systems

Over half the world's population live in cities. They consume 75% of the world's energy and produce 80% of all greenhouse gas emissions. Cities need to reduce their environmental impact to be more sustainable.

We can think of a city like London as a **system**. Most cities are a linear system with **inputs** and **outputs** (Figure 1). To be more sustainable they need to become circular systems where resources are recycled, with fewer inputs and outputs.

Goods are made in factories. Many goods are imported, especially from China.

Food is mostly grown on farms outside London. Much of it is imported.

Inputs

Water comes from rivers or groundwater and is stored in reservoirs around London.

Energy comes from fossil fuels, often imported, or renewable sources in the UK.

Solid waste ends up in landfill sites or is burnt in incinerators.

Sewage is treated at a sewage works before the water returns to the river.

Outputs

Air pollution from burning fuel or waste is carried by wind beyond London.

Figure 1 London as a linear system

London's ecological footprint

We can measure the environmental impact of a city by its **ecological footprint**. This is the total area of land or sea required to supply its resources and absorb its waste anywhere in the world. It is measured in global hectares (gha) per person.

London's ecological footprint is 5.8 gha per person. Multiplied by its population, this is an area larger than the whole of the UK. There is only 1.9 gha available for each person on the planet. That is what we need to aim for to be sustainable.

Six Second Summary

- Most cities work as linear systems, using inputs and producing outputs.
- Our ecological footprint is the area required to produce our resources and absorb our waste.
- London's ecological footprint covers an area larger than the whole of the UK.

Over to you

Draw a large footprint. Divide it into the ways we use space to supply our resources or absorb our waste. You need to think of all the resources we use (e.g. food) and the space required to produce each one (e.g. farmland). Then show all the areas on your footprint.

You will find out:

- how sustainability is measured on the Green City Index
- how London compares with Copenhagen on the GCI
- what Copenhagen did to become more sustainable.

Your key question

How could living in London be more sustainable?

Making cities more sustainable

Cities like London can become more sustainable by reducing the size of their ecological footprint. They can do this by:

- reducing the resources they consume
- recycling more resources
- using renewable energy
- producing less waste.

The European **Green City Index** is used to compare sustainability between cities. It includes eight indicators (Figure 1). London is ranked 11th of the major European cities and Copenhagen is 1st (Figure 2).

Figure 1 *The Green City Index*

Copenhagen's good example

Copenhagen expects to become the world's first **carbon-neutral city** by 2025. Carbon emissions will be reduced to zero, or balanced by removing CO_2.

Improvements Copenhagen has made include:

- **Water pollution** – a modern sewerage system improves water quality
- **Water supply** – better management of water resources to reduce waste
- **Cycling** – new cycling lanes make cycling safer
- **Public transport** – an integrated public transport system, so fewer people drive
- **Waste** – more waste is recycled; less than 2% is sent to landfill
- **Heating** – a combined heat and power system supplies 98% of the city.

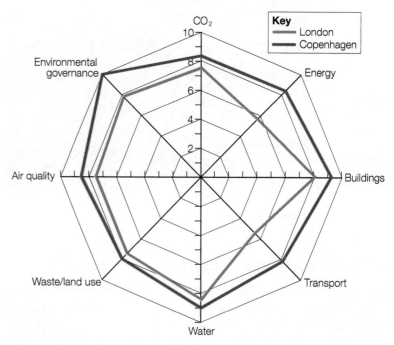

Figure 2 *London and Copenhagen compared on the Green City Index*

 Six Second Summary

- The European Green City Index is used to measure a city's sustainability.
- Copenhagen is Europe's most sustainable city; London is 11th.
- Copenhagen expects to be even more sustainable, and carbon-neutral by 2025.

Over to you

Make eight flash cards, one for each of the Green City Index indicators. On each card, write at least one improvement cities could make to be more sustainable. You could use Copenhagen as an example. If you can't think of any ideas, come back to it later, when you have finished the chapter.

You will find out:

- why London's transport system is struggling
- how the new Crossrail route will help
- what the benefits are of reducing traffic.

Your key question

How could living in London be more sustainable?

London's transport system

London has a well-integrated public transport system. But, it is struggling to cope with the number of passengers as the population grows. 75 million passengers use buses and trains in London each week.

Crossrail

Crossrail is a new, high-speed, east-west route across London that opens in 2019 (Figure 1).

It will bring a number of benefits to London, including:

- increase the number of passengers the network can carry
- reduce east–west journey times by half
- bring an extra 1.5 million commuters into London each day
- raise property values and create new jobs around stations on the route.

Figure 1 *The Crossrail route through London*

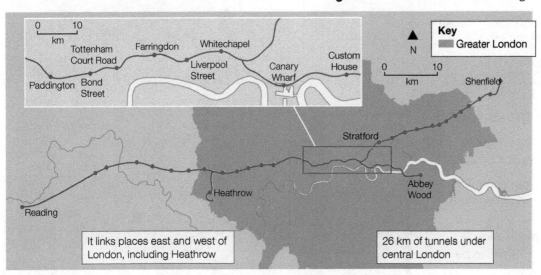

It links places east and west of London, including Heathrow

26 km of tunnels under central London

Benefits of reducing traffic

By encouraging people to use public transport, Crossrail will help to keep cars off the road in London. This, in turn, will help to:

- reduce congestion
- speed up road journey times
- cut the number of road accidents
- reduce air pollution
- cut CO_2 emissions (Figure 2).

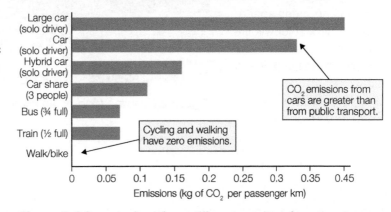

CO_2 emissions from cars are greater than from public transport.

Cycling and walking have zero emissions.

Figure 2 *CO_2 emissions from different modes of transport*

 Six Second Summary

- London's transport system struggles to cope with an increased number of passengers.
- Crossrail is a new high-speed route that will help carry more passengers.
- It will also help to reduce traffic, bringing other benefits.

Over to you

Draw a simple flow diagram, making connections to show how Crossrail will help to reduce carbon emissions in London.

You will find out:

- how much green space there is in London
- the benefits of green space
- why people use allotments to grow food.

London – a green city

London is one of the world's greenest cities. 47% of the city is green space (Figure 1). Green spaces include:

- parks
- gardens
- woodland
- cemeteries
- playing fields
- allotments
- farmland

Key
- Open green space 38%
- Domestic gardens 24%
- Open water 2%
- Footpaths 1%
- Railways 1%
- Roads 12%
- Domestic buildings 9%
- Non-domestic buildings 5%
- Other land uses 8%

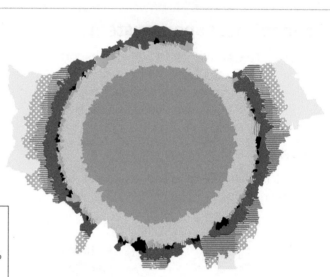

Figure 1 Land use in London

Benefits of green spaces

There are many benefits to having green spaces in cities;

- Trees produce oxygen, helping us to breathe, and absorb CO_2
- Trees and plants reduce the danger of flooding by absorbing water.
- Woodland and green space provides a habitat for wildlife.
- People enjoy activities in green spaces to keep fit and healthy.
- People use green spaces for growing food (Figure 2).

There has been an increase in the popularity of allotments in the 21st century.

There are over 700 allotments sites in London, with 20 000 individual plots.

Allotments began in the early 20th century as a way for families feed themselves.

People produce their own food and so reduce the distance their food travels.

Figure 2 Growing food on an allotment in London

Six Second Summary

- London is one of the world's greenest cities with 47% of land green space.
- Urban green spaces have benefits, including the reduction of carbon emissions.
- People in cities can use green spaces to grow food to feed themselves.

Over to you

Show the data in the graph in Figure 1 in a different way. Which of the two ways is the best for you to learn the information? Use that one to revise from.

You will find out:

- about East Village, a new community in London
- what features make East Village sustainable.

East Village – a sustainable community

East Village is the former Athletes Village from the London 2012 Olympics (Figure 1). It was designed as part of the Olympic legacy to become a sustainable new community.

2800 new homes were built on a 27-hectare site. There is a 50/50 mix of privately rented homes and cheaper, more affordable rented homes.

Buildings
- The buildings are high-rise so use less land.
- They are well insulated and don't have boilers.

Transport
- A light railway station links to the London Underground.
- There are bus connections to other local areas.

Water
- Buildings have green roofs to absorb water.
- Water is recycled to irrigate plants and flush toilets.

Energy
- The energy comes from a combined heat and power (CHP) station.
- It burns biomass which is a renewable source of energy.

Waste/land use
- The village was built on a derelict brownfield site.
- There are 10 ha of green space.

CO_2
- Homes use 30% less energy than normal homes.
- Trees have been planted to absorb CO_2

Environmental governance
- Two organisations own the homes and manage the area.
- There is strict environmental management.

Air quality
- Hundreds of trees produce oxygen and absorb CO_2
- Reduced traffic means less harmful gases.

Figure 1 *Sustainability in East Village*

Six Second Summary

- East Village is the former Athletes Village from the London 2012 Olympics.
- It was designed as part of the Olympic legacy as a sustainable new community.
- A combined heat and power station (CHP) provides all the energy for the village.

Over to you

Make a large copy of a kite diagram like this. Give a score for each aspect of sustainability for East Village and draw the kite on the diagram (see Figure 2, 11.2). Then, draw another kite for a place you know. Compare the two kites. How does your place compare with East Village?

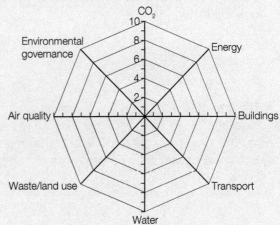

You will find out:

- how China's economy compares to the USA's
- how China has changed in the past 30 years
- how fast China's economy is growing.

Your key question

Which way should China develop now?

China – the world's largest economy?

For the past 30 years China's economy has been growing rapidly. Measured by GDP, China is the second largest economy after the USA. But, measured by **purchasing power parity (PPP)**, it has already overtaken the USA (Figure 1). PPP is a more true reflection of actual wealth than GDP.

Changes in China

China has come a long way in a short time.

- From 1949 to 1978 it was a **centrally planned economy** under the control of a communist government.
- In 1978 the government switched to a **market-based economy** with more control by companies and individuals. China was still a LIDC.
- Today, China is an EDC. More than 500 million people have been lifted out of poverty. But, about 100 million people remain in poverty.

China's economic growth

Economic growth in China has averaged about 10% a year since 1978 (Figure 2). The average rate in the UK over the same period was below 1%.

Economic growth has brought some challenges:

- growing inequality between rich and poor, urban and rural
- rapid urbanisation
- environmental pollution
- imbalances in the world economy, with China growing faster.

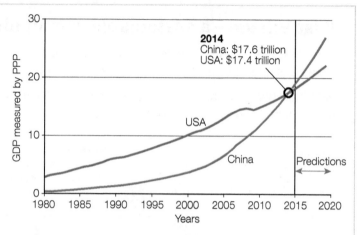

Figure 1 *Economic growth in China and the USA compared, using PPP*

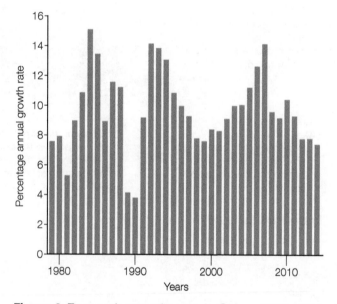

Figure 2 *Economic growth rates in China, 1979–2014*

 Six Second Summary

- The size of China's economy has overtaken the USA's, measured by PPP.
- In 1978 China was still a LIDC, but today it is an EDC.
- Economic growth in China has averaged about 10% a year since 1978.

Over to you

GDP, PPP, LIDC and EDC are terms you have learnt before. Try to write a definition for each one. If required, go back to Chapter 6 to remind yourself.

You will find out:

- how China's carbon emissions have grown
- what China's contribution is to global emissions
- why China still depends on coal.

Your key question

Which way should China
develop now?

China's contribution to global emissions

China now consumes more energy than any other country. Economic growth has led to rapid increases in the country's energy consumption and carbon emissions (Fig 1).

China is often blamed for the global increase in emissions. This might be unfair because:

- China is trying to develop as advanced countries like the UK did in the past
- it has developed manufacturing industries as we did during the 19th century
- many of the goods we buy are now manufactured in China
- the cumulative (total) emissions over the past 250 years are less for China than for the USA and Europe.

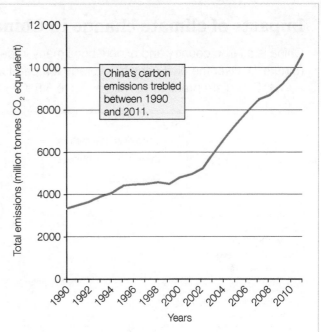

China's carbon emissions trebled between 1990 and 2011.

Figure 1 *Growth of China's greenhouse gas emissions, 1990–2011*

China's dependence on coal

66% of China's energy comes from coal, the most polluting fossil fuel of all. As well as burning coal in power stations, coal is also used by many of China's manufacturing industries, especially steel (Figure 2).

China produces 50% of the world's steel.

Each tonne of steel requires 0.7 tonnes of coal.

Steel manufacturing uses coal; there are no low-carbon alternatives.

China's steel industry uses 7% of all the world's coal.

Figure 2 *A steelworks in China*

 Six Second Summary

- China's carbon emissions trebled from 1990 to 2011.
- It is unfair to blame China for global emissions, as we buy the goods they produce.
- 66% of China's energy comes from coal which is essential for the steel industry.

 **Over to you**

Make a list of all the evidence on this page that China is to blame for global carbon emissions. Then, list the reasons that it is not to blame. Decide whether China is to blame or not.

You will find out:

- what impacts climate change have in China
- how temperatures have changed
- what other environmental problems China faces.

Your key question

Which way should China develop now?

Impacts of climate change in China

China is a large country and experiences many impacts of climate change (Figure 1). Over the past century, average temperatures in China have risen by 1.1 °C and are predicted to rise by up to 3.5 °C in the 21st century.

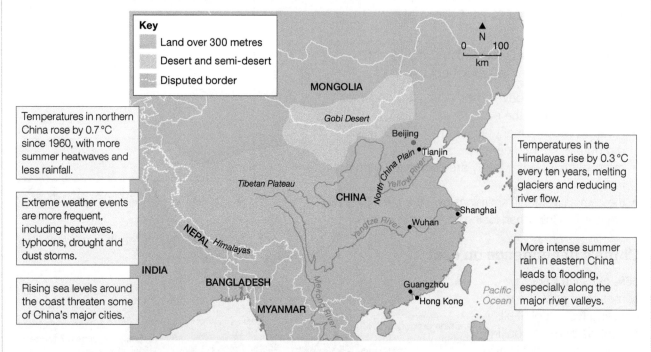

Figure 1 *Impacts of climate change in China*

Map annotations:

Key
- Land over 300 metres
- Desert and semi-desert
- Disputed border

Temperatures in northern China rose by 0.7 °C since 1960, with more summer heatwaves and less rainfall.

Extreme weather events are more frequent, including heatwaves, typhoons, drought and dust storms.

Rising sea levels around the coast threaten some of China's major cities.

Temperatures in the Himalayas rise by 0.3 °C every ten years, melting glaciers and reducing river flow.

More intense summer rain in eastern China leads to flooding, especially along the major river valleys.

Map labels: MONGOLIA, Gobi Desert, Beijing, Tianjin, North China Plain, Yellow River, Tibetan Plateau, CHINA, Shanghai, Wuhan, Yangtze River, NEPAL, Himalayas, INDIA, BANGLADESH, Guangzhou, Hong Kong, Pacific Ocean, MYANMAR, Mekong River

Other environmental problems

For years, China's priority has been economic growth. The policy was, 'grow first, clean up later'. But, now environmental problems are making the government think again:

- Ecosystem loss – due to dam building, farming improvement and urbanisation.
- Air pollution – due to more cars and burning coal, leading to more lung and heart disease.
- Water pollution – due to sewage and waste from industry being poured into rivers, leading to higher cancer rates.
- Desertification – due to drought, so land is no longer suitable for habitation or farming.

Six Second Summary

- Average temperatures in China have risen by 1.1 °C in the past century.
- Climate change brings different impacts in each part of the country.
- Ecosystem loss, air and water pollution and desertification are problems in China.

Over to you

Match each of the environmental problems in China with one or more of these causes – *cities, industry, farming, climate change*. In each case, explain the connection.

You will find out:

- why China has a water crisis
- how the South–North Water Transfer Project works
- what the drawbacks of the project are.

Your key question

Which way should China develop now?

Solving the water crisis

China has a water shortage crisis. More than half of China's rivers have disappeared and half of those remaining are polluted. The problem is more severe in the dry North China Plain, where economic growth uses more water.

The government's solution to the crisis is the South–North Water Transfer Project (SNWTP) (Figures 1 and 2).

Key features

- SNWTP is the world's largest water transfer scheme. It cost more than US$62 billion.
- Water is moved from the humid south (with high rainfall) to the drier north.
- It supplies Beijing and other northern cities with water for industry and farms.

Drawbacks

- Water evaporates from canals and this is wasteful.
- Focusing on water for cities means that villages and farms miss out.
- Changing climate might mean that the south will have less water to share.

Figure 1 A canal moving water for the SNWTP

How the project works

The idea of the scheme is to transfer water along three routes between China's two largest river basins – the Yangtze in the south to the Yellow River in the north (Figure 2).

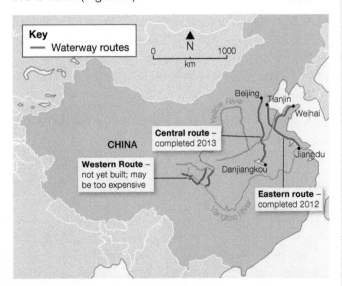

Key
— Waterway routes

N
0 ——— 1000
km

CHINA

Beijing Tianjin
Yellow River
Weihai

Central route –
completed 2013

Western Route –
not yet built; may be too expensive

Danjiangkou

Jiangdu

Eastern route –
completed 2012

Yangtze River

Figure 2 China's South–North Water Transfer Project

Six Second Summary

- China has a water shortage problem, particularly in the North China Plain.
- The SNWTP moves water between China's two largest river basins.
- It supplies cities such as Beijing and Tianjin with water for industry and farms.

Over to you

Draw a sketch map of China to explain the SNWTP. Mark and label the Yangtze River and Yellow River, Beijing and Tianjin on the map. Then, annotate your map (using 3 colours) to explain:

a why the project was necessary
b how the project works
c what the drawbacks are.

You will find out:

- how China's priorities are changing
- the environmental consequences of economic growth
- what options China has for sustainable development.

Your key question

Which way should China develop now?

Economic growth and the environment

China's priorities are changing. The Chinese government now emphasises the 'quality of growth', not simply the economic growth rate. People in China are concerned about the environment. For many years, their government ignored, or even denied, China's environmental problems.

So, is it possible to have both economic growth and sustainable development? The graph in Figure 1 gives us a clue.

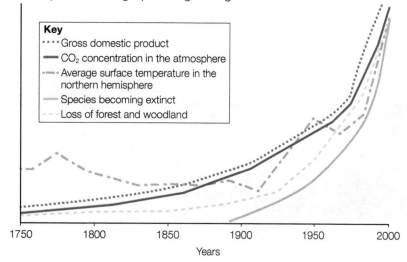

Key
···· Gross domestic product
▬▬ CO_2 concentration in the atmosphere
▬·▬ Average surface temperature in the northern hemisphere
▬▬ Species becoming extinct
- - - Loss of forest and woodland

This graph shows that, as GDP rises:

- CO_2 levels in the atmosphere go up
- surface temperatures rise (global warming)
- more species become extinct
- forest and woodland disappear.

Figure 1 *Global changes over the past 250 years*

Sustainable options for China

There are ways in which China could develop more sustainably. These would involve making difficult decisions.

Economic growth

- Switch from manufacturing to services, closing factories and opening offices, or
- Keep factories open but switch to cleaner fuels and technology where possible.

Energy

- Switch from burning coal to cleaner non-renewable energy sources like gas, or
- Switch from burning coal to renewable forms of energy like wind and solar.

Water

- Transfer water from wetter to drier regions of the country by canals and tunnels, or
- Charge more for water and use the money to repair leaks and clean up pollution.

Transport

- Ban cars in cities and make people ride bicycles or walk instead, or
- Improve public transport so people will use trains and buses rather than cars.

 Six Second Summary

- China now emphasises 'quality of growth', not simply economic growth.
- Historically, environmental problems get worse with economic growth.
- Sustainable development will mean that China has to make difficult decisions.

Over to you

Make four flash cards (labelled Economic growth, Water, Energy, Transport). Write the two options for each on either side of the card. For each case, decide what the best option is and turn your cards that way up. Compare your ideas with a partner. Justify your decisions to each other.

A

abrasion the process of erosion in which rocks and other hard materials in water wear away the water channel or coast

adult literacy rate the percentage of adults able to read

advanced country (AC) country that is wealthy, has a wide range of jobs and many services

afforestation planting trees to create new forest

agribusiness farming by large companies that grow food for profit on huge areas of land

agroforestry growing trees and crops together

albedo effect the amount a surface reflects the Sun's rays back into space

attrition the process of rocks in water bashing into and wearing each other down into smaller, rounder particles

B

backwash the movement of waves down a beach

bi-lateral aid international aid given by one country to another

biodiversity variety of plant and animal species

biofuel fuel made from renewable plant material

biological weathering breaking up of rock caused by plants or animals

biomass the mass, or weight, of living material

biome large ecosystem characteristic of a specific part of the world

bottom-up aid/development aid/development funded and carried out by NGOs in co-operation with local communities

brownfield site a site in an urban area, either derelict or with old buildings, that could be used for future development

by-catch the unwanted fish and animals caught in huge fishing nets

C

carbon footprint the amount of carbon emissions produced by individuals, organisations or communities

carbon sink an area, such as rainforest, that uses up carbon dioxide in the atmosphere

chemical weathering the breakdown of material caused by the action of rainwater in rock

climate change the long-term change in global or regional climate due largely to increased levels of CO_2 in the atmosphere

collision boundary where tectonic plates move towards each other, creating mountains

colonialism the ruling of one country by another country

composite volcano a steep volcano formed by alternate layers of lava and ash on destructive plate boundaries

conservation protection

conservative boundary where tectonic plates move alongside each other

constructive boundary where tectonic plates move apart and new land is created

continental crust the part of Earth's crust that makes continents

convection current pockets of warm air or liquid that rise, then cool and fall, in a circular motion

convectional rainfall rainfall, often heavy, that occurs when thick clouds form because of warm air rising quickly

core the centre of Earth

coriolis effect the way the spinning of Earth makes winds veer to the right in the northern hemisphere and to the left in the southern hemisphere

counter-urbanisation the movement of people out of cities into the countryside and smaller towns

D

debt relief the total or partial cancellation of debts owed by LIDCs

deep focus earthquake an earthquake that starts 70–700 km below Earth's surface

deforestation the clearing of trees to transform forest into cleared land

Demographic Transition Model a model that shows the changes a population is likely to go through over time

dependency ratio the proportion of people under 16 or over 65 who depend on the working population

deposition occurs when material carried by the sea/river is dropped when the sea/river loses energy

destructive boundary where tectonic plates are forced together

development an improvement in living standards through better use of resources

drought a period when there is much less precipitation over a specific time than is usual for an area, leading to water shortages

dry valley valley left after the river that formed the valley has disappeared

E

economic development an increase in the total goods and services a country produces

economic hub the focal point for the economy of a country or region

ecosystem a community of plants and animals, and the environment in which they live

ecotourism travel that aims to conserve the natural environment and local communities

El Niño an event that occurs when weak trade winds blowing east to west allow surface temperatures to increase

emerging and developing country (EDC) country that is in transition from being a low-income developing country to an advanced country

emissions greenhouse gases put into the atmosphere

employment sectors different types of industry that employ people

enhanced greenhouse effect the trapping of more of the Sun's energy because of the cumulative effect of greenhouse gases, causing Earth's temperature to increase

epicentre the point on Earth's surface directly above an earthquake's focus

ethical consumerism buying products that do not have negative social, economic or environmental impacts

evapotranspiration evaporation of water from plants and soil

eye of the storm the area of calm, clear conditions where cool air sinks at the centre of a tropical storm

F

fairtrade trade that gives farmers a fairer price for their products

fault a crack in the Earth's crust

fauna animal life

flash flooding flooding that appears very quickly as a result of heavy rain

floodplain flat land, along the sides of a river, formed by silt and clay when the river floods

flora plant life

focus the source of an earthquake beneath the Earth's surface

fold mountains mountains formed when continental plate buckles

food chain producers and consumers linked within an ecosystem

food web interconnected food chains that make up a large ecosystem

food security when all people at all times have access to sufficient, safe, nutritious food to maintain a healthy and active life

Glossary

fracking the method of obtaining gas and oil by blasting huge amounts of water mixed with sand and chemicals into the ground

freeze-thaw weathering the breakdown of rock caused by large variations between day and night temperatures

front the boundary at which warm air and cool air meet

frontal rainfall rainfall that occurs when warm air rises over cool air

G

genetically modified (GM) crop a crop developed by taking DNA from one species and inserting it into another

gentrification the improvement of areas, leading to the influx of wealthier people to replace poorer residents

geographical information system (GIS) a computer system that stores, analyses and presents different types of geographical data in map form

geomorphic processes the ways in which the landscape is shaped

glacial period a colder period in Earth's history

global circulation system the movement of air around the world

global warming an increase in the average temperature of Earth's atmosphere and oceans

GNI/capita gross national income divided by the population

gorge a valley with high, steep sides

green belt open space around cities on which no further development is allowed

Green Revolution a period in the 1960s when scientists produced rice and wheat seeds by cross-breeding, which gave very high yields

greenhouse gas a gas in the atmosphere, such as CO_2, that acts like the glass roof on a greenhouse, increasing temperature

gross national income (GNI) the sum of all the money earned in a country

growth corridor a region of economic growth

H

hard engineering human-made structures that help to deal with natural hazards, e.g. sea walls to stop coastal flooding

herbicide chemical used to kill weeds

high pressure (belt) a cold air mass pressing down on Earth

hotspot a place where lava rises up through very thin oceanic crust

Human Development Index (HDI) a measurement of development based on the indicators of wealth, health and education

hydraulic action the process of rock being broken up by air being forced into cracks

hydroponics growing plants indoors in water

I

ice age an period of time when Earth has permanent ice sheets

ice core a tube of ice drilled out from the depth of an ice sheet

indigenous people the people who originated in a particular place

infrastructure a country's transport and communication networks and essential services, such as train routes, water supply and hospitals

insolation the radiation from the Sun that reaches Earth

intensive farming farming that uses large amounts of machinery, chemicals or labour to maximise the amount of food produced

interglacial period a warmer period in Earth's history

internal growth growth of a population as a result of a higher live birth rate than death rate

international aid help that one country gives to another in times of need, taking the form of food, technology, money or advice

international migration the movement of people from one country to another

J

jet stream strong wind high in the atmosphere

L

La Niña an event that occurs when strong trade winds blowing east to west reduce surface temperatures

lahar a mudflow of melted snow and volcanic ash released from a glacier melted by a volcano

landslide a large body of soil and rock that slides down a steep slope

levee a river embankment caused by material deposited by river floods

life expectancy the average age to which people can expect to live

lithosphere the outer part of Earth, consisting of the crust and upper mantle

litter rotting leaves on the ground below growing vegetation

longshore drift the process by which pebbles and sand are transported along a beach

long-term development assistance international aid to help people to improve their lives and develop their country

low-income developing country (LIDC) a country that is poor, has a narrow range of jobs and few services

low pressure (belt) a warm air mass rising up from Earth

M

mantle the layer of very hot rock below Earth's crust

meander a bend along the course of a river

mechanical weathering the breakdown of rock caused by temperature changes, especially on mountains

megacity a city with a population over 10 million people

mid-ocean ridge a ridge of new rock under the ocean formed by eruptions of lava

migrant a person who moves from one place to live in another

Millennium Development Goals (MDGs) minimum acceptable standards of living agreed by world leaders from 189 countries in 2000 to cut world poverty in half by 2015

mitigation action taken to make something less severe

multi-lateral aid international aid given by countries through international organisations like the International Monetary Fund

N

natural greenhouse effect the natural process by which Earth is kept warm by gases that trap the Sun's energy in the atmosphere

net migration the different between immigration and emigration

nutrient cycle the stores and flows of nutrients in an ecosystem

O

oceanic crust Earth's crust beneath the ocean

organic farming the method of farming that bans the use of chemical fertilisers and pesticides

overseas development assistance (ODA) international aid given by governments and paid for by taxes

oxbow lake a crescent-shaped lake formed when a river meander is cut off from the river and isolated

P

peak oil when oil production reaches its maximum level before declining

periglacial around the edge of areas covered with ice

permaculture a way of growing food that tries to achieve food security by copying nature

permafrost ground that is frozen throughout the year

pesticide chemical used to kill insects

plate boundaries where the edges of tectonic plates meet

political unrest protest or violence arising from dissatisfaction with the government

population density a measure of the number of people who live within a given area

population pyramid a graph showing population structure, including the breakdown of age and sex within a population

prevailing wind wind from the most common direction in any given place

pull factor a factor that encourages people to move to a place

push factor a factor that encourages people to move from a place

pyroclastic flow torrent of hot ash, rock, gas and steam from a volcano

Q

quaternary industry industry based on high-level information and research

Quaternary period the time period in Earth's history that began about 2.6 million years ago and continues today; includes the Pleistocene epoch and the Holocene epoch

R

rain shadow the leeward side of mountains, where there is little rain

rejuvenated river a river that has eroded down into its old floodplain due to a fall in sea level

relief rainfall rainfall that occurs when clouds rise up over mountains

re-urbanisation the process of people moving back into city centres

rift valley a block of land that falls between fault lines when tectonic plates pull apart

river terrace an old floodplain of a rejuvenated river

Rostow's model a model of the stages of economic development

rural–urban migration movement of people from the countryside to cities

S

saltation the process in which pebbles and small stones are bounced along in flowing water

sanitation infrastructure for drainage and sewerage

sea ice maximum/minimum the maximum/minimum area of the Arctic Ocean covered in ice in any year

secondary industry manufacturing industries

seismic gap an area along known faults that has not experienced earthquake activity for a long time

seismic (shock) wave fast waves of energy generated from the focus of an earthquake

shallow focus earthquake an earthquake that starts within 70 km of Earth's surface

shield volcano a gently sloping volcano formed by runny lava, usually at a constructive plate boundary

shifting cultivation a sustainable way for farming in a forest by moving from one area to another

short-term emergency relief international aid to cope with the immediate problems caused by disasters like earthquakes and wars

social development an improvement in human welfare to meet people's needs

soft engineering adaptations to work with nature to limit damage from natural hazards

soil profile different layers within soil

solution the process in which rocks slowly dissolve in water

spit a long ridge of sand, shingle and/or pebbles attached to the land at one end but not at the other

stack column of rock surrounded by sea, once but no longer attached to the mainland

storm surge abnormal rises in sea level that occur when low air pressure raises sea levels, especially when a tropical storm nears land

subduction when a dense oceanic plate is forced under a continental plate at a destructive boundary

subsistence farming when farmers grow crops and animals to feed their own families

suburb residential areas outside the centre of a city

suburbanisation the process by which suburbs grow as a city expands outwards

sun spot a temporary dark spot on the Sun's surface caused by magnetic storms

suspension the way tiny particles of sand and silt are carried along, suspended in water

sustainable development economic, social and environmental development to meet people's needs now without compromising the ability of future generations to meet their needs

sustainable management using resources carefully so that future generations can also use them to meet their needs

swash movement of waves up a beach

T

tectonic plates the huge segments of Earth's crust

tertiary industry service industries

top-down development strategy development funded and carried out by government or a large international organisation like the World Bank

tornado a very strong rotating wind

traction the process in which boulders and large stones are dragged along a river bed or sea floor

trade the buying and selling of goods and services

trade winds winds that blow from high- to low-pressure belts

trans-national company (TNC) a large company that operates in more than one country

tropical rainforest large expanses of lush forest growing in the tropics in high temperatures and very high rainfall

tropical storm a powerful, rotating storm in the tropics (also known as a cyclone, hurricane or typhoon)

tundra areas in polar regions with cold winters, cool summers and low rainfall

U

urbanisation growth in the proportion of people living in towns and cities

W

water cycle the stores and flows of water in an ecosystem

water stress when the demand for water uses up a high proportion of the rainfall

water transfer scheme an infrastructure project for moving water from areas with lots of water to areas of shortage

weathering the breakup of rocks, often due to the weather

world city one of the most important cities in the global economy

Symbols on Ordnance Survey maps

ROADS AND PATHS

M I or A 6(M)	Motorway
A 35	Dual carriageway
A 31(T) or A 35	Trunk or main road
B 3074	Secondary road
	Narrow road with passing places
	Road under construction
	Road generally more than 4 m wide
	Road generally less than 4 m wide
	Other road, drive or track, fenced and unfenced
>>>	Gradient: steeper than 1 in 5; 1 in 7 to 1 in 5
Ferry	Ferry; Ferry P – passenger only
	Path

PUBLIC RIGHTS OF WAY

(Not applicable to Scotland)

1:25 000	1:50 000	
-----------	....	Footpath
— — — —	-.-.-.-.-	Road used as a public footpath
+++++	— — — —	Bridleway
-+-+-+-+-	-+-+-+-+-	Byway open to all traffic

RAILWAYS

	Multiple track
	Single track
	Narrow gauge/Light rapid transit system
	Road over; road under; level crossing
	Cutting; tunnel; embankment
	Station, open to passengers; siding

BOUNDARIES

+ — + — +	National
+ — + — +	District
— · — · — ·	County, Unitary Authority, Metropolitan District or London Borough
	National Park

HEIGHTS/ROCK FEATURES

Contour lines	
· 144	Spot height to the nearest metre above sea level

outcrop cliff scree

ABBREVIATIONS

P	Post office	PC	Public convenience (rural areas)
PH	Public house	TH	Town Hall, Guildhall or equivalent
MS	Milestone	Sch	School
MP	Milepost	Coll	College
CH	Clubhouse	Mus	Museum
CG	Coastguard	Cemy	Cemetery
Fm	Farm		

ANTIQUITIES

VILLA	Roman	✕	Battlefield (with date)
Castle	Non-Roman	✶	Tumulus/Tumuli (mound over burial place)

LAND FEATURES

	Buildings
	Public building
	Bus or coach station
	Place of Worship {with tower / with spire, minaret or dome / without such additions}
∘	Chimney or tower
	Glass structure
Ⓗ	Heliport
△	Triangulation pillar
	Mast
	Wind pump / wind generator
	Windmill
+	Graticule intersection
	Cutting, embankment
	Quarry
	Spoil heap, refuse tip or dump
	Coniferous wood
	Non-coniferous wood
	Mixed wood
	Orchard
	Park or ornamental ground
	Forestry Commission access land
	National Trust – always open
	National Trust, limited access, observe local signs
	National Trust for Scotland

TOURIST INFORMATION

P	Parking
P&R	Park & Ride
V	Visitor centre
i	Information centre
✆	Telephone
	Camp site/Caravan site
	Golf course or links
	Viewpoint
PC	Public convenience
	Picnic site
	Pub/s
	Museum
	Castle/fort
	Building of historic interest
	Steam railway
	English Heritage
	Garden
	Nature reserve
	Water activities
	Fishing
☆	Other tourist feature
	Moorings (free)
	Electric boat charging point
	Recreation/leisure/sports centre

WATER FEATURES